The Rise and Fall
of Chilean Christian
Democracy

The Rise and Fall
of Chilean Christian
Democracy

« »

MICHAEL
FLEET

Princeton University Press
Princeton, New Jersey

Copyright © 1985 by Princeton University Press

Published by Princeton University Press, 41 William Street,
Princeton, New Jersey 08540
In the United Kingdom: Princeton University Press,
Guildford, Surrey

Library of Congress Cataloging in Publication Data will
be found on the last printed page of this book

ISBN 0-691-07684-7 (cloth)
ISBN 0-691-02217-8 (paperback)

Publication of this book has been aided by the Whitney
Darrow Fund of Princeton University Press

This book has been composed in Century Schoolbook

Clothbound editions of Princeton University Press books
are printed on acid-free paper, and binding materials are chosen
for strength and durability. Paperbacks, while satisfactory for
personal collections, are not usually suitable for library rebinding

Printed in the United States of America by Princeton
University Press, Princeton, New Jersey

al pueblo chileno

CONTENTS

LIST OF TABLES

LIST OF ABBREVIATIONS

ANEF	Associación Nacional de Empleados Fiscales
CDU-CSU	Christian Democratic Union-Christian Social Union
CEPCh	Confederación de Empleados Particulares de Chile
CERA	Centro de Reforma Agraria
CFDT	Confédération Française Démocratique du Travail
COPEI	Comité de Organización Política Electoral Independiente
CORA	Corporación de Reforma Agraria
CUT	Central Unica de Trabajadores
DC	Democrazia Cristiana
ECLA	United Nations Economic Commission for Latin America
FRAP	Frente de Acción Popular
INDAP	Instituto de Desarrollo Agropecuario
MAPU	Movimiento para Acción Popular Unitario
MIR	Movimiento de Izquierda Revolucionaria
PADENA	Partido Democrático Nacional
PANAPO	Partido Nacional Popular
PDC	Partido Demócrata Cristiano (Chile)
PDC	Partido Demócrata Cristiano (El Salvador)
PDC	Partido Demócrata Cristiano (Peru)
PIR	Partido de Izquierda Radical
PN	Partido Nacional
SNA	Sociedad Nacional de Agricultura
SOFOFA	Sociedad de Fomento Fabril
SPD	German Social Democratic Party
UP	Unidad Popular
USEC	Unión Social de Empresarios Cristianos

PREFACE

I have written this book in the hope of contributing to a fuller understanding of both Christian Democracy and Chilean politics. While both subjects have been widely studied, neither has been approached in a way that captures the often subtle interplay of political, ideological, and class forces. Attempting to provide such an analysis, I have used a modified class perspective in which ideological and institutional structures are seen as channels through which class interests and relationships are shaped, conditioned, and played out.

At another, related level, this is a study of Catholic politics in contemporary Latin America. Here I am concerned with describing and accounting for the seemingly endless and often harmful divisions within a party claiming inspiration in the social teaching of the Catholic Church. How is it, I ask, that the values and ideals of the progressive Catholic tradition can be so variously understood, given such different weights, mediated through such diverse sociological perspectives, and applied in practice with such dissimilar strategies and purposes.

As a "progressive" Catholic myself, I have been doubly interested in these matters. I had the good fortune to live, study, and teach in Chile for three years in the late 1960s and to return for extended visits on two occasions since then. Over the years I have spoken with hundreds of people—intellectuals, priests, party militants, social activists, and relatively passive followers—who have sought to work out a social Christian politics they believed to be adequate to the challenges of Chilean society. Some were fully conscious of their efforts in this regard. Others were not but were nonetheless helpful and informative. Over time I came to know many of these people personally and was able to watch them evolve politically in various ways and directions.

My own values, feelings, and friendships have thus no doubt affected what I understand and what I have written here. On occasion they may even have prevented me from seeing or assessing things that would have been painfully obvious to others. I believe, however, that for the most part they have strengthened my work by providing me with a feel for the issues I have studied and for Chilean politics generally.

I first went to Chile in 1966 as a graduate student on an educational exchange program. I returned later that year to undertake dissertation research and to study at ILADES, the Latin American Institute for Doctrine and Social Studies in Santiago. At ILADES, where I spent 1967, I had access to a faculty that included Panamanian Christian Democrat Ricardo Arias Calderón, Jesuits Gonzalo Arroyo, Pierre Bigó, Paulo Meneses, Renato Poblete, Roger Vekemans, and Mario Zanartu, and German-born economist Franz Hinklehammert. I remained in Chile until May 1969 doing library research and conducting interviews while teaching at the School of Political and Administrative Science of the University of Chile under the auspices of the University of California-Universidad de Chile Cooperative Program. There my faculty colleagues included Clodomiro Almeyda, José Miguel Insulza, and Jaime Suárez.

Thanks to the help of these colleagues and to students and friends in these institutions I wrote and successfully defended a dissertation on the *Ideological Tendencies within Chilean Christian Democracy*. But my debt to them is even more extensive, for much of what I have learned then and since about Chilean and Catholic politics is the result of our discussions and debates during this very formative period. I hope that each of them knows how grateful I am for the time, the friendship, and the political education they so graciously provided me.

I returned to Chile in 1972 to study the Allende government, in which former Christian Democrats were playing important roles. During a five-week period, I gathered Popular Unity (UP), Christian Democratic, and other materials (formal documents and statements, internal reports, media materials, etc.) and conducted additional interviews of both government and opposition personalities. The money for this research was generously provided by the (then) School of Politics and International Relations (SPIR) Research Fund of the University of Southern California. To the SPIR officials and to the University's Haines Faculty Fellowship Program, which enabled me to spend the summer of 1974 working with these materials, I am most appreciative.

I also wish to acknowledge the singular assistance of Professors Brian Smith of M.I.T. and Eduardo Hamuy of Santiago's Centro de Opinión Pública. Professor Smith's research on the Chilean Catholic Church brought him into possession of four of

Hamuy's attitudinal surveys of Greater Santiago, those for 1964, 1970, 1972, and 1973, which he graciously shared with me. Their importance to this book is substantial and so too, therefore, is my indebtedness to him and to Professor Hamuy. In this connection I must also thank the Marquette University Graduate School's Faculty Development Fund for its assistance in acquiring Hamuy's 1958 survey and in defraying related computing costs.

I did not return to Chile until May 1981 when I made a visit of two weeks thanks in large measure to the support and hospitality of the Maryknoll Fathers. During this visit, I was able to resume relationships with many colleagues and friends and to interview Christian Democrats and former Christian Democrats whom I had not seen since the late 1960s or early 1970s. Though brief, this trip helped enormously in piecing together and assessing the impressions I had formed at a distance, and in contact with Chilean exiles, during the years since 1972.

I would be remiss if I did not also acknowledge the help of Professor Jack Stebbins of the University of Wisconsin-Milwaukee, who introduced me to the wonders of SPSS, of Sandra Brown, Frances Johannes, and Robert Smith of Marquette's Computer Services Division, whose patient and gracious assistance helped me to overcome countless SPSS and word-processing problems, and of Cathy Thatcher of Princeton University Press, whose editing skills have helped me to think and write more clearly.

Lastly, and most importantly, I would like to thank those whose encouragement and constructive criticism during the past four years have helped me to write and to improve this study. I am especially grateful to my wife Jean, to my Marquette colleagues James Rhodes and Matthew Lamb, to Lars Schoultz of the University of North Carolina, and, again, to Brian Smith. Each read all or part of earlier drafts, made insightful observations and suggestions, and helped me to persevere in my instincts and arguments. For their advice, their companionship, and their patience I am most appreciative.

The Rise and Fall
of Chilean Christian
Democracy

INTRODUCTION

When the Christian Democrats first emerged as a significant force in Chilean politics almost thirty years ago, they seemed an ideal ideological and political alternative to the left and right. Vowing to do away with capitalism but to preserve freedom and generate social and economic development, they won the support of peasants, workers, the urban poor, petit bourgeois groups, and even progressive entrepreneurial elements. Eduardo Frei's election to the presidency in 1964 was hailed as the opening of a new Christian Democratic era in Latin America. Since then, however, the party has suffered a series of disappointments and setbacks and has lost much of its reforming zeal.

During its years in power, Frei's government failed to bring about its much vaunted Revolution in Liberty. Although among the country's most effective and progressive governments, it failed to revitalize the Chilean economy, to follow through on promised structural reforms, or to head off the unrest that swept the country during the last two years of its term. As a result, Frei's political support diminished steadily, and in 1970 the party lost the presidency itself, with Christian Democrat Radomiro Tómic finishing a poor third behind the victorious Salvador Allende and runner-up Jorge Alessandri.

At the time, Allende's victory was widely regarded as evidence of a radicalization of Chilean politics. In fact, however, most of those abandoning the Chilean Christian Democratic party (PDC) went over (or back) to Alessandri and not Allende, and had Frei been eligible to run for a second term he might have been reelected. Moreover, although the party helped to secure Allende's confirmation, it was critical of his government from the beginning, eventually joining with the right in blocking his policies and ultimately undermining his economic and political base. In so doing it retained and even expanded its own following, although it also encouraged military conspirators and helped to usher in the ensuing military dictatorship under which its own fortunes would decline dramatically.

Today, almost fifteen years after Frei relinquished the presidency to the Socialist Allende, the Chilean Christian Dem-

3

ocratic party is experiencing a species of political resurrection. Following Allende's overthrow, the party's influence, adherents, and morale fell to unprecedentedly low levels. Since 1982, however, the once seemingly invincible Pinochet government has been rocked by economic and political crises, and its critics, including the Christian Democrats, have become newly active and assertive. Christian Democrats, for example, are among the most popular and influential leaders of the revitalized Chilean labor movement. Neighborhood organizations of Catholic and other Church-fostered social organizations have become bastions of antijunta resistance. The party itself appears to have regained some of its lost credibility, seems revitalized in spirit, and has developed decent working relationships with both right- and left-wing groups.

With these signs of apparent renaissance, can it be proper to speak of the rise *and* fall of Chilean Christian Democracy? I believe so. The party's strength today is largely apparent and is not likely to endure beyond the early stages of the transition to civilian rule, if or when it comes. Since 1973 the PDC has lost touch and credibility with its once substantial public following. Further, with the death in 1982 of Eduardo Frei it has lost the figure with whom it rose to national political prominence. Finally, it has been badly weakened by internal divisions, defections, and changes in the composition of both activists and followers, originating in some cases even before the coup.

Polarizing class and political pressures have long been sources of tension and occasional crisis for the party. Nonetheless, it maintained its multiclass, multitendency character for many years and often made positive use of its internal divisions. In the present context, however, these divisions appear to be a virtually fatal liability. In the past a substantial constituency of inexperienced and strongly anticommunist workers, slum dwellers, and peasants provided reliable support for the party's moderately reformist petit bourgeois leadership. Most were content with the centrist policies and strategies that it offered, while the more progressively minded appeared to have no alternative but to stay with the party. They neither trusted the left nor their own ability to survive or prosper politically on their own. Since the coup, however, these forces have undergone important formative experiences, developing ideas, organizational capabilities, and political relationships of their own. As a result, they are no longer the docile or compliant followers of earlier periods. Many are

4

unlikely to accept either secondary roles or the policies espoused by the party's more conservative faction. Rather, they are likely to move the party in a more progressive direction and failing that to strike off leftward on their own. Were the party to remain in the middle of the road, they would probably stay, but it is not likely to do so once the transition to civilian rule takes place, and at some point relatively soon the Christian Democrats will have to choose between the left and right, i.e., between center-right and center-left coalitions. Whatever its choice, the PDC seems destined to split into roughly equal and increasingly class-based political forces, each of which will play a secondary or at best coequal role within its respective coalition.

Christian Democratic parties have been somewhat more successful in other countries in recent years. In Latin America, Christian Democrats have only recently left power in Venezuela and Ecuador, are important albeit uncertain factors in El Salvador and Peru, and are likely to play prominent roles in any transition to civilian rule in Uruguay and Guatemala. In Europe, Christian Democratic parties head up the West German, Italian, Irish, and Luxembourgian governments and are a significant force in both Belgium and the Netherlands.

These more successful parties have prospered under relatively conservative banners, however, and have abandoned reformist tenets and commitments with which the Christian Democratic movement was once associated historically. Those currently or recently in power are more eager to defend the rights of the private sector and to pursue growth, stability, and harmony within existing economic structures. They are less inclined to press for the reform, much less the elimination, of capitalist structures or forces. Those who have not yet achieved power are waiting expectantly in the wings and seem intent on winning the trust or indulgence of conservative and/or military forces.

The rightward drift of these Christian Democratic parties reflects changing political, ideological, and class contexts. Several of the Latin American parties operate under regimes (military and civilian) in which leftist forces are proscribed, severely restricted, or hopelessly fragmented. As a result, these Christian Democrats are neither challenged nor prodded by the left. In France, Italy, and Germany, on the other hand, it has been the moderation of Social Democratic, Socialist, and Communist parties that has pushed most Christian Democrats further rightward. Finally, many European and Latin American Christian

5

Democrats have drawn neoconservative lessons from experiences in which their "third-road" alternative (their own or that of confreres elsewhere) was found (or seen) to be wanting.

The rightward drift of the European parties has been explained largely in terms of changing political contexts and strategies (Irving 1979a; Pridham 1977; and Kogan 1981). Class considerations, while conceded a certain relevance, have been relegated to a secondary plane, more useful, it seems, in accounting for the success or failure of particular strategies than the choice of strategy as such. In dealing with the Chilean PDC, analysts have been more polemical and one-dimensional. Critics (Altamirano 1977; Stallings 1978) have attacked it as a bourgeois force committed to the defense of the existing order by any and all means necessary, while apologists (Arriagada 1974; Sigmund 1977) blame Marxist totalitarianism for forcing the party into the arms of forces with whom it shared only a concern for democratic politics. Other analysts (Garcés 1976; Garretón and Moulián 1979; Roxborough 1976 and 1979; Valenzuela 1978) offer more balanced approaches, attributing the social and political polarization to conflicting class interests and to the mistrust, shortsightedness, and partisan self-interest of the two sides.

None of these analyses adequately captures the character of the Christian Democratic party or Chilean politics during this period. Those stressing either class or institutional factors alone are unduly one-dimensional and prejudgmental. Those attempting to blend class and nonclass considerations, while more enlightening, pay insufficient attention to the Christian Democrats and either fail to place the Allende period in proper historical context or are insufficiently clear as to the reasons why class interests did not play a more determining role at certain junctures.

The following chapters offer a modified class analysis of Chilean Christian Democracy, one that sees its evolution in terms of interrelated class, cultural, ideological, and institutional political factors. They trace the movement's origins and early character, its rapid growth and expansion prior to the 1964 election, its years in power under Frei, and its subsequent opposition to the Allende government. They stress and seek to account for the party's retention of substantial working-class and popular support through 1973, even as polarizing trends intensified and its own political fortunes began to decline. They then turn to the years of military rule since September 1973, attempting to explain how and why this support unravels and what these developments portend for the party's future.

In dealing with these phases of the PDC's development I bring together evidence of various sorts. Fortunately, substantial material and information concerning the Christian Democrats are available to the moderately industrious researcher. For much of the party's history its spokespersons have written books, published journals, and engaged in internal and public debate on a variety of issues. From the late 1940s until its closure by the military in 1975 the semiofficial journal *Política y Espíritu* served as a forum in which theoretical and practical issues were aired and debated. These materials were written in contexts and for specific purposes that are not always as clear in retrospect as they may have been at the time. But if read carefully and in conjunction with news and other accounts of the period, they can provide reliable and useful indications of party thinking and sentiment at crucial junctures.

Another important source of information and perspective has been the largely conversational interviews with Christian Democratic leaders and activists that I conducted during my initial stay in Chile from 1966 to 1969 and during return visits in 1972 and 1981. These interviews provided me with clearly stated positions on various intramural and extramural issues. They also clarified numerous ambiguities and mistaken impressions, provided insight into some of the subtleties of Chilean politics and party dynamics, and generally helped me to understand and assess material whose significance I would otherwise have missed.

A third data source are the attitudinal surveys taken by Dr. Eduardo Hamuy's Centro de Opinión Pública. Drawn from very similar samples of the Greater Santiago population in 1958, 1964, 1970, 1972, and 1973, they proved in each instance to be remarkably accurate predictors of voting behavior or general political trends. They also provide valuable data on the political preferences, occupational statuses, and opinions and judgments of both members and supporters of the country's major political parties. Recent studies of Chilean politics have characterized the Christian Democrats in varying terms, tying their leaders to certain interests, pressures, and ulterior objectives. Much has been alleged or asserted regarding its "hegemonic" as opposed to allied and supporting forces. Rarely, however, have these characterizations been supported by more than fragmentary empirical evidence, nor have patterns been traced over an appreciable period of time. The Hamuy data presented and analyzed in Chapters 2, 3, and 4 provide an empirical base from which to test leading claims and presumptions in this regard.

The opinions, strategies, and political relationships that emerged from these various materials should not be dismissed as superstructural or secondary phenomena. They are constitutive political features of "objective" social reality. They reflect, mediate, and help to condition class interests and relationships.

Chapter 1 sets forth the framework of analysis. It defines the basic building blocks of class, politics, ideology, and culture, and then describes the forms and relationships that they assumed in Chile during the 1960s and 1970s.

The PDC's development prior to 1964 is the subject of Chapter 2, which describes the party's origins and early years, the social forces to which it successfully appealed, the impact of Frei's rise to national prominence, and its attitudes and relationships vis-à-vis other political forces. This chapter is an attempt to show that the party was not the strong, well-disciplined, cohesive organization it seemed to be at the time and that Frei's mandate for reform was neither strong nor likely to endure.

Chapter 3 deals with the Frei government, using survey and other data to challenge the analyses of both its critics and apologists. On the one hand, it relates its problems and shortcomings to the PDC's own internal divisions and to its inability to achieve understandings with key working-class or entrepreneurial forces. On the other, it argues that while Frei failed to get the economy moving again, or to deliver on his various reform commitments, most of those abandoning the PDC turned to the candidate offering a more conservative and not a more radical approach to national problems.

The ensuing Popular Unity period and the party's drift into increasingly uncompromising opposition is explored in Chapter 4. Against various one-dimensional analyses, it stresses the interaction of class interests, institutional political considerations, and grass-roots mobilization and polarization that neither side could control or deflect.

Chapter 5 covers the period of military rule since Allende's overthrow, a time in which the party's sentiments, fortunes, and taste for confrontation with the military government have varied considerably. Here I stress the divisions between leaders, labor militants, and other social activists sharply critical of the junta and those less hostile elements who remain committed to negotiating differences and building a center-right alliance despite the harshness of military policies and practices. And here too I emphasize the importance of new extraparty experiences and relationships for many formerly docile Christian Democratic workers and marginals.

Chapter 6 offers a brief overview of the experiences of other Christian Democratic parties. These are compared in terms of their political evolution, their social base and composition, their ideological orientation, and their political ties, positions, and strategies. I then define and attempt to account for their common and distinctive features. And finally, with these matters in mind, I return to the Chilean case, drawing together a number of loose strands and offering reasoned speculation regarding the party's political future.

« 1 »

UNDERSTANDING
CHILEAN POLITICS

Recent studies of Chilean politics offer the reader a plethora of perspectives, sympathies, and assessments with which to analyze the breakdown of democratic politics. Some Marxist analysts (Altamirano 1977; Boorstein 1977; Castells 1974; Stallings 1978) stress structural processes, conflicting class interests, and the "bourgeois" character of forces opposing the ill-fated Allende government. Institutional and ideological considerations are either ignored or treated as matters of tactical calculation or manipulation. In contrast, pluralist and anti-Popular Unity analysts (Alexander 1978; Arriagada 1974; and Sigmund 1977) confine themselves to partisan maneuvering, institutional and policy conflicts, and largely ideological representations of reality. They blame the "totalitarian" designs of the left for upsetting the consensus on which Chilean politics rested prior to 1970.

Analysts falling between these poles (Garcés 1976; Garretón and Moulián 1979; Roxborough 1976 and 1979; Valenzuela 1978) offer a mixture of class and nonclass considerations, and I share many of their views and judgments. While they are correct in holding both sides responsible for the tragic turn of events, however, their eclecticism prevents them from clearly characterizing the experience or fully elucidating its implications.

With this thought in mind, I offer a modified class analytical perspective from which to look at Chilean Christian Democracy. My foundational assumption is that political phenomena are best understood in terms of class. Social experiences, relations, and understandings are all conditioned by class status and interests, and political events themselves are most meaningfully described in terms of the struggle for class hegemony. While the single most important determinant of social and political life, however, "class" is itself affected by contingent cultural, ideological, and political factors. These are part of the setting in which labor is performed and are thus constitutive features of one's objective class status. They also provide the terms, organizational dynamics, and institutional context in which that status is acquired and can facilitate or stifle the subjective process by which class

11

is understood and acted on. The entire process is contingent, not determined. Human will and consciousness are free and decisive historical phenomena, not the predetermined externalizations of irresistible material forces.

This perspective differs from leading pluralist and Marxist analyses. For pluralists, power is variously rooted in economic, ideological, institutional, and other sources and is dispersed among forces that contain and dilute one another. No one aspect or combination of these forces, it is claimed, enjoys enduring control over the social or political process. In recent years pluralists have helped other social analysts to see the potentially cross-cutting impact of nonclass forces, the contestability of the state, and the largely contingent character of the struggle for it. In opposition I would argue 1) that power can but *need not* be widely dispersed or evenly balanced; 2) that power rooted in the production process is ultimately more decisive than that stemming from other sources; and 3) that economic and noneconomic power sources may reenforce one another, producing concentrations of power not always visible at the institutional political level.

Among Marxists, views as to how class should be related to and weighed against other experiences and relationships vary considerably. Following Marx's death, and with the rise of Bolshevism and Stalinism, economic and productive relations were viewed as determining all superstructural phenomena. Later, however, others (Korsch, Lukacs, Gramsci, and the Frankfurt theorists) began to argue that cultural and political factors might both reflect and affect class interests and consciousness. Although it has made fewer inroads among the leaders of ruling and nonruling Marxist parties, this "dialectical" perspective has been embraced by virtually all contemporary Marxist theorists.[1]

The dialectics have been variously understood, however. For Marxist "structuralists," for example, the "mode of production" (a combination of forces and relations of production) is rooted in roles that are essentially material in nature. Nonetheless, it generates economic, ideological, and political "instances" (expressions) that serve to strengthen and preserve the prevailing relations of domination.[2] These instances are relatively au-

[1] Only the Italian, and to a lesser extent the Spanish, parties show signs of embracing these frankly revisionist views at even the theoretical much less the practical political level.

[2] Among the better known Marxist structuralists are Louis Althusser, Nikos Poulantzas, Manuel Castells, and Perry Anderson. These theorists draw on ear-

UNDERSTANDING CHILEAN POLITICS

tonomous, i.e., in keeping with their own particular laws and dynamics. In this way ideology and politics are included as elements of the productive process and class struggle and yet seen as "determined" by them. As "instances" they (alone) are real and concrete but cannot be understood except as rooted in and linked together by underlying structures, i.e., the dominant mode of production. Class ties and relations are thus "objective" material features of that mode of production and its division of labor. They are independent of the wills and understandings of the people occupying them, informing those wills and understandings but in no sense depending on them.[3]

"Cultural" or "political" Marxists,[4] on the other hand, see political and cultural factors as constitutive, not epiphenomenal, and as contingent, not determined, aspects of the productive process. In their view productive relations are defined by both material *and* social factors. At any given moment, property laws, labor codes, corporate statutes, and the balance of political and class forces will condition, if not alter, strictly material relations of production and thereby help to define productive relations

lier structuralist work in psychoanalysis, anthropology, and linguistics in opposing both economic determinism and contemporary Marxist humanism. Poulantzas' views evolved considerably between the late 1960s and his death in 1982. Meiksins Wood (1983) argues that in the process he abandoned a materially rooted conception of class and the concept of class struggle as well. Skotnes (1979) contends that his concessions are minimal (i.e., limited to the single case of the petite bourgeoisie) and that they do not compromise his overall structural conception of class. An excellent review of structuralist analysis in contemporary Latin America is Harris 1979, 76-79.

[3] Structuralists attempt to remain flexible. Although insisting that under the capitalist mode of production the economic instance ultimately prevails (literally "in the final instance"), they concede that at certain stages (as when several modes of production combine and coexist), and within certain classes or class fractions, ideological and/or political relations may actually be more decisive (Poulantzas 1979, 56). Further, structuralists concede that social behavior and developments at the "conjunctural" (the concrete historical) level may or may not conform to the determinations of productive relations and interests. The political and ideological vestiges of previous periods, for example, may continue to influence hearts, minds, and actions although they are not considered important in themselves and are not seen as enduring long in the face of countervailing structural forces.

[4] Among the more prominent political or cultural Marxists are E. P. Thompson, Leszek Kolakowski, Roger Garaudy, and Stanley Aronowitz. A social historian currently employing political Marxist analysis in dealing with modern European history is Robert Brenner (1976). Among Latin Americanists the most systematic and widely read statement of political or cultural Marxism is found in Roxborough (1979).

generally (Brenner 1976, 52). But they are also features of historical conjunctures in which subjective consciousness and contingent political dynamics have played decisive roles. They are not simply passive or secondary "specifications" of some underlying process but rather constitutive and determining factors within it.[5]

The perspective from which I have approached the Chilean Christian Democrats draws from these cultural or political Marxists. I too view class status as both an objective and a subjective condition. Roles and claims vis-à-vis the productive process are initially and essentially material, i.e., based on the power to extract surplus labor, separate workers from the means of production, and subject them to a disciplined and rationalized labor process (Meiksins Wood 1983, 259). While these material relations imply certain social experiences, concrete interests, and historical potential, however, they can be compounded, mitigated, cut across, and even redefined by other, nonmaterial relations such as labor codes, property laws, the balance of political forces, cultural and political relations among workers, and other contingent phenomena. One's relationship to the means of production thus constitutes the material dimension of a productive role that is also defined nonmaterially; and although this broader class "situation" carries a potential for consciousness and development, its tapping and fulfillment require the mediation of nonmaterial and largely contingent forces and processes (Roxborough 1979, 71).

Political forces thus condition one's class situation and what is made of it. Similarly, classes exist as operative social forces to the extent that they become conscious of themselves as a class and undertake action against their antagonists. Class consciousness thus entails a new understanding of one's interests, allies, and enemies and is the product of a process in which competing

[5] Not all who would reclaim the political dimension of Marxist thought qualify as either political or cultural Marxists. Meiksins Wood, for example, concedes that productive relations are socially (and politically) "shaped" but insists that the core of class status is essentially material, i.e., rooted in material relations of exploitation (1981, 75). Accordingly, she believes that ideological and political differences among workers, along with those reflecting the dynamics of a particular work place, are secondary and will wane and ultimately fade away as the uniformizing impact of capital takes its toll (1983, 259). Class ties and consciousness thus should not be understood as political or ideological phenomena but as "material" relations established and confirmed by political and ideological factors.

14

cultural, ideological, and political influences have played a part. These influences, in turn, are reflections and constitutive elements of the productive process and the structures through which its social significance is mediated.

This conception of class obliges one to take a closer look at a society's political institutions and relationships, ideological tendencies, and cultural traditions. By political institutions I refer to governmental institutions, the size and strength of social and class forces, property laws and labor relations codes, the appeal of dominant political personalities, and time-honored political practices and behavioral patterns. Each of these factors helps to define productive relations and the process by which class consciousness and forces arise. In effect, a class's sense of itself and its mission depends in part on the institutional structures and organizational options available to it. Although pushed and pulled by materially rooted experiences, sentiments, and energies, political institutions and dynamics are the channels into which these various forces flow and take form.

In turn, institutions and dynamics are affected by both structural and contingent forces and processes. Politics involves efforts to create, sustain, and channel support for positions and courses of action with which not all are initially in agreement. Such efforts are invariably uncertain as to outcome. Particular forces may be more or less likely to respond given their class situations, their material circumstances, and other factors, but the end result is never "predetermined." Conscious human agents assess their circumstances in light of their relations and expectations and these, in turn, in light of their circumstances. Such dynamics cannot be predetermined on either an individual or social level. People with similar class situations embrace different visions, priorities, and strategic perspectives with respect to their interests; those with quite different class situations and interests (e.g., independent as opposed to industrial blue collar workers) are even more likely to do so.

Relations between class situations and political forces are thus problematic. They are all the more so in social formations in which several modes of production coexist, or where the capitalist labor process is not fully extended. In such cases forces in similar class "situations" are less likely to identify or act as a single class. They are rather inclined to think and act in terms of political ties and concerns and are likely to view multiclass political parties as more useful in the promotion or defense of their interests than strictly class formations.

In identifying with a particular party, classes and class fractions enter into coalitions in which they play dominant, allied, and/or supporting roles (Poulantzas 1973, 229-252). Classes and class fractions that divide along ideological lines often remain subordinate partners in the blocs and parties of which they are a part. The political dynamics and power relationships in such cases are complex and difficult to identify, much less predict in advance.

At another level the state itself becomes a "contestable" object of class struggle, although its individual branches or agencies may be controlled by particular classes or class fractions. The nature and functions of the state have been hotly debated by Marxists in recent years. So-called "instrumentalists" view it as an instrument of ruling-class domination, one controlled by ruling-class elites or those sharing their inclinations (Miliband 1969, 146). Structuralists, on the other hand, see no need for direct or overt class control, emphasizing rather the imperatives of the structures in which the state is "embedded." These imply systemic constraints and functions that the political apparatus must respect and/or perform, whatever the preferences of its personnel or political constituency. In fact, Poulantzas (1973, 190) specifically provides for the state's carrying out of policies contrary to the short-term interests of the dominant class(es) but compatible with its (their) political interests and continued hegemony.

Both views are deterministic. Instrumentalists assume that a ruling class actually controls the state, which cannot but reflect and serve its concerns and interests. Structuralists consider the state to be passive and in unavoidable conformity with underlying systemic urges or mandates. Neither regards institutional or contextual details as significant.[6]

[6] More recently Miliband has argued that the state can be an instrument in either a direct or indirect sense: direct insofar as the ruling class supplies its personnel or its immediate political constituency; indirect in view of the concessions to be made if the economy is to remain strong and a government's political position secure (Miliband 1977, 68-72). Gold, Lo, and Wright (1975, 48) go further, proposing criteria by which to determine when and where the instrumental or structural perspective would be more appropriate. Drawing on Offe (1975), they argue that "allocative" (budgetary) decisions are more susceptible to direct economic determination and thus more likely to exhibit the state's instrumental character. Productive decisions, on the other hand, are less directly linked to ongoing struggles and interests and involve questions on which little or no rul-

My sense of the state is of something that is at once an object, a product, and a determinant of class struggle. In each respect it is affected by contingent cultural, ideological, and political factors. Its institutional characteristics are the product of previous struggles and an important factor in those currently taking place. All states are subject to systemic pressures, and in any given instance these may coincide with the interests of sectors of capital that are not in control of any of its branches or agencies. They are the beneficiaries of a system whose maintenance and/ or expansion is in their interest, even though they may not be politically responsible for it. The state, in other words, may be "capitalist" even though government personnel may not be, and may not wish it to be either.

The divisions existing between the fractions and individual interests within capital provide a government with room for maneuver and initiative. These include divisions of ideological orientation, material interest, political strategy, and/or personality. Class fractions may or may not overcome their rivalries and conflicts to form a single class: contingent factors affecting levels of consciousness, organizational cohesion, and popular support will play decisive roles. Unless they do overcome these problems, however, capital interests may have to endure governments they cannot control and whose policies are detrimental to them. Similarly, governments themselves possess varying degrees of cohesion, administrative effectiveness, and broad public support. Those enjoying more of each are clearly better able to resist or endure the pressure of such interests and thus carry their efforts through to a successful conclusion.

Culture and ideology affect both the politics and class structure of a society. They are closely related phenomena. An ideology is that set of perspectives and judgments which define a person's social relationships and political options. Ideally, at least, it consists of explicit and systematically structured normative values, analytical judgments, and strategic orientations. However, such highly developed ideologies are normally confined to a movement's leaders or intellectual elite, whose education and political experience exceed those of their followers. Few of the latter are moved by such refined considerations. They are drawn

ing-class consensus exists. In such instances the state enjoys a "relative autonomy" in choosing its method or strategy of action for meeting systemic (and ruling-class) needs.

instead by vague representations or distortions thereof, by slogans, symbols, and arguments that are supportive of their immediate concerns and/or interests. However crudely, such ideologies provide adherents with a political identity. They dispose them to embrace certain goals and to ally with or support certain forces while challenging or opposing others. They offer them a way of assessing social reality and choosing from among competing political options.

In these ways ideology is essential to the full tapping of class potential. Whether those sharing a common class situation see themselves as comrades or rivals in struggle, as having or not having a common historical project, depends on their ideological perspective.[7] In this sense class is a product of ideological consciousness. But at the same time class also contributes to this consciousness, prompting it and setting the limits within which it operates. Ideological currents are not abstract or ahistorical phenomena. They are more likely to emerge and take hold at certain stages and in certain contexts than others. They are most likely to appear when and where there are interests at stake of the sort for which they can provide legitimation and support.

Ideologies are thus rooted in particular social contexts. They lend meaning, direction, and support to groups struggling for survival and advantage within these contexts. A given mode of production and set of social conditions can thus offer fertile ground, a constituency, and an accommodating environment for certain ideologies. In the case of revolutionary socialism, class potential is a function of the extent to which industrialization and the capitalist labor process have developed. Industrial workers must be brought together in large numbers and subjected to labor discipline if they are to perceive their class interests and potential class power. In addition, changes in the productive and distrib-

---

[7] Ideologies, it might be noted, may be true or false. They may provide an adequate (true) or inadequate (false) sense of a particular class's interests and an adequate or inadequate strategy for defending and promoting those interests. In practice, most people have a false sense of their interests and how to promote them. Many are the victims of ideological forces that prevent them from forming a correct understanding; others are indirectly conditioned and constrained by their general culture. Because of such phenomena some analysts would limit the concept of ideology to that of false consciousness. I prefer to retain the broader meaning, that of values, beliefs, etc., that provide an understanding of social relationships and political options, be that understanding true or false. I consider "false" consciousness to be as "real" and as likely to endure and define crucial relationships and possibilities as if it were "true."

utive processes affecting labor relations, wage levels, profits, employment opportunities, etc., may further clarify the interests at stake, the nature of their conflict, and the means necessary for resolving such conflicts.

Not all ideologies are simply "instruments" of contending classes, however. Among those competing for hegemony at any moment will be forces attempting to advance the interests of particular classes or class fractions while seeking to obscure or discredit those of antagonistic groups. But they will be joined by independent and/or less immediately involved forces (multiclass parties, the Church, etc.) seeking to reconcile the interests of diverse classes and sectors. These groups can be "used" by one of the dominant or contending classes but can also force them to adjust their strategic objectives and alliances.[8]

Marxist structuralists such as Castells do not take such ideologies seriously. They do not regard ideology as descriptive of a movement's "real" line or class character, or as having an enduring hold over those whose interests it may be obscuring. In their view ideologies are at best idealized aspirations and at worst cynical posturings. In either case they distort a group's "real" interests, which are expressed in its actual choices amidst the conflicts, constraints, and contingencies of political life (Castells 1974, 367).

To stress what is done (the action itself) as opposed to what is said (ideology), however, is to underplay the extent to which the conscious understanding of an act affects its character, extent, and impact. Political options are always limited, and diverse forces are frequently compelled into similar courses of action. In such cases important political differences will be clear only if positions and actions are viewed against intentions and rationales.

[8] Ideologies are frequently dismissed as unreal abstractions that prevent workers from making the most of their class situation. Not all ideological divisions need be creations or instruments of capital, however. In fact, many grow out of productive and/or political relations among workers themselves or between workers and forces outside the work place. Because of them workers may become political rivals with differing and even opposing political and strategic goals and with very different and opposing class interests. Whatever their origins, moreover, these divisive relations become constitutive of one's "class situation." They become the objective terms by which this situation is differentiated from that of others and by which workers are denied a "conventional" and ultimately unifying class experience and consciousness. Finally, such divisions do not readily wane or fade away but tend to become self-perpetuating unless the broader political context within which they are rooted is changed.

These may well be self-serving but are nonetheless significant for being so. The judgment that a specific group's support is essential, or that a particular sort of posturing will obtain it, sets a movement apart from others in politically important ways. Further, a movement's ideological self-understanding and/or rationale color the perceptions and responses of both its rivals and supporters.

A culture, on the other hand, consists of the values, attitudes, beliefs, sensibilities, and practices that structure the life of a people. More particularly, a political culture consists of values, etc., that relate to political relationships and phenomena, e.g., the state, law, the nature of society, social obligation, and so on. In most instances these notions are less explicit and less coherent than in an ideology. But they do condition expectations, judgments, and behavior in social and political matters, give them meaning, structure, and coherence, and therefore help to frame a people's social and political understanding.

The values, attitudes, beliefs, etc., of any political culture are embodied in and conveyed through the media, religious organizations, literary and intellectual circles, the educational system, and occupational and residential structures. They are transmitted with varying degrees of directness and explicitness and generally evolve over time. Political cultures permeate all reaches of a national society, both reenforcing and cutting across class, regional, and political lines. Although differing in other ways, people formed within that society are likely to share common orientations regarding authority, hierarchy, leadership, social and political participation, the importance of material well-being, and justice.[9]

Chilean Class Structure

During the 1960s and early 1970s in Chile, class consciousness and solidarity remained at relatively low levels due to the diversity of class "situations" and to the political, ideological, and cultural factors that affected both the situations and consciousness

[9] Among the more useful studies of Latin American political culture are Moreno 1969, Dealy 1977, and Wiarda 1982. After characterizing the region's dominant values and attitudes each of these analysts questions both the possibility and the desirability of a radical redistribution of power and wealth. I note this not to dismiss their views but to underscore the need for class analysts to take them more seriously.

of them. Breaking down the country's economically active population along occupational lines points up the structural basis of its class fragmentation (see Table 1-1).

Although further distinctions will be in order, class groupings can be collapsed into five categories: the bourgeoisie, the petite bourgeoisie, the working class, the marginal class, and the peasantry.

THE BOURGEOISIE

The Chilean bourgeoisie consisted of landed aristocrats (*latifundistas*), large commercial farmers, the industrial and financial bourgeoisie, and a "bureaucratic oligarchy." In very large part it was an unimaginative and unenterprising bourgeoisie, whose members opposed moderate reforms, failing to grasp their potential for expanding demand and raising profits. In some instances the lack of drive and vision reflected a preoccupation with family, professional, and other extraeconomic interests. In most cases, however, neither drive nor vision were needed for continued prestige or prosperity.

Until the mid-1960s, the agricultural sector was characterized by highly unequal land distribution patterns and general inefficiency.[10] The large, extensively exploited holdings of the *latifun-*

TABLE 1-1
Occupational Breakdown of Chile's Economically
Active Population, 1970

Administrative, executive, and managerial personnel	50,000	1.9%
Professional or technical workers	185,000	7.1
Clerical workers	249,000	9.5
Sales workers	214,000	8.2
Industrial and independent workers	1,050,000	40.6
Domestic workers	303,000	11.6
Farm workers, fishermen, etc.	550,000	21.1

SOURCE: Wilkie 1977, 192.

[10] In 1955 some 1,464 farms (.7 percent of the country's total) encompassed 61 percent of the land, while 168,000 farms (83.3 percent of the country's total) accounted for only 11 percent. In 1952 the entire agricultural sector, while employing close to 30 percent of the labor force, accounted for only 18 percent of the

distas were worked profitably but inefficiently. They typically produced beef cattle and wheat, but much of their land lay fallow or was worked by tenants or sharecroppers. The surpluses went into travel, second homes, and financial or industrial investments in which the landowner played a similarly inactive role. This aristocracy continued to prosper, thanks to cheap labor and abundant agricultural resources. Although no longer the dominant economic and political power of previous times, it was still a force with which to be reckoned: it could affect agricultural production, it politically controlled the peasant population in most areas, and it maintained close ties with urban economic and political elites.

The less numerous but more dynamic commercial farmers were a more significant economic force. They invested more capital (in machinery, irrigation systems, a year-round work force, etc.) and energy in their land, producing cotton, sugar beets, fruits and vegetables, dairy cattle, and wine grapes for the domestic and international markets. Many of them were linked to groups in other sectors who looked to agriculture as a source of raw materials and/or diversified investment opportunities.

The bulk of Chile's industrial entrepreneurs were as lacking in initiative and imagination as the *latifundistas*. They were at once contributing factors and victims of the country's modest level of industrial development and of its persistent stagnation in recent decades.[11] Highly dependent on state-granted tariffs, credits, and subsidies for profitability, they were also little inclined to innovation or to risk taking.

In general, ownership and control of Chilean industry was concentrated in relatively few hands. One or two very large firms

Gross Domestic Product; by 1969, it constituted 25 percent of the labor force but provided only 7.5 percent of the GDP. The vast majority of the country's farms (90.3 percent) were less than 200 hectares in extent and thus either small- or medium-sized. Of these, most were subsistence plots of less than 2 hectares. The remaining 9 percent were divided more or less equally between inefficient *latifundia* and more intensively worked commercial farms (Lagos 1965, 94).

[11] As recently as 1970 the industrial sector accounted for only 30 percent of the Gross Domestic Product (Stallings 1978, 22). Between 1940 and 1970 the economy grew by an average of only 1.4 percent per capita per year and the manufacturing sector by only 2.5 percent. The latter increase was due largely to growth in consumer durable and capital goods production between 1960 and 1970, but even with this spurt 77.5 percent of the value added in manufacturing came from the less dynamic traditional and intermediate sectors.

tended to dominate each of the various areas of production,[12] and they usually had close ties to firms dominating the equally concentrated financial or banking sector.[13] In fact, "interlocks" between the agricultural, industrial, and financial sectors were such that some observers (Zeitlin, Ewen, and Ratcliff 1974) have insisted on speaking of an integrated, and not a fragmented, bourgeoisie.[14] Lagos (1965, 121-173) identifies eleven groups as dominating the country's economic life. Typical of them was the powerful Edwards group, which controlled a commercial bank, five insurance companies, seven financial or investment corporations, thirteen industries, and two publishing houses. These groups were linked with one another in direct and indirect ways and dominated or decisively influenced 290 of the 1,300 incorporated firms in the country, with 70.6 percent of all capital assets (Lagos 1965, 164).

Despite the relative integration and financial power of this bourgeoisie it played a lackluster role in the country's development and would make even less of a contribution in the 1960s and 1970s. During the years 1961 to 1969, public investment as a percentage of total fixed capital investment rose from 46.6 percent to the almost incredible figure of 74.8 percent. During roughly the same period (1962 to 1970), more than U.S. $1,450 million in foreign capital was invested (Stallings 1978, 248; Molina 1972,

[12] A handful of large firms easily dominated the industrial sector. Of the more than 35,000 in the country fewer than 850 (2.4 percent) accounted for two-thirds of the industrial output, and of these fewer than one-third (271) accounted for 82 percent of all capital stock. These dominant firms were controlled by a handful of large shareholders. As few as ten owned over 90 percent of the shares in 60 percent of the public stock firms and over 50 percent of the shares in 85 percent of these firms (de Vylder 1976, 18). And yet as few and as dominant as they were they were not large firms by normal standards. As late as 1960 only 190 employed 2,000 or more workers, and only 1,700 (5 percent of the total) employed even 200 (Angell 1972, 69).

[13] One bank alone, the Banco de Chile, accounted for 32 percent of the credit, 42.8 percent of the capital assets, and 29.3 percent of the national currency deposits in the country. The seven leading banks accounted for 58 percent of the credit, 74.4 percent of the capital assets, and 65.8 percent of the domestic currency deposits.

[14] Many industrial firms were established by groups whose initial fortunes and relationships were in banking activities (the Banco de Chile, the Banco Sudamericano, the Banco Español, and the Banco Edwards). In other cases groups with roots in industrial activities saw fit to establish their own banking, credit, and insurance operations (the Banco Panamericano, the Banco Continental, and the Banco de Credito e Inversiones). See Lagos 1965, 114-119.

82). Private sector investment declined, tending to remain in the less dynamic consumer goods area and in those intermediate and capital goods areas in which either the state or foreign capital had taken risks and provided leadership.[15]

A final segment of the bourgeoisie must also be mentioned, if only in passing. The administrative or bureaucratic bourgeoisie consisted of party politicians and/or bureaucratic officials whose positions of influence made them valued friends or contacts for the bourgeoisie as such. Thanks to their good offices and timely mediations, banks, firms, and landowners received important price hikes, credits, subsidies, or privileged information. For their efforts they were rewarded with outright bribes, consultant fees, and even directorships or partnerships in the ventures they helped to start or sustain.[16] Government officials willing to accommodate the petitions of business interests became adjunct "bureaucratic" members of the bourgeoisie (Urdemales 1970, 30-31). If defeated for reelection or displaced by a change in administration, they moved fully into the bourgeoisie themselves, drawing profitably on the contacts and debts accumulated during their years of "public service."

THE PETITE BOURGEOISIE

Petit bourgeois elements occupied the strata between the bourgeoisie and working class, providing nonproductive services in either the private or public sectors.[17] They consisted of profes-

[15] The increase in public investment during the Frei period would have been substantial whatever the private sector's response, as state-financed expansion or development of the copper, petrochemical, steel, and cellulose industries were part of the Christian Democratic program from the beginning. In fact, when viewed in absolute terms, private investment remained at prevailing levels in most areas, although it clearly failed to respond as Frei had hoped and even expected. For investment figures for the period see Ffrench-Davis 1973, 278; Aranda and Martínez 1970, 162.

[16] Lagos (1965, 168) cites the case of one Chilean congressman who was a member of the board of directors of twelve firms and another case of one hundred public stock firms that had at least one congressman on their boards. He also points to the Compañía de Acero del Pacífico (CAP), the Industria de Azúcar Nacional (IANSA), and the Chilean Electric Power Company (CHILECTRA) as examples of enterprises financed and developed by the government and then taken over by politically well-connected private sector groups. Urdemales (1970, 31-32) details the case of Cemento Melón, a large cement producer, as representative of the many industrial ventures that were beneficiaries of concessions, subsidies, and regulatory policies that effectively undermined their competitors.

[17] Because the petite bourgeoisie hold positions of both economic and political

sionals, upper- and intermediate-level government functionaries, educators, merchants, small businessmen, and small- and intermediate-sized farmers. These groups performed key economic functions (the case with merchants, independent truckers, and wholesale distributors), were an important electoral force, and played a disproportionately influential role within the country's political parties and bureaucratic agencies.

Historically, they were a service class that had grown up with urban and governmental expansion, one that produced little but lived relatively well. Its members seemed progressive but were often more interested in imitating than in displacing the old aristocracy. The substantial political weight of the petite bourgeoisie hung heavily over any government not meeting its high material and status expectations.

Some professionals (doctors, lawyers, architects, civil engineers, economists, and administrators) had independent, family-based financial resources, and as such actually belonged to the bourgeoisie. Most did not, however, although they did live comfortably on their salaries or fees, viewing themselves as aristocrats of talent, taste, or vision, if not material wealth. Independent professionals tended to identify with the views and interests of their clients. Those who worked in the public sector (civil servants and school teachers), or were currently training for a profession (university students), on the other hand, usually held more progressive views.

The typical small businessman owned a small machine shop, a construction firm, a retail store, or a firm that provided special services to the public. None employed more than ten salaried workers. The economic well-being of most depended on the vitality of the economy as a whole and was always somewhat precarious. Small businessmen were distinguishable chiefly by their lack of influence within the state bureaucracy, without which they were cut off from credit, denied lucrative tax breaks, and encumbered by burdensome regulations (Urdemales 1970, 46-55).

The petite bourgeoisie's relationship to the bourgeoisie and to wage workers could be complementary, competing, or conflictive, depending on conjunctural circumstance and ideological orien-

significance virtually all theorists concede their importance in a society's class struggle and political life. But they are widely viewed as an unpredictable force, and even Poulantzas (Skotnes 1979, 42) concedes that their class interest is more a function of their ideological or political practice than their productive status or relationships.

tation. Those who saw themselves engaging in "mental labor" often identified with management and capital and saw workers as adversaries. Others saw themselves as part of a state apparatus or political movement that transcended class considerations and served the interests of all. Still others simply identified with other wage earners.

Given their structural fragmentation, petit bourgeois elements lacked a "natural" setting in which to come together. Accordingly, they were influenced by a variety of ideological and political currents, thereby further dividing their ranks. While many were drawn to "progressive" ideas because of their education or cultural activities, most also feared the challenge to their social status and living standards posed by the emergence of the "masses." Hence they found it difficult to continue supporting initially attractive reform programs once the reality of popular mobilization and its potential costs were made clear.

THE WORKING CLASS

The largest and most fragmented of Chile's social forces was its working class. While for years the Chilean labor movement was one of Latin America's strongest and most militant groups,[18] it was hampered by the high percentage (55 percent) of industrial firms that employed fewer than twenty-five workers, making them ineligible for organization.[19] Another inhibiting factor was the very slow rate of growth in industrial employment in the manufacturing sector during the postwar period. The perennial presence of a "reserve army" of unemployed workers made organizing difficult and militance hazardous (de Vylder 1976, 11).

The most telling weakness of Chile's working class, however, was its fragmentation, a consequence of both economic structure and conscious government policy. The Chilean working class included sales, clerical, industrial, independent, and domestic workers, few of whom were directly involved in production as such. Most were engaged in the organization of production (white collar workers), in clerical or service activities, or as independent

[18] In 1969 the central labor confederation (the Central Unica de Trabajadores, or CUT) was credited with bringing together roughly 20 percent of the country's 2.6 million urban and rural workers. The actual figure was probably closer to 30 percent (Angell 1972, 43-45) and within the industrial sector included between 70 percent and 80 percent of those eligible for unionization.

[19] According to the Chilean labor code, only those work forces of more than twenty-five workers were eligible for unionization (see Angell 1972, 50).

tradesmen. Moreover, the legal distinction between white collar (*empleados*) and blue collar (*obreros*) workers affected their wages, fringe benefits, and social status.

Among blue collar workers one must further distinguish between industrial, independent, and domestic workers. Industrial workers were largely production workers employed in larger factories (of more than 25 workers) under conventional work conditions and discipline. While some of the roughly 600,000 workers in this category possessed specific skills and were not easy to replace most were either minimally skilled production workers or unskilled laborers. Labor organizing efforts had focused on the skilled and minimally skilled who worked in foreign or monopolistic industries such as cement, paper, copper, beverages, cigarettes, motor vehicles and motor vehicle parts, and in textiles and construction. Some 220,000 of these workers were unionized, with the minimally skilled thereby afforded a degree of job security they would not otherwise have enjoyed. Not surprisingly, they were also the most successful in pressing for improved wages and working conditions. Their earnings were often twice, and in some cases five and ten times, those of the average industrial worker.

Most of these industrial workers along with the 200,000 independent workers and 300,000 domestic workers constituted a relatively silent majority of the work force. Among the unskilled and weakly or nonunionized workers were construction laborers, small shop workers, store and restaurant employees, and small- and intermediate-sized mine workers. Their lack of skills and the insolvency or instability of the firms and areas in which they worked made them vulnerable to dismissal and replacement, skeptical of their class potential, and willing to endure difficult work conditions and low wages. Under the right combination of economic prosperity and government encouragement or tolerance they could be mobilized in support of bread-and-butter and broader political demands. It was typical, however, that their enthusiasm and determination waned in the face of resistance, and they remained submissive and relatively unexpectant.

Independent workers included plumbers, carpenters, electricians, gas appliance repairmen, and other tradesmen who were either self-employed or worked for private contracting firms, effectively functioning on their own. Although some earned decent money, most did not, and virtually all had to put up with both uncertainty and seasonality. Working alone and largely free of

27

supervision, independent workers were less likely to identify with other workers. Domestic workers (house maids, gardeners, man-servants, and maintenance employees in both the public and private sectors), on the other hand, were more likely to identify with the ideas and/or interests of their employers.

White collar workers further complicated this already fragmented mixture. They included both "privileged" and "undifferentiated" subgroups (Urdemales 1970, 56-66). Some privileged *empleados* were actually skilled blue collar workers given employee status in earlier negotiations with management. Others (some 200,000) held intermediate positions in public and private institutions and were really members of the petite bourgeoisie. Their wages were good by Chilean standards and their fringe benefits (pensions, family allowances, job security, etc.) even better. Many were involved in the administration of policies and regulations of interest to politicians and businessmen and were frequently objects of their attention and considerations. In fact, some held their positions because of party loyalties or ties, displacing those appointed under previous administrations. The latter would retain their positions and salaries but were excluded from politically sensitive projects and decisions. In either case, an *empleado*'s concern was with keeping his or her position and thus remaining loyal to the party and not to other workers.

Undifferentiated white collar workers, including clerks, sales-persons, and lower-level administrative and clerical workers, were more numerous and much less comfortably situated. They had decent educational backgrounds, but their tasks required little or no skill and could easily be performed by others. Harboring conflicting feelings of ambition (*arribismo*) and resentment (Urdemales 1970, 65), they often earned less and had a lower standard of living than blue collar workers, whom they both disdained and feared.

White collar workers were encouraged to see themselves as "intellectual" or mental, not "manual," workers with interests and prospects different from others in their firm or agency. Most belonged to white collar "craft" as opposed to "plant" unions, although some (in small private sector firms) joined both blue collar and management personnel in broad, though usually weaker, company associations.

Chilean workers were thus numerous and to some extent organized but hardly a "class" in either situational or consciousness terms. Only the industrial production workers constituted a potential "proletariat"; and only about 220,000 of these actually worked in the larger establishments likely to breed working-class consciousness and solidarity. The rest of the country's blue and white collar workers labored in very different capacities, under different conditions, and with very different senses of themselves and their interests.

THE MARGINAL CLASS

This group consisted of unemployed or irregularly employed people, many of whom were relatively recent arrivals from the countryside. Living on the margin or fringes of the national economy and society, they were exposed to, though not a part of, the money economy. Some had never worked, and those who had worked did so only periodically and usually in the vast "informal" sector as sidewalk or street vendors, porters, handymen, and general laborers. Many worked fifty to sixty hours a week for less than minimum wages and lacked the social standing, identity, and organizational experience that came with regular employment. In fact, if they had a social identity at all, it was likely the product of neighborhood associations and relationships that included industrial workers, lower-level public sector employees, and even small businessmen.

Since 1958 the marginal population had become an important political constituency and was courted by diverse candidates and movements, including Christian Democracy. At first glance it seemed an ideal support base. Its needs and wants were largely material and relatively modest, i.e., jobs, running water, electricity, health services, and minimal housing accommodations. Its members seemed far more interested in entering society than in transforming it. Presumably their demands could be met and their support retained with little effort and without jeopardizing other objectives or commitments.

THE PEASANTRY

The final social force to be considered is the peasantry, whose support and forebearance was crucial in any agrarian reform effort. Here again, the dominant characteristic was diversity. According to the Inter-American Committee for Agricultural Development (CIDA), eight distinct subgroups made up Chile's rural social structure in the 1960s (see Table 1-2).

Those comprising these various subgroups had different relationships to the land and would view agrarian reform and its

29

TABLE 1-2
Rural Population by Subgroup, 1960s

latifundistas (large landowners)	2%
rich peasants	7
middle peasants	21
minifundistas (small plot holders)	20
foremen and custodians	7
inquilinos (workers living on farms)	12
medeiros (sharecroppers)	4
afuerinos (migratory workers)	27

SOURCE: Steeland 1974, 132-133.

attendant phenomena in varied lights. *Latifundistas*, for example, were obviously one, albeit not the lone, privileged stratum. Foremen and custodians, rich peasants (who employed wage laborers on medium-sized pieces of land), and middle peasants all had a considerable stake in the existing social order and would be socially and economically threatened by almost any redistributive agrarian reform. On the other hand, as far as the "underprivileged" majority (comprising 63 percent of the rural population) was concerned, there was insufficient land to meet either its needs or its expectations. Difficult and divisive decisions would have to be made regarding the form of tenure to be established (e.g., individual, cooperative, or collective ownership and management) and the groups to be given land. Many would simply not get the land they hoped for, and disappointment, frustration, and hostility were virtually inevitable.

The structural diversity of the Chilean economy was thus an obstacle to class formation and development during this period. Workers found themselves in different "class situations," as did petit bourgeois elements. Only the bourgeoisie had a sense of itself as a class, and even it remained dependent on the state and lacking in both dynamism and confidence. There was thus little structural or material basis from which a sense of common experience, interest, or objective could emerge among large numbers of people. These material relationships were further affected, however, by political, ideological, and cultural factors. In some instances they cut across formal class lines, effectively redefining productive relationships. In others they affected consciousness of those relationships and their implications. In either event they placed additional barriers between those holding the same occupational position.

Chilean Politics

The institutions, practices, and dynamics of Chilean politics were the structures within which class struggle took place and by which its outcome was partially determined.[20] The more important of these included the formal and effective divisions of power between branches of government, the nature and role of the Chilean state, and the roles of electoral politics and public opinion.

Prior to the 1950s Chilean politics had been the purview of bourgeois and petit bourgeois groups, with only modest participation by the industrial working class. Unorganized workers, marginals, and peasants were effectively excluded, thereby contributing to the system's remarkable consensus and stability.

Beginning in the 1950s, however, forces were set in motion which would challenge that consensus and stability. These included a period of sustained economic stagnation following on the Korean War boom, the rapid expansion of the urban population, the tripling in less than twelve years of the national electorate, the increased power of organized labor, the arousal of the peasantry, and the intensification of inflationary and other social pressures.

These developments aroused and strengthened those groups demanding greater well-being and a broadening and restructuring of the system. The pressures proved excessive for both the Ibáñez (1952-1958) and Alessandri (1958-1964) governments and fueled a radicalization of Chilean politics of which first Frei and then Allende were beneficiaries.

During the period, party strengths and loyalties remained remarkably constant. Of the country's six largest parties in the mid-1960s all but the Christian Democrats had been major political forces since the 1930s. Further, the same basic distribution of power and support had prevailed among them in all but one or two elections. Until 1965, in fact, no party had ever polled more than 25 percent of the vote in a congressional election, and except for the Socialists in 1947 and 1953, none had fallen below 10 percent. Over the years, tripartite division characterized the party system. The left and right wings, despite occasional oscillations, maintained their core constituencies, although the right did lose some working-class and petit bourgeois followers.

On the left were the Marxist-Leninist Communist and Social-

---

[20] See Brenner (1976) cited in Meiksins Wood (1981, 79).

31

ist parties, each of which claimed to be a working-class political force. This was truer of the Communists, whose constituency and leadership were predominantly from that sector. The Communists were also the more organizationally solid of the two. While the Socialists tended to be a loosely knit, electorally oriented alliance of left-wing notables, Communist party members and supporters were integrated into party structures at factory and neighborhood levels and were deeply involved in the party's work, familiar with its positions, and responsive to its leadership.

The Socialists had both blue collar support and a substantial following among white collar workers and the petite bourgeoisie, from which most of their leaders were drawn. In the late 1950s they adopted a more aggressively revolutionary line, while the Communists grew more conciliatory, expressing a willingness to work with bourgeois and petit bourgeois forces on common "intermediate" goals. To the left of the Socialists was the Movimiento de Izquierda Revolucionaria (MIR). It was composed of former young Radicals and Socialists whose largely university student followers fancied themselves the conscience of the left. The MIR would be an important destabilizing force under both the Frei and Allende governments.

On the right were the Partido Nacional, a 1965 fusion of the old Liberal and Conservative parties, and the Democratic Radicals, a splinter group of conservative ex-Radicals unhappy with that party's leftward drift in recent years. Although it had declined as the size of the electorate expanded, the right's support was still broad, encompassing peasants, marginals, some blue collar and white collar workers, petit bourgeois elements, and leading sectors of the agricultural and urban bourgeoisies. Much of its strength among "popular" circles was a function of the charismatic appeal of local and national personalities.

Between the left and right was the volatile political center, where party and personal fortunes had fluctuated since the 1930s. The rise of Frei and the Christian Democrats in the late 1950s and early 1960s was but the most recent instance of this phenomenon. In 1952, following fourteen years of Radical-led coalitions, middle and popular sector groups rallied around former military strongman Carlos Ibáñez, forming several mass-based but short-lived *ibañista* parties. The same forces helped rightist Jorge Alessandri gain a winning plurality in 1958. In each case the political conquests were short-lived and never consolidated. Enthusiastic supporters quickly became disenchanted with the new government, and their efforts to find someone or something else on which to place their hopes set up the 1964 election that brought the Christian Democrats to power.

These political structures were among the agencies available for awakening and channeling class-based interests. Although at odds on many issues, most of the country's agricultural, industrial, and financial bourgeoisie identified with the traditionally conservative Partido Nacional. For them, the neocapitalist reformism of Christian Democracy was but the first step on the road to certain ruin. Only an isolated minority saw it as an enlightened strategy for strengthening both themselves and the system on which their interests and privileges depended. And its numbers would dwindle with time.

Petit bourgeois elements were a more unstable and fragmented force. While sharing a common concern for their social status and influence, they were drawn to diverse ideological and partisan political orientations. Independent professionals were more likely to favor traditionally conservative parties, although the Christian Democratic and leftist parties drew some support from them as well. Among public sector professionals, many engineers, administrators, economists, and other *técnicos* were drawn to the PDC during the 1950s and 1960s and became a major force within the bureaucracy during the Frei years. While the *técnicos* of previous administrations had been willing to accommodate the powers that were, the Christian Democrats appointed under Frei were determined to pursue their own not always consistent visions and goals and to resist the blandishments offered by interested parties.

The vast majority of Chilean workers were not revolutionaries. They were primarily concerned with wage and cost-of-living issues, although the governments to which they addressed their demands were usually rightist and as a result made them appear to be more radical than they actually were. Their gains over the years had been the fruit of arduous struggle, effective organization, and good leadership, coming despite generally adverse economic and social conditions and a host of restrictions and restraints that inhibited organizing efforts. Because of the workers' vulnerabilities and the difficulty of predicting political trends and relationships their leaders devoted most of their attention to their own immediate interests. Occasional militance and rhetorical flourishes notwithstanding they did little on behalf of the less skilled and more vulnerable workers in other sectors.

Partisan ties and sentiments were decisive factors in the labor movement at all levels. In fact, most labor organizations were led by loyalists operating under general instructions from party superiors, and questions of party rivalry and interests frequently arose between workers affiliated with the Socialist and Communist parties, and between these workers and those affiliated with Christian Democracy. Their skepticism regarding one another's motives and long-term objectives ran deep, often reducing commonality of interest to a very narrow range of general issues.

Most blue and white collar workers were allied with the Socialist and Communist parties. However, the Christian Democrats constituted a third up-and-coming force, particularly among white collar employees and blue collar workers whose plants or shops were previously unorganized. Undifferentiated white collar workers (clerks, shop attendants, etc.), in turn, were drawn to parties and candidacies projecting a strong populist image. Whether the populism was of a radical or conservative character did not seem to matter. But their attachment was not likely to endure hard times or failed promises either.

Also notoriously fickle were the *marginados*. Their lack of social identity and organization made their support easy to obtain but difficult to use effectively and even easier to lose. In practice, they were not easy to please or to continue pleasing. Though not of society they lived in it and experienced the frustration of exposure to the prosperity enjoyed by others. The crowded huts and neighborhoods in which they lived threw them into close contact with one another. Their frustration and denial were experienced collectively, if not as a class at least as a whole whose members shared and reenforced one another's attitudes and anxieties. The possibility of losing their support and incurring their wrath was substantial.

In terms of constitutional prerogatives Chile was clearly a strong presidential regime. The president's broad decree-making and legislative powers made him the most powerful political figure in the country and the principal source of policy initiatives. The presidency was thus an objective around which political forces could be rallied, as its capture meant access to the substantial resources and jurisdictions of the Chilean state.

The presidential office was by no means an unchallenged power, however. The constitution of 1925 had intended to do away with the parliamentarism introduced in 1891, but vestiges survived in the form of the politically independent Supreme Court and contraloría, a system of "disproportionate representation" that favored numerically small but economically powerful rural interests while further fragmenting "popular" forces, and the appropriation and censure powers of the legislature itself. Traditionally, in fact, because of their lack of majority support in the legislature no twentieth-century Chilean government had succeeded in carrying out the program on which it had been elected. All were forced to make concessions and agree to modifications in order to "govern" at all.

Also of importance to the course and outcome of class struggle were the restrictive features of the labor code, the quasi-absolute character of private property rights prior to the reforms of the mid-1960s and early 1970s, and the active involvement of the state in productive activities, in important resource allocation decisions, and in the setting of wage and price levels (Gil 1966, 92-106).

The extensive economic resources and jurisdiction of the Chilean state made it an object of expectation and reliance for all social and economic forces. It financed a great deal of the new investment, controlled the allocation of credit, and virtually determined wage and price levels, thus playing a major role in the accumulation process. As a result, it was more likely to be the direct object of working-class resentment and resistance than in more advanced capitalist countries in which the functions of production and accumulation were taken care of in the relatively decentralized private sector.[21]

The Chilean state also appeared to be less neutral than more developed capitalist states, although it may well have been more so. It was linked in various ways to powerful economic groups, but these often offset one another or were balanced by countervailing political forces. Public sector jobs were among the rewards awaiting winning coalitions and their supporters. Normally, however, these were permanent civil service posts, and new appointees had to share space and influence with their coalition partners and holdovers from previous periods. As a result, the bureaucracy harbored groups of varied persuasions and loyalties, no one of which could fully capture or appropriate it. An object and arena of struggle, its considerable powers were seldom

[21] Under such circumstances the state was more likely to be(come) the principal antagonist of working-class organizations than either capital or management (see Meiksins Wood 1981, 93).

used in a concerted or consistent manner. Administrative reform, coupled with more purposeful and coherent coalitions, might have allowed for greater executive control but would have eliminated an important source of patronage for all political forces and would have been met with fierce resistance.

A final feature of Chilean politics was the frequency and importance of elections, which provided indications of the support enjoyed by the various political parties and were a major bargaining point in their discussions and negotiations. The stronger a party's electoral base, the better was its bargaining position with both rivals and allies. In some instances elections were extremely helpful in clarifying such matters, but in others they needlessly obstructed and poisoned developing political relations. Representatives to the Chamber of Deputies were chosen every four years, as was roughly half the membership of the Senate. In addition, nationwide municipal elections were also held every four years (between congressional elections), and vacancies occurring in either legislative house would be filled through the holding of by-elections at the earliest possible convenience. In any given year there might be as many as three or four elections of a regular, extraordinary, or strictly local character. But whatever their nature, they were seized upon and converted into national plebiscites. Political forces were encouraged to think almost constantly in terms of their differences and relative standings vis-à-vis one another. Those engaged in sensitive rapprochement or dialogue had to break off such talks and take up adversarial style electioneering in order to preserve or improve their standing in the political arena.

Ideology

In addition to these institutions and practices Chileans were exposed to and conditioned by a variety of ideological perspectives. Ideologies are ways of looking at social reality. They help to define the interests, relationships, and political options of those embracing them. They also aid in defining productive relationships and can stifle or stimulate solidarity among persons sharing a "class situation" by preventing them from seeing their common interests or pointing to ways of serving those interests so diverse as to effectively redefine them. One's ideology is not something apart from class interest, something that is worn down as it asserts or imposes itself. It is rather the viewpoint from

36

which that interest is experienced and understood and is thus a constitutive element of it.

Ideological struggle is thus not only part of class struggle it is a factor on which the outcome of class struggle depends. In Chile a number of ideological currents competed with one another. They were "products" of cultural, socioeconomic, and political forces that had certain needs and potential for stimulus. Among such forces were the country's long-standing economic stagnation and popular desires for increased political participation, social well-being, and general mobility. Each of Chile's major ideological tendencies endured because it was able to orient, legitimate, and promote the interests of important class and social forces.

One such tendency was populism.[22] Although useful in countering class-based appeals, populism exerted a hold on leaders and followers all along the ideological spectrum, coexisting with and diluting their formal tenets and convictions. Central to it was the notion of an undifferentiated "people," an amalgam of virtuous, hard-working but underrewarded social forces whose needs were both legitimate and reconcilable. For the populist the resolution of social problems was less a matter of changing structures or choosing between interests than of governing more responsively and determinedly, of getting the system to produce more and distribute more rationally and equitably. Whatever redistribution was necessary would be at the expense of a small, inefficient, and corrupt minority, not the hard-working, conscientious, or patriotic entrepreneur. In Chile these populist currents penetrated the Marxist, social Christian, and traditional conservative traditions. Although occasionally in conflict, in most instances they generated a diluted "populist" version of each.

Chilean Marxism had arisen with the labor-organizing efforts in northern nitrate and copper mines in the 1910s and 1920s, spreading to the country's urban areas with the growth of industry during the 1930s. From the beginning it stressed class struggle, defense of working-class interests (wages and working conditions), and militant antiimperialism. Beyond these basics, however, its content depended on party affiliation. Communist, Socialist, and Popular Socialist party members proclaimed dif-

---

[22] Di Tella (1965, 43) has defined populism as "a political movement which enjoys support of the masses of the urban working class and/or peasantry, but which does not result from the autonomous organizational power of either of these two sectors, and which is also supported by non-working class sectors opposed in some sense to the status quo."

ferent strains of Marxism and Marxism-Leninism at various times. Within the 1950s alone the Socialist party flirted with Titoism, Maoism, and Social Democracy. Communists, on the other hand, particularly copper and coal miners and industrial production workers, tended to be stolid Marxist-Leninists.

Despite these distinctions, the Marxism of most Chilean workers was heavily populist in both tone and content. However Marxist-Leninist their leaders, most rank-and-file Communists and Socialists viewed themselves as part of a relatively undifferentiated people, or *pueblo*. Although impatient with workers of differing ideological views, they thought less of crushing class foes or changing structures than of winning wage and other concessions from their employers (Landsberger, Barrera, and Toro 1967; Portes 1971). They assumed that current economic and administrative resources were more than adequate and needed only to be reorganized in order to produce or function more equitably and more efficiently. The *pueblo* itself lacked only a leader genuinely committed to its liberation and possessed of the political skills needed to achieve it.

Social Christianity offered an even more congenial home for populist sentiments. Emerging in the late 1920s and early 1930s, it drew on the social encyclicals of Popes Leo XIII and Pius XI and the efforts of European-educated priests active among university students and working people. Although calling for new social and economic structures, social Christianity insisted that existing class distinctions could be "transcended" and the rights of both capital and labor respected. It also stressed the sufficiency of moral suasion (as opposed to coercion) in the transition to new structures and argued that technological innovation and superior organization would lead to abundance and would make choosing between classes and groups unnecessary.

Chilean social Christianity was closely identified with the Falange Nacional and Christian Democratic party but was also embraced by independents and by segments of the old Conservative party. It enjoyed a broad following in petit bourgeois, white collar, and some blue collar circles and among women beginning to participate politically for the first time during the 1950s and 1960s.

Traditional conservatism, which posited an unequal distribution of responsibilities and rewards within any well-ordered and prosperous society, offered a third outlet for populist instincts and sentiments. Though rarely practicing or fulfilling what they preached, Chilean conservatives were staunch defenders of the free market and trickle-down economics. Popular well-being would be a by-product of economic growth, which in turn required a climate conducive to private initiative and investment, i.e., ample public credit, low wages, free-floating or subsidized prices, tax breaks, etc.

These various sentiments and convictions exerted an important influence in the country's board rooms, offices, and work places. They gave their adherents a sense of their experiences, their social relationships, and their political options. At the same time they also encouraged skepticism and hostility toward competing groups and tendencies, literally creating antagonisms and inhibiting solidarity among those in similar circumstances.

Chilean Culture

A country's political culture is at once a reflection, a medium of expression, and a conditioning factor of its class structure. Cultural values and attitudes are by-products of social experience and of efforts to rationalize or legitimate that experience. Those that endure or prevail are usually formed and conveyed through institutions dominated by leading or ruling classes. These institutions defend ruling-class interests and thus reflect and help to perpetuate existing class relationships. At certain junctures, however, values and attitudes can escape the pull of a ruling class or classes. Preserved by other institutions (the Church, parties, etc.), they can suddenly "catch on," be put to critical use, and challenge existing structures and relationships.

During the 1960s and 1970s, Chilean culture affected class consciousness and development directly and through ideological and political phenomena. It both reflected and cut across class distinctions and relationships. Chilean conceptions of authority, leadership, personal and social ties, appropriate social goals, etc., were those of a predominantly Catholic patrimonial society (Dealy 1977, 4-32). Chileans were imbued with a nominalist notion of authority and social obligation, one in which a law's compulsory character stemmed from its author's status and the threat of sanction, not its inherent reasonability or propriety. Such a notion colored the experience and relationships of most Chilean workers, marginals, and peasants, placing a premium on obtaining concessions, special arrangements, and mercy or sufferance from people in high places.

Paternalism and *caudillismo* were also deeply rooted in Chile, despite the country's reputed ideological and political sophistication.[23] They permeated social and political life at all levels and at all points along the political spectrum. Most social and political movements, whatever their class composition or ideological orientation, revolved around powerful, charismatic leaders, who were relied on more for their will and guile than for the content of their programs or their political capabilities or constancies. In effect, these movements brought together relatively passive retainers looking to leaders who had their interests at heart and who somehow would reconcile, promote, and defend them. For their members political struggle consisted in placing the right leader in power, not in supporting or working with him or in carrying out projects for which they were also responsible (Stephens 1957). Among other consequences this made it difficult for Chilean workers to see themselves as a self-reliant or potentially self-liberating force, whether they worked in small workshops alongside their employers or in large, impersonally structured factories.

However situated on the political spectrum, Chileans were also imbued with corporatist sentiments and inclinations. They were inclined to link their identities and fulfillment with membership in associational groups such as universities, guilds, ethnic clubs, churches, and industrial or commercial firms. These were seen and valued as both outlets for sociability and mechanisms for representing needs and interests within the political process.[24]

The corporatist spirit was also reflected in an attachment to harmony, hierarchy, the "common good," and the moral agency of the state. These had been cornerstone values in Thomistic social and political philosophy and have retained a strong appeal in almost all Hispanic and broader Catholic cultural circles. In

[23] See Stephens (1957) for a study of the Ibáñez government (1952 to 1958) that emphasizes the tendency of Chileans to rely on the paternal instincts and power of an authority figure to resolve personal and social problems. See also Dealy (1977) who focuses at length on the phenomenon of *caudillismo*.

[24] See Stepan (1978, 48-52). In corporatism the state gives representational status to groups in exchange for their acceptance of constraints conducive to, or required by, the good of the larger social whole. Distinct class and other components within corporations are to work with, and not against, one another. They are to avoid defining their interests narrowly or conflictually and to give greater weight to the common stake they share together. And, finally, they are to keep their corporate interests in proper relationship to the more urgent or higher priority interests of other sectors or of the nation as a whole.

Chile they permeated traditional conservative and Christian Democratic movements, melding with both hierarchical and liberal democratic political traditions. They also gave rise to full-fledged corporatist tendencies. Whatever the movement, stress was placed on the use of official channels and structures of representation, the illegitimacy of "narrow" or sectarian demands, and the obligations as well as rights of citizenship. In each, moreover, partial or private interests were to be subordinated to those of larger functional associations and society as a whole.

Mention should also be made of the "revindicationist" tendencies of Chilean workers, including those identifying with the Marxist left. Over the years organizations of all levels and ideological persuasions found wage demands an effective basis on which to appeal for support. Because the governments with which the labor movement struggled were of the right and center-right and because its leaders generally couched their appeals in radical tones and terms, the movement's narrow, short-term, and self-interested character generally escaped attention, although it continued to blunt impact and revolutionary potential.[25]

Summary

The effect of these political, ideological, and cultural features of Chilean life during the 1960s and 1970s was to further fragment the country's social forces. In some instances groups with similar class situations and material interests defined one another as antagonists and not allies. In others differences in both class interests and levels of consciousness were lost amidst the common endorsement of a leader or a set of party slogans or symbols. As structures through which class identity and interests were awakened and at least partially channelled, political institutions and organizations thus conditioned class interests and helped to determine what was made of them.

During the 1960s and 1970s, material class situations were not a consistently decisive factor among either Chileans generally or Christian Democrats in particular. In fact, the absence of any significant patterns along class lines among Christian Democrats suggests the greater importance of partisan political, sociopsychological, and cultural forces. As the party developed, it

[25] Two notable exceptions are Landsberger, Barrera, and Toro (1967) and Portes (1971).

drew to its ranks progressive and maverick entrepreneurs, blue and white collar workers, professionals, merchants and small businessmen, peasant proprietors, agricultural laborers, and slum-dwelling marginals. In later years, even as its fortunes declined and the country's social and political forces polarized, it retained its broad base and its working-class support in particular.

These forces were conditioned by their respective class situations. The individuals within them often worked alone or in enclaves that were set apart physically from others in similar situations. The blue collar recruits included as large a proportion of skilled (as opposed to unskilled) workers as did the more militant Marxist workers, although fewer belonged to plant or craft unions or had previous political experience. Whether alone or with others, moreover, these new recruits were closely identified with the party's positions, personalities, and meteoric political rise, all of which divided them from their fellow workers, employees, and/or students. This was particularly apparent among industrial production workers, where ideological and political forces were at work from very early on, forming and fueling antagonisms that would block the development of working-class consciousness and solidarity. In some instances political and ideological concerns merely precluded workers from seeing or accepting the implications of their common class situation and interests; in others they altered their very class situations, in effect displacing conventional relations of exploitation with politically and/or ideologically rooted antagonisms toward one another.

Because of this formative influence, politics and ideology play a central role in the following analysis. The ensuing chapters deal successively with the party's early development, its years in power under Eduardo Frei, and its subsequent opposition to the Popular Unity and military junta governments. In each, strictly "class-based" and institutional analyses will be challenged. In each, the interdependence of class, cultural, ideological, and political factors will be stressed. In each, finally, an attempt is made to capture the complex character of Chilean politics and Christian Democracy more generally.

CHRISTIAN DEMOCRACY PRIOR TO 1964

During the late 1950s and early 1960s, the PDC experienced spectacular growth, drawing former Liberals, Conservatives, and Radicals, one-time followers of former President Carlos Ibáñez, and a high percentage of first-time voters[1] to its ranks. Between 1957 and 1964 the party increased its membership and broader public following more than fivefold. Once confined to professionals, white collar workers, and small businessmen, its social base expanded to include women, blue collar workers, slum-dwelling marginals, and peasants. By 1963 it was the country's largest single political grouping.

This expansion helped to create widespread optimism and expectation regarding the incoming Frei government. It also placed considerable strain on the party's organizational and ideological cohesion, however. Newer arrivals were more interested in Frei's personal qualities, in a piece of the growth and prosperity he promised, and/or in a more viable alternative to (i.e., defense against) the Marxist left (the Frente de Acción Popular, or FRAP) than in the PDC or its ideal "communitarian" society. Their incorporation had a conservative effect on the movement as a whole, diluted the reformist thrust of Frei's 1964 campaign, and exacerbated the party's developing ideological crisis. In fact, as it prepared to assume power, Christian Democracy was less a unified party than an amorphous electoral coalition whose diverse ideological and policy orientations would affect its fate as a governing force.

The Beginnings

Christian Democracy played a distinctively minor role in Chilean politics until the late 1950s. During the 1930s, 1940s, and early 1950s, it offered itself as an alternative to the traditional left and right but failed to win many converts from the estab-

[1] The Chilean electorate more than tripled in size between the years 1952 and 1964, expanding from 907,351 to 2,917,121. A disproportionately large number of the new voters were women, who were first permitted to vote in 1949. Their incidence in the electorate rose steadily thereafter, surpassing male voters for the first time in 1964.

lished parties. Its following oscillated between 2 and 4 percent of the electorate and was largely confined to petit bourgeois and white collar circles, from which its leaders came as well.

The origins of the movement can be traced to the early 1950s to a group of Catholic university students that included Frei, Radomiro Tómic, Bernardo Leighton, Rafael Agustín Gumucio, and Manuel Garretón. Like their counterparts in Europe, these young petit bourgeois Catholics were attracted by recent developments in Catholic social thinking. The encyclicals of Popes Leo XIII and Pius XI and the writings of Jacques Maritain and others provided progressively oriented Catholics with encouragement and legitimation. Greater importance was given to the temporal order and to efforts to remake it. Notions of fatalism and other-worldliness were set aside, and Catholics were encouraged to involve themselves politically in defense of the common good. Many young Chilean Catholics were drawn to these new currents and to the many study groups and social action projects that they inspired.

Despite the skepticism, if not hostility, of the Chilean Catholic bishops, individual Jesuit and secular priests were instrumental in awakening student interest in these new trends. Fathers Francisco Vives and Jorge Fernández Pradel, who had been exposed to social Christianity while studying in Europe, became active in youth circles upon returning to Chile, fostering an interest in Catholic social teaching and its application to national problems. Their recruits, most of whom were university students, were members of such organizations as the Asociación Nacional de Estudiantes Católicos (ANEC), Acción Católica, the Círculo de Estudios, and the Liga Social.[2]

Most of the students shied away from political involvement, however. They viewed Chile's existing parties as sterile and opportunistic and many were suspicious of politics as such. They were drawn into the political arena by their opposition to the dictatorial Ibáñez government, but after aiding and abetting its

[2] The Liga Social sponsored seminars and research projects that focused on social problems and organized assistance projects directed at the poor. The ANEC, on the other hand, arranged for the publication (in Spanish) and circulation of Pius XI's encyclical *Quadragessimo Anno* and further succeeded in obtaining a Vatican pronouncement to the effect that no single Catholic party could claim to represent the Church and its teaching, thus challenging Conservative party pretensions in this regard. See Silva Bascuñán 1949, 15-23; Grayson 1968a, 88-90 and 99-104; and Larson 1967.

overthrow, they resumed their apolitical stance, refusing to endorse or affiliate with any group.

Their abstention from politics ended in 1934 when the young social Christians joined the youth sector of the Conservative party. The Partido Conservador was the political home of the country's agricultural and urban bourgeoisies, together with their peasant, working-class, and marginal clients. A highly traditionalist Catholic party, its spokesmen were visibly uncomfortable with the new social Christian ideas, viewing efforts to eliminate poverty and injustice as defiant of divine will and wrath.[3]

Nonetheless, the students believed the party to be the most appropriate available vehicle for the achievement of their goals. First, it was a solid, well-financed party, commanding the loyalty of most politically active Catholics. This augured poorly for the building of a rival Catholic formation but not badly for those willing to work within its ranks. Second, despite their backwardness on social issues, Conservatives stood for things to which the students were also committed: the principles of law, order, and hierarchy, the preservation of a constitutional political order, and defense of the prerogatives and interests of the Church.[4] Finally, Conservatism's nominal beholdenness to papal authority and Catholic social teaching provided a platform and a justification for pressing their reformist views from within.[5]

The future Christian Democrats joined the Partido Conservador indirectly, constituting its new youth branch, the Juventud Conservadora. Almost immediately they issued an eighteen point declaration of principles in which they stressed the interdependence of freedom, social justice, and what was termed "natural" hierarchy. They also called for an "ethical and dynamic politics which would assure appropriate decisions without denying es-

[3] Conservative party leaders not only objected to the content of the so-called "social" encyclicals but for a time successfully prevented their publication and circulation within the country (Silva Bascuñán 1949, 10-21).

[4] Among these were religious education, clerical immunity, and the indissolubility of marriage. A Conservative leader who explicitly appealed to the youths in the name of Christian values was Rafael Luís Gumucio, whose son, Rafael Agustín, was an active member of the group. The elder Gumucio wrote a pamphlet, *El Deber Político*, in which he argued that Conservatism was the only viable defense against an allegedly imminent renewal of militant anticlericalism.

[5] Few Conservatives were willing to repudiate papal authority or general Christian principles, and some were trying to push the party in a more progressive direction. See, for example, Palacios 1932.

45

sential rights and freedoms" and proposed corporatist economic institutions as a means of overcoming the conflict between capital and labor (*Lircay* 1935b, 1).

The declaration reflected a concern for both individual and societal values. Like Catholic groups elsewhere during the 1930s, Chilean social Christians opposed right- and left-wing perspectives as one-dimensional. The right's lack of social consciousness left it indifferent to the welfare of others, while the left's class-based politics, its encouragement of conflict, and its advocacy of a state-controlled economy gave undue primacy to historical and societal forces at the expense of the individual. According to the young Christian Democrats, the legitimate claims and interests of all were fully compatible. Profound social changes were possible without compromising individual rights and liberties. The common good was consistent with individual interests and freedoms as long as "certain adjustments" were made and the freedoms "rightly exercised" (*Lircay* 1935a, 1).

How this would be accomplished was left unclear both in this initial declaration and for much of Christian Democracy's early period. Its leaders spoke of "jan organic democracy" that would be authoritative and yet respectful of personal freedom (*Lircay* 1938b, 1-2; and 1938c, 3), and until the mid-1940s they clung to the notion of a corporatist economy. But these positions were more abstract expressions of what one hoped to achieve than strategies or proposals for immediate action. In this sense the Christian Democratic "alternative" remained an aspirational, if not rhetorical, set of goals with various interpretations and a variety of implications for practice.

Despite their imprecision, however, the young Christian Democrats held progressive positions on many issues. Largely because of this, they were perpetually at odds with Conservative leaders and were forced to abandon the party in 1938. One source of conflict was the Juventud's critique of capitalism, which was seen as "tyrannical," as "responsible for existing poverty and misery," and "an institutionalized form of the materialistic individualism vigorously condemned by the encyclicals" (*Lircay* 1936, 1). In fact, it was capitalism's inability or unwillingness to restrain the pursuit of individual self-interest, not the regime of capital as such, with which most young Christian Democrats took issue (*Lircay* 1938b, 1-2; and 1938c, 1). But such distinctions were lost on Conservative elders, whose land and commercial interests gave them an abiding stake in the status quo.

A similar conflict developed with respect to communism. The young Christian Democrats were adamantly opposed to Marxist values, political methods, and social analysis but viewed the Communist party's critique of existing socioeconomic conditions as essentially valid. Indeed, the Juventud saw frank recognition and resolution of these problems as essential if the communist threat were to be effectively met, a view that to most Conservatives amounted to consorting with the enemy.

Party-youth relations were further strained with the emergence in 1936 of the Falange Nacional, an organization through which the Juventud hoped to enhance its independent identity. It did just that. Within a year of its founding, Manuel Garretón ran and was elected to the Chamber of Deputies as a *falangista*, Bernardo Leighton was named minister of labor by President Arturo Alessandri, and six Conservative party deputies declared their formal allegiance to the new organization.

The Falange Nacional was no conventional political formation. Its more zealous members wore military style uniforms and engaged in fitness and paramilitary training activities "not only to make our internal hierarchy and discipline more efficient, but also to prepare them to serve the country were any event to require it" (*Lircay* 1937a, 4).

Its emergence was a concession to the growing appeal of fascist ideas and trappings at the time. During the 1930s, political struggle moved to the streets, frequently ending in brawls between opposing groups. Several of the country's political parties had paramilitary units, and the government itself maintained a "political" militia in addition to the regular military and national police forces. The Falange's martial tone and trappings helped to attract recruits who otherwise might have gone elsewhere, although most party members appear to have been either mildly amused or embarrassed by these fascist overtones. For their part party spokesmen stressed that the corporatist notions to which the Falange was committed were democratic and pluralist in character and emphatically condemned the doctrines and movements associated with Hitler, Mussolini, and Franco.[6]

This quasi-fascist phase, although brief, provided the increased visibility and independence the Juventud sought. And

[6] See *Lircay*, nos. 9, 10, 11, 40, 62, 88, 89, 113, 126, and 140 for articles in which Falange spokesmen sought to dissociate Catholic social teaching from Franco, Mussolini, Portugal's Salazar, Belgian "Rexism," and both German and Chilean National Socialism.

as it did, Conservative leaders grew increasingly more anxious and impatient. The 1938 presidential campaign brought matters to a head. Liberals and Conservatives jointly nominated former Finance Minister Gustavo Ross, despite vigorous opposition from *falangistas*, who subsequently refused to endorse his candidacy. Ross's narrow defeat at the hands of the Popular Front's Pedro Aguirre Cerda prompted Conservative leaders to order a reorganization of the Falange and the disciplining of its leadership. The Falange-Juventud rejected these moves, declared its political independence, and left to find its own way and place in the Chilean political arena.

Independent Political Life

During the next two decades, Christian Democrats sought to establish the Falange Nacional as a viable alternative to the country's left- and right-wing forces. Politically, it remained a minor force, never exceeding 4 percent of the national electorate. Ideologically, the Falange's "third-way" position remained vague through the late 1940s, at which point various internal groupings began to define themselves more clearly, giving rise to a left-right division within party ranks.

Although it had vigorously opposed the Ross candidacy, the Falange resolved to oppose the Popular Front government of Radical Pedro Aguirre Cerda as well. It did so primarily to avoid association or identification with the left, although it appeared to share many of the concerns and commitments underlying the Front's program. The Falange was on record, for example, for calling for the transformation of capitalism and the "redemption" of the proletariat (*Lircay* 1938a, 1; and 1938d, 1-2). Further, it continued to distinguish between communism as such and Communist party positions that it considered legitimate and appropriate.[7] And finally, it endorsed policies of minimum wage, worker profit sharing, and worker participation in company own-

[7] The group argued that social reform, and not repression, was the only way to fight communism effectively. "Actually, the most effective propagandists for communism are reactionary rightists. . . . Anti-communism only exacerbates the danger of social revolution in Chile because its relies entirely on the use of repressive measures . . . which merely awaken in the masses an even more intense class hatred. . . . We are its only real enemy because we fight with ideas and reasons, and [because] we work for a new order which, producing peace and true social revolution, will contain the revolutionary advance" (*Lircay* 1937b, 3).

ership and decision making, all of which were either consistent with, or in advance of, Popular Front positions.

These commitments remained rhetorical, however. The Falange gave little indication as to how they would be fulfilled and was unwilling to work with those of like mind to bring them about. It refused to support the Popular Front's programs because of its inclusion of Marxist parties. In effect, it was more concerned with preserving its independent image and with avoiding potentially compromising political commitments than with accomplishing anything concrete.[8] During these initial years of independent political life, the party's progressive political commitments functioned more as theoretical credentials than as guides to political action.

Aguirre Cerda died suddenly in 1941, bringing the struggling Popular Front experiment to an end. He was succeeded by Radical Juan Antonio Ríos, who moved quickly to the political center. As he did so, the Falange agreed to enter his government, accepting secondary administrative posts, although remaining a relatively inconspicuous political force. During Ríos's years in office, however, the movement experienced an ideological radicalization that caused it to abandon the center and align itself with the left.

This shift was the outgrowth of developing wartime solidarity among "democratic" forces. In Chile, as in Europe, the war brought Christians and Marxists together in defense of democratic institutions and in opposition to both fascism and "world capitalism."[9] Shortly after the war began, the Falange joined the new Marxist-dominated national labor confederation, abandoning previous efforts to promote "parallel" unions and weaken Marx-

[8] Although it urged the "redemption of the proletariat," for example, the party proposed to achieve this not by supporting the claims of the existing labor movement, which represented the majority of the country's industrial workers, but by promoting parallel union organizations in an effort to weaken existing structures (Lircay 1938a, 3).

[9] The October 1945 edition (number 32) of Nuestro Tiempo (a monthly publication that succeeded Lircay) carried an article entitled "The War was not Waged to Perpetuate the Wicked Capitalist System." In Nuestro Tiempo, number 33 (1945b), an editorial spoke of a universal popular movement "to realize the principles and ideals for which the workers of the world had fought and given their lives. They participated in the conflict not only to liquidate the worst enemy humanity has ever had, but also, and very especially, to obtain their complete liberation, that is to say, to liquidate international capitalism, the cause of their unhappy condition and the principal factor responsible for the catastrophe."

ist influence within the working class. Subsequently it worked with Communists, Socialists, and Radicals in helping to relocate Spanish Republican refugees, in gaining diplomatic recognition of the Soviet Union, and in marshalling political support for the allied war effort.[10]

A key factor in these developments was Bernardo Leighton, who was elected president of the Falange in October 1945. Leighton and others had come to see the movement's traditionally independent stance as practically supportive of the right. Under his leadership the party abandoned the Ríos government, joined the ranks of the opposition, supported leftist candidates in several by-elections, and committed itself to the building of a "proletarian democracy."[11]

These initiatives were strongly opposed within the party. At its Fourth National Congress in 1946 Leighton was challenged by those favoring the earlier appeal to all classes and interests for whom the Falange was "not a purely working class party" but one "of essentially national content, open to all groups desirous of transforming existing capitalist disorder for a more efficient and just social Christian order" (*Nuestro Tiempo* 1946, 2).

Group spokesman Radomiro Tómic narrowly defeated Leighton for the party presidency and led the Falange back to the independent center. Two months later the party again divided along these lines, this time over the 1946 presidential election. The Leighton camp urged joining together with Communists and Socialists in support of Radical Gabriel González Videla; the Tómic group supported "progressive" Conservative Eduardo Cruz-Coke, hoping to forge closer ties with social Christian elements within the Conservative party. Centrist forces again prevailed, and the

---

[10] The Falange also joined the Unidad Nacional, an informal confederation of Communists, Socialists, and Radicals that held meetings, rallies, and other activities in defense of democratic institutions and social reform.

[11] *Nuestro Tiempo* 1945c, 4. In the struggle between capital and the proletariat Leighton stated flatly, "we must be with the proletariat." Its special suitability as the social base of the new order was its status as the "victim of the capitalist regime," which made it "free from the sin of exploitation of man by man" and "the carrier of moral reserves entitling it to a special mission with respect to the new world." Leighton qualified these views by speaking of the proletariat as all workers, manual or intellectual, who labored for a salary and by stressing that the party's commitment was not to the interests of one segment of society as opposed to another but "to those working for the whole society as opposed to those guided by political or class interests."

party formally endorsed Cruz-Coke, although many *falangistas* worked and voted for the victorious González Videla.

The Leighton-Tómic confrontation provided the first instance of significant political division within Christian Democratic ranks. Tómic and others minimized the differences as "tactical" or "merely strategic," insisting that unity prevailed with respect to the party's fundamental vision. This appeared a plausible claim at the time, in light of the unanimous approval given statements of principle at the 1946 and 1948 party congresses and in view of Leighton's subsequent return to the centrist mainstream.[12]

The choice of constituency and allies was nonetheless an important matter. It raised very basic questions about the movement's identity and sense of purpose and about the conditions, measures, and commitments believed essential for their fulfillment. On these matters disagreement was substantial and would resurface in the years to come whenever political ties and strategies were discussed.

Internal Polarization

Following González' election, party leaders spent most of their time pursuing closer ties with "social Christian" Conservatives. Their interest reflected both expediency and ideological affinity. Social Christian Conservatives could plausibly claim half of the Conservative party's still considerable public support and were thus politically attractive to a party whose electoral following still had not surpassed the 3 percent figure.[13] Moreover, the two held similar views on a number of issues, and, like the Falange years earlier, social Christian Conservatives had run afoul of their more traditional party colleagues in attempting to instill greater social conscience.

During this period, *falangistas* and social Christian Conservatives worked closely on a variety of issues and served together

[12] In 1950 Leighton supported the party's decision to enter the González government and served as minister of education despite its increasingly conservative policies.

[13] Frei's appeal for social Christian unity was expressive of Falange concerns in this regard: "We know our limitations. We have struggled hard with scarce resources, with reduced expression. ... We know we have advanced; but the advance is slow and the multitude's anxiety has exhausted its patience. Many would come, but for something larger. This is precisely what we wish to do, enlarge our actions. ... We are open to agreement on action of larger proportions" (*Ercilla* 1949, 5).

in several of González Videla's cabinets once his administration abandoned its left-wing allies and programs. During the late 1940s, the two groups called for the creation of an *economía humana* as an alternative to capitalist and communist economic structures. This would entail: 1) the ordering and regulation of production in line with consumption needs; 2) the subordination of profit to moral considerations; 3) the primacy of labor over capital; and 4) worker sharing in managerial responsibilities, profits, and company ownership.[14]

Unfortunately such commitments were phrased ambiguously and dealt with ultimate goals. No mention was made of the methods or timetable for their realization. Nothing was said of the role of the state in the transition period, of how resistance would be dealt with, or of the rights, interests, and functions to be assigned workers and capitalists. In short, there was little indication of what a "human economy" would look like or of how it would come into being. As it stood, it could be endorsed with equal conviction by persons of widely differing views and thus provided no assurance of ideological unity either within the Falange or between it and social Christian Conservatives.

In fact, substantial problems in both regards were already apparent. During the late 1940s, there reemerged within the Falange a vocal left wing at odds with other *falangistas* and the social Christian Conservatives. It was led by younger Christian Democrats who had joined the movement during the period of wartime solidarity. Like Leighton earlier, this group pressed for closer ties with the left and saw pursuit of social Christian unity as an obstacle to that end.

Most of them were university students and active in the Asociación de Jóvenes de la Acción Católica (Young Catholic Action). As they pressed their views within both party and university circles they pulled the Falange into open conflict with Chile's Catholic hierarchy. In 1947, for example, Auxiliary Bishop of Santiago, Monsignor Augusto Salinas, publicly assailed their "extreme" views and singled out their advocacy of cooperation with the Chilean Communist party despite repeated hierarchical prohibitions thereof.[15]

[14] The notion of an *economía humana* was endorsed simultaneously by the Falange's Fifth National Congress and the Partido Conservador's Sixteenth Congress. For the Falange's declaration see Falange Nacional 1948.

[15] The controversy was given extensive coverage in the Falange's semiofficial journal *Política y Espíritu* (1947).

The underlying issue concerned whether the Church's jurisdiction was confined to official Catholic organizations (like Young Catholic Action) or extended to Catholics belonging to independent political parties as well. While Church authorities insisted that relations with atheistic movements like the Communist party raised moral issues over which they held legitimate jurisdiction, Falange officials saw this as a contingent matter in which the party was properly autonomous. At the same time, however, as they claimed inspiration in the Church's social teaching, they did not wish to be at odds with the hierarchy, much less be condemned by it.

Conciliatory spirits prevailed, and an open break was averted. Falange leaders acknowledged episcopal authority, offering to dissolve the party if it were formally condemned by the bishops. The latter reaffirmed Monsignor Salinas's initial charges but made no mention of either condemnation or dissolution. Apparently, in their view, the censure of a particular act did not entail condemnation of the party itself, and though they wished to affirm certain general principles, the "noble task of searching for their applications and determinations in the middle of contingent circumstances" was to be left to the laity (*Política y Espíritu* 1947, 167).

Party radicals remained undaunted by these difficulties. Two of them, Julio Silva Solar and Jacques Chonchol, had been at the center of the controversy from the beginning as university students and members of Young Catholic Action. Drawing on Catholic thinkers like Lebret and Mounier,[16] and on Marx as well, they espoused a communitarian form of socialism, offering a distinctively radical Christian Democratic "alternative" to capitalism.[17]

---

[16] Louis Josef Lebret was a French Dominican priest who was both a sociologist and economist. He founded the Institute Economisme et Humanisme in Lyons and edited a journal of the same name devoted to the study of Third World problems from a social Christian perspective. Emmanuel Mounier was a leading French Catholic philosopher, editor of *Esprit*, and founder of the philosophical movement of personalism, which combined elements of Christian existentialism and Marxism.

[17] Major statements of their views during this period were: *Qué es el Socialcristianismo?* (Silva Solar and François 1948) and *Hacia un Mundo Comunitario* (Silva Solar and Chonchol 1951). Chonchol wrote the first of these works under the pseudonym of Jacques François in an effort to keep his Jewish father from learning of his conversion to Catholicism and of his involvement in Christian Democratic politics.

According to Silva and Chonchol, a truly human society required abolition of private ownership of the means of production. In their view private ownership meant the primacy of self-interest, which invariably resulted in poverty, injustice, and class exploitation. Moreover, proposals of the sort advanced by social Christian Conservatives, e.g., social legislation, higher salaries, profit sharing, and improved working and living conditions, left the "structural disorder" of capitalism intact and were ultimately counterproductive.

In place of mere reforms Silva and Chonchol proposed communitarian structures in which workers themselves would own the means of production and make corporate decisions. As workers had been the principal victims of exploitation, they were more aware of the evils of capitalism and more qualified to construct the new society. They would thus be the agents and principal beneficiaries of the revolutionary process. During a transition period, the state would orient, coordinate, and assist workers, promoting greater communitarian consciousness and creating "from above the framework within which the new institutions could develop." Full respect for worker autonomy and initiative would be assured through decentralized worker-managed factories of the sort then emerging in Yugoslavia.

Such notions proved a stumbling block to Falange-social Christian unity. For their part Silva and Chonchol saw social Christian Conservatives as "well intentioned rightists" with whom the Falange had (or should have) little in common. Conceding a shared commitment to broad social Christian ideals, the two felt closer to Marxists with whom they shared an understanding of social reality and of what was needed to change it.[18]

Silva and Chonchol's advocacy of worker revolution and communitarian socialism did little to alleviate the fears of social Christians concerning the Falange's character and ultimate objectives. Their impact was effectively countered, however, by other party leaders and by the influence of Eduardo Frei. During this period, party spokesmen softened their critique of capitalism and conception of social change. The latter came to be regarded as

[18] In *Hacia un Mundo Comunitario* Silva and Chonchol argued that the bond uniting social Christians "is not the belief in the same religious faith, but a common criterion with respect to the things of the temporal world, to the things of political and economic organization of historical dynamism" (Silva Solar and Chonchol 1951, 9). See also a later discussion of the same issue in *Política y Espíritu* 1959a, 15-16.

"an effort to raise the standard of living of the lower classes" in which "ample guarantees . . . to all those who worked in an enterprising manner, and who managed their economic dealings humanely" (*Política y Espíritu* 1953a, 27) would be given. In effect, all social forces, including capital, were to be part of a broad coalition, provided they accepted the principles and objectives "analogous to those of the Falange" (*Política y Espíritu* 1953b, 32).

Also helping to allay Conservative fears was Eduardo Frei, whose election to the Senate in 1949 brought him new prominence in party and national political circles. Resolutely anti-Marxist and anticommunist, Frei defended the party's traditional independence from left and right. In recent years he had embraced the developmentalist perspective of the United Nations Economic Commission for Latin America (ECLA), which he used effectively in countering party radicals.

Citing a common stake that all social forces had in growth and development, Frei called for the formation of a broad national and popular movement. Development, he argued, was the basis of all progress, the most effective guarantee of greater equality and social justice. "A country," he contended,

> which achieves a high level of economic development needs thousands of skilled workers, more culture, and more organizations, all of which almost automatically produce better human conditions, eliminate differences, and create equality upwards, rather than leveling poverty, misery, and backwardness. [Frei 1956b, 30]

For Frei such development was most effectively pursued within existing structures and with the collaboration and sacrifice of all interests. Given the country's limited capital resources and the state's already burdensome responsibilities, business community support (i.e., productive investment) was essential; the state should seek to encourage, not restrict, its activities. But long-term success would also depend on the austerity, hard work, and large-scale infrastructural investments endured or generated in the short run, and these things should be given priority over immediate income redistribution or improved living standards. As Frei put it, "One must first build the spring" and then drink the water (Frei 1955, 61).

In this connection Frei termed the views of Silva and Chonchol "naive" and overly idealistic. On the one hand, he argued, the moral principles governing social life could not be applied literally. They had to take into account technical limitations and "the requirements of their concrete circumstances" (Magnet 1951). On the other hand, he claimed, socialist "schemes" of the sort proposed by Silva and Chonchol would merely add a new political inferiority to already burdensome psychological, economic, and legal inferiorities. And in any case, he added, they would trigger social conflict of such intensity as to outweigh any benefit they might bring (Frei 1955, 15).

Frei's developmentalism thus offered an alternative to the communitarianism of Falange radicals. It also embodied the fulfillment of a long-standing Christian Democratic aspiration: the formulation of a position theoretically reconciling the interests of competing classes and social forces, and thus potentially appealing to all. Arguing that an expanding economy made it unnecessary to choose between diverse interests, Frei offered something to everyone: to workers, professionals and middle-class groups, and to small- and large-scale businessmen, to haves and have-nots, and to those both desirous and fearful of social change. Over the next ten years his views would enjoy increasingly broad appeal, drawing many new recruits to the Christian Democratic fold.

For the moment they helped to allay Conservative reservations regarding social Christian unity. Active negotiations were begun in July 1953, and in October the Social Christian Federation was formally established. The Falange and social Christian Conservatives would remain separate entities but would coordinate policies and function as a united force. They were joined shortly by members of the Movimiento Nacional Cristiano, a group of former Conservatives who had supported the 1952 presidential candidacy of Carlos Ibáñez.[19]

While failing to push the Falange leftwards or prevent merger with social Christian Conservatives, the party's radicals remained an influential minority, having considerable appeal among second-generation *falangistas* who were active in university-level politics during these years.[20] In addition, the party's ideological

[19] The MNC's leading figure, José Musalem, was to become a powerful force and vote-getter for the PDC, and until September 1973 was a senator from Santiago province.

[20] In 1953, while still a relatively insignificant force nationally, the Falange

pronouncements and resolutions often embraced or reflected radical views, despite the fact that Frei and others were visibly uncomfortable with them.[21] This tolerance reflected a general indifference to "theorizing," a need to be identified with a concrete socioeconomic ideal, and a confidence that such notions could be redefined or interpreted in more congenial terms at some future point. But the dichotomy between formal commitment and practical political position would remain an enduring party characteristic and the occasion, if not the cause, of recurring controversy.

With the establishment of the Social Christian Federation Frei and the Christian Democratic movement rose steadily in prominence. Both were beneficiaries of disenchantment with the Ibáñez government. Elected in 1952 thanks to a campaign in which he attempted to project a strongman image, Ibáñez proved a weak and ineffective leader and was soon embroiled in the internal bickering and inaction that had plagued most recent governments. By mid-1954 his momentum was gone, and former supporters began to look with interest at Frei and the social Christian movement among other alternatives. Earlier that year Ibáñez invited Frei to join his government at the head of a cabinet of his choosing. The prospect elicited favorable reaction in many quarters, and although the offer was later withdrawn, it revealed substantial public respect for Frei and his associates.[22] Among other consequences it left party leaders impressed with

---

won control of the powerful student federation of the University of Chile (FECh) and in 1958 of the student federation of the Catholic University of Santiago (FEUC). These successes reenforced the party's image as an up-and-coming force and helped to extend its support among the electorate at large.

[21] At its first National Congress in 1959 the newly founded Christian Democratic party committed itself to the creation of economic structures that "tend to group men in communities of workers who own capital and the means of production, and to convert the state, as rector of the common good, into the maximum expression of communitarian life." In terms of property it supported "a community or cooperative system with respect to the means of production requiring the work of many." See *Política y Espíritu* 1959b, 14-18. Frei opposed the notion of communitarianism, terming it one of several "interesting but untested aspirations whose operationality and productive efficiency would have to be demonstrated before they could be included in a social Christian platform" (Frei 1956a, 43). He was apparently too busy with more important (i.e., more practical) matters to engage in ideological debate, however.

[22] Among these were Sergio Molina (later finance minister under Frei), William Thayer (Frei's labor minister), and Sergio Ossa Pretot, Domingo Santa María, and Alejandro Hales, all of whom held important posts in Frei's administration.

the possibilities of building a Christian Democratic base among independents and others attracted to Frei.[23]

During the next several years, Frei was given maximum public exposure through party organs and media. His speeches and essays appeared frequently in the journal *Política y Espíritu* and were reprinted and distributed nationally and internationally by the Editorial del Pacífico, the party's unofficial publishing house. When Frei sought reelection to the Senate in 1957, he ran in populous Santiago province in hopes of gaining wider recognition and a larger number of votes for the Falange and the Federation. The strategy worked well. He won an impressive victory, receiving the most votes of any of the five winning candidates and helping the Falange to win 9 percent of the national vote and fourteen seats in the Chamber of Deputies.[24]

Frei's rising political stock also prompted the Federation partners to consummate their union. In June 1957 a joint committee of *falangistas* and social Christian Conservatives was appointed to draw up a declaration of principles, and in July the *Partido Demócrata Cristiano* (PDC) was founded.

Growth and Expansion, 1957-1964

Between 1957 and 1964 Christian Democracy grew rapidly in size and political importance. Closely identified with the person and views of Frei, the Christian Democrats offered a reformist alternative to "Marxist dictatorship." During the period, they drew to their ranks those committed to far-reaching reform and democratization, others seeking a more viable defense against such things, and yet others simply looking for lower inflation rates, a better job, or extended social programs. In the process the party's already problematic organizational and ideological unity was further aggravated.

With its foundation the PDC was thrown into a presidential

[23] In the words of Falange and Social Christian Federation president Rafael Agustín Gumucio, the country "was ready to support a movement with a clear, non-sectarian national policy." What was needed were programs of practical action, and in this regard the Falange "was fortunate to have in its ranks capable and creative men whose technical knowledge guarantees a rectifying turnabout in national life" (*Política y Espíritu* 1954, 27-33).

[24] The party was aware of its debt to Frei. In Gumucio's words, ". . . as his figure rose to become the most prominent in Chilean politics, . . . at the same time the Falange's position was becoming more understood by the great mass. . . . Our candidates for deputy were discerned by the electorate as key men on a team . . . whose first representative was Frei" (*Política y Espíritu* 1957, 31).

campaign in which it was closely identified with its candidate Eduardo Frei. Frei's campaign sought to hold a middle ground between what he termed the right's insensitivity to social problems and the "dangerous extremism" of the left. Stressing the compatibility of all interests, he promised higher productivity, more jobs, public housing, broader social services, and greater political participation for workers. He also sought Liberal and Conservative party backing, pulling Christian Democratic trade unionists out of the Marxist-dominated central labor confederation (the Central Unica de Trabajadores, or CUT) and choosing not to press for an agrarian reform in an effort to make his candidacy more palatable to these groups. His efforts were to no avail, however, as both groups swung their support to independent rightist Jorge Alessandri, son of former president Arturo Alessandri and a wealthy businessman. Alessandri narrowly defeated the Socialist Salvador Allende, with Frei finishing third with nearly 21 percent of the vote.

Frei's 255,769 votes were more than twice the number *falangistas* and social Christian Conservatives received in congressional elections the year before and thus marked Christian Democracy's emergence as a significant political force. Electoral analyses appearing shortly thereafter indicated that Frei's support was evenly distributed throughout the country and drawn proportionately from men and women and from all social strata.[25]

Chilean sociologist Eduardo Hamuy's survey of Greater Santiago a month before the election (Hamuy 1958) provides even more useful information concerning Frei's expanded support base.[26] The survey shows it to be both broader socially and more conservative politically than in earlier years. Prior to 1958 the party's small following had been predominantly petit bourgeois in character.[27] But of the 305 respondents indicating a preference just prior to the presidential election, 20.8 percent favored Frei,

[25] See *Chile, Election Fact Book* 1965, 34-35.

[26] The survey is entitled *Political Behavior in Chile*, hereafter referred to as Hamuy 1958. For details on the sample see the Appendix. The survey turned out to be a reliable predictor of voter behavior as far as Frei and the Christian Democrats were concerned. Among those expressing preferences in the survey sample, Frei received 20.8 percent of the total. In the election itself, in the three Santiago districts covered by the sample he polled 21.3 percent.

[27] Leading histories of Chilean Christian Democracy (Silva Bascuñán 1949; Boizard 1965; and Grayson 1968a) all convey this impression but offer no real substantiation for it. The most informative discussion is Smith (1982, 95-97), who quotes those directly involved as conceding that the Falange and social Christian parties failed to attract more than minimal working-class support.

and of these only 39.1 percent were from professional or independent worker backgrounds, while 40.6 percent were from white collar worker and 20.3 percent from blue collar worker backgrounds.[28]

Frei's relative success among workers appears to have been a function of both personal appeal and positive identification with leading "bread-and-butter" concerns of the day (jobs, housing, control of inflation, and educational opportunity).[29] It was also, in part at least, a function of his close association with the Catholic Church. As Table 2-1 indicates, he enjoyed disproportionately strong support among regularly practicing Catholics, while other candidates did well among Catholics who did not practice their religion or did so only irregularly.

Frei's supporters held moderate or centrist views on most ideological issues. The great majority of them (63.1 percent) placed themselves in the center of the political spectrum as opposed to the left (9.3 percent) or right (27.8 percent). On specific ideological issues most held views falling between those of the Marxist left and the conservative right. On questions dealing with the legal status of the Communist party, possible redistribution of

TABLE 2-1
Extent of Religious Practice of Prospective Catholic Voters
by Candidate Preference, August 1958

Candidate Preference	Non-practicing	Irregular	Regular	All Catholics
Alessandri	34.0%	43.0%	43.0%	40.9%
Allende	28.1	29.3	11.1	22.8
Bossay	17.2	6.5	8.6	10.1
Frei	20.3	20.7	37.0	26.2
n	64	92	81	237

SOURCE: Hamuy 1958.
NOTE: $x^2 = 18.4$, p = .005
KEY TO SYMBOLS: In this and all subsequent tables x^2 refers to the chi square test factor, tau b to the tau beta test factor, and p to the probability value obtaining for a particular x^2 or tau b value.

[28] The x^2 factor of 33.8 is significant at .001.

[29] When asked to indicate the most important problems that their candidate would deal with if elected, 43.8 percent of Frei's supporters mentioned the cost of living, 20.3 percent mentioned unemployment, and 17.2 percent mentioned housing. Those planning to vote for other candidates responded along much the same lines.

agricultural lands, use of surpluses, worker participation, worker-management relations, and worker power, respondents were asked to choose between clearly progressive and conservative options.[30] Table 2-2 indicates the percentage of those supporting the major candidates that chose the progressive options with respect to these issues.

On almost all issues Frei supporters fall to the right of Allende supporters (by an average of 27 points) but to the left of Alessandri and Bossay supporters (by an average of 19 points and eight points respectively).

When Christian Democrats and Frei supporters are broken down in terms of party status and length of association,[31] similarly

TABLE 2-2
Progressive Ideological Views of Prospective Voters
by Candidate Preference, August 1958

Candidate Preference	Communism	Land Redistribution	Surplus	Worker Participation	Worker-Management Relations	Worker Power
Alessandri	38.6%	22.5%	61.3%	39.8%	27.1%	32.6%
Allende	94.0	75.5	91.4	82.7	79.2	81.8
Bossay	65.8	40.5	66.7	41.7	34.6	40.0
Frei	71.0	37.1	72.1	62.5	50.0	45.5
x^2	65.8	55.5	21.8	39.8	53.2	39.3
p	.000	.000	.000	.001	.000	.000

SOURCE: Hamuy 1958.

[30] The "clearly progressive" options favored the Communist party being treated as any other party (and not "outlawed"), the redistribution of land (rather than the aiding of farmers), the use of surpluses for increasing worker and employer salaries (as opposed to reinvestment in the firm), worker participation in management decisions, consistent support of workers in labor conflicts or strikes, and greater worker power and influence in government.

[31] Of the 807 persons responding to the survey 12 indicated membership in the PDC, another 109 ("supporters") expressed an affinity for the party, and 64 indicated that they planned to vote for Frei. Unfortunately, the survey asked for the respondent's present political affiliation, and only if none were indicated, whether he or she had ever been affiliated with a party. It thus provides no direct indication that members of the PDC had previously been affiliated with the Falange, although it can be assumed that most had been. All 12 PDC members were old enough to have been *falangistas*, and 9 actually voted in the 1952 presidential election (4 for Alfonso, the candidate officially endorsed by Falange leaders, 2 for Ibáñez, whom many *falangistas* had supported, 2 for the Liberal Matte, and 1 had submitted a blank ballot). Furthermore, most appear to have

61

TABLE 2-3
Occupational Statuses of Christian Democrats
and Frei Supporters, August 1958

Subgroup	Employers	Professionals, Independent Workers	White Collar Workers	Blue Collar Workers	Domestic Workers	
Falangistas	—	50.0%	37.5%	12.5%	—	n = 8
Christian Democratic supporters	6.3%	—	68.8	18.8	6.3%	n = 16
Unaffiliated *freístas*	—	50.0	50.0	—	—	n = 6

SOURCE: Hamuy 1958.
NOTE: x^2 = 11.9, p = .15

significant differences emerge. As Table 2-3 shows, for example, most newer PDC (87.6 percent) and Frei supporters were blue and white collar workers, in contrast to the predominantly petit bourgeois *falangistas*.[32]

While claiming more "popular" occupational status, however, the newer arrivals were significantly more conservative in terms of ideological self-placement, i.e., they were more likely to place themselves to the right, and less to the left, of the political spectrum (see Table 2-4).

As there is no indication of what each respondent understood by the various alternatives, the precise import of these patterns is unclear. The lack of significant correspondence between left-

---

been affiliated with the organization for some time. Only 3 were too young to vote or eligible but not registered to vote in the 1946 election. Of the other 9, 2 voted for Cruz-Coke (the candidate officially backed by the party), 1 for González Videla, and 1 for Bernardo Ibáñez; the remaining 5 were women, who had still not been granted franchise. Nine of the 12 party members may thus be taken for *falangistas* and can be compared and contrasted with the 38 newer arrivals, i.e., those who had not voted in the preceding election but who expressed sympathy for the PDC and were eligible to vote in 1958. Eighteen of the 64 respondents indicating plans to vote for Frei were neither members nor supporters of the PDC and may be seen as representative of the political independents attracted to Frei.

[32] The x^2 factor of 11.9 is only significant at .15, although if one compares *falangistas* to the two other categories combined, the x^2 of 6.4 is significant at .09. Hamuy (1958) employed a fairly simple occupational classification system in his survey. Its categories were public employee, private employee, worker, employer, independent worker, professional, and domestic employee. I have collapsed them into five groups: managers-owners (employers), professionals-independent workers, public and private employees (white collar workers), blue collar workers, and domestic workers.

TABLE 2-4
Ideological Self-Placement of Christian Democrats
and Frei Supporters, August 1958

Subgroup	Left	Center	Right	
Falangistas	28.6%	42.9%	28.6%	n = 7
Christian Democratic supporters	12.1	66.7	21.2	n = 33
Unaffiliated *freístas*	—	60.0	40.0	n = 15

SOURCE: Hamuy 1958.
NOTE: tau b = .21, p = .046

right classification and one's views on ideological issues strongly suggests that the labels may have had different meanings for different respondents.[33] So too does the weak correspondence between the several subgroups of Christian Democrats and Frei supporters and their responses to specific ideological issues. Table 2-5 indicates that relationships run in the expected direction (longer-standing members tended to choose the more "progressive" option), but in only one instance (whether workers should be given control of the factories in which they worked) were the patterns strong enough to compensate for the relatively small number of *falangistas* in the sample.

Relationships are stronger, however, with attitudes on more immediate political questions, including one's reasons for supporting Frei, one's preference for Alessandri or Allende, one's expectations of an Alessandri government, and one's sense of the party (or parties) most likely to collaborate with that government. Here it is reasonable to consider those supporting Frei because of his party or platform (as opposed to his personality or religious convictions), those who preferred Allende to Alessandri, those who opposed any collaboration with Alessandri's government, and those who judged that government more negatively to be more progressive. Table 2-6 compares responses for the three subgroups. On three of the issues the percentage of those making "progressive" responses is given. For the last, the figure is the mean score on a scale of from 1 (very good) to 4 (bad).

[33] The x^2 factor for communism was significant at .15, those for land redistribution, surplus, worker participation, worker-management relations, and worker power were significant at levels ranging from .40 to .56. For Alessandri versus Allende, expectations of Alessandri, and party alliance with Alessandri the x^2 factors were significant at levels of .80, .74, and .90 respectively.

63

TABLE 2-5
Progressive Ideological Views of Christian Democrats
and Frei Supporters, August 1958

Subgroup	Commu- nism	Land Redistri- bution	Surplus	Worker Partici- pation	Worker- Management Relations	Worker Power
Falangistas	77.8%	50.0%	77.8%	66.7%	66.7%	62.5%
Christian Democratic Supporters	66.7	34.2	75.0	64.9	44.4	31.3
Unaffiliated *freístas*	72.2	47.1	64.7	58.2	47.1	62.5
n	63	63	62	63	53	56
x^2	.48	1.2	.75	.22	2.5	5.4
p	.78	.54	.68	.89	.86	.07

SOURCE: Hamuy 1958.

TABLE 2-6
Progressive Political Views of Christian Democrats
and Frei Supporters, August 1958

Subgroup	Reasons for Support	Alessandri- Allende	Alessandri Government	Party Collabo- ration
Falangistas	75.0%	66.7%	*2.7	85.7%
Christian Democratic supporters	43.3	83.9	*2.1	41.2
Unaffiliated *freístas*	23.5	94.1	*1.9	33.3
	n = 55	n = 57	n = 57	n = 36
	$x^2 = 10.3$	tau b = − .20	$x^2 = 14$	$x^2 = 9.9$
	p = .03	p = .05	p = .001	p = .04

SOURCE: Hamuy 1958.
NOTE: Values preceded by an asterisk (*) are measured on a scale of from 1 (very good) to 4 (bad).

More recent "converts" to Frei and Christian Democracy were thus more conservative than longer-standing *falangistas*. The more pragmatic thrust of party positions and strategy since 1953 may have had something to do with this phenomenon. In addition, the fact that differences among the three subgroups were sharper on issues of alignment and expectation may mean that self-placement on the ideological spectrum has more to do with parties and personalities than with principles or convictions. Or, for that matter, it may simply reflect the conservative political origins of many newer arrivals or the general political climate of the period.

The effect that these newer arrivals would exert on the Christian Democratic movement in the years to come was remarkable. In the space of a few years those recruited in a political context dominated by Frei's personality and pragmatic views became the principal base of a party that for many years had the stamp of more ideologically oriented leaders and spokesmen. They helped to make Christian Democracy a more formidable, more representative, and yet more conservative force, and doubtlessly encouraged its leaders to remain on the current pragmatic course.

Although many newly acquired followers had previously supported Alessandri, the PDC resolved to oppose the new Alessandri government from the beginning. It went to considerable pains, however, to keep its distance from the Marxist left as well, thus continuing its efforts to build an "independent" centrist force. Party leaders were apparently convinced that Alessandri's traditionally conservative policies would not work and that with the right discredited the country would favor the PDC over the Marxist left. In pointing toward the next presidential election, therefore, the middle of the road appeared to hold considerable political promise.

To make a viable bid for the presidency in 1964 the party would have to absorb and further extend Frei's current 20 percent following. Accordingly, recruitment efforts were focused on independent Frei supporters and newly registered voters.[34] In July 1959 party president Patricio Aylwin reported a doubling in the number of party members since the election and urged a continuation of these and other recruiting efforts.

The question of Frei's "independent" followers, and particularly the political notables among them, quickly became an issue within the party. Frei loyalists and enthusiasts (*freístas*) urged their incorporation without question or delay. Others, however, were worried about their effect on ideological and organizational cohesion. The controversy carried over to the party's first National Congress, at which issues of party identity and mission were discussed. Frei partisans favored the notion of a broad reform movement appealing to all sectors and representative of

---

[34] Of the respondents indicating sympathy for the Christian Democratic party, 56 were unable to vote (presumably for Frei) because they were not registered. This suggests the existence of a sizable but as yet untapped segment of the country's population on which the party could draw for future support.

their various interests (*Política y Espíritu* 1959c, 17-18). A second group of so-called "purists" urged that the party remain "a small, efficient, and ideologically homogenous unit devoted to the uncompromising propagation of its own doctrine" (*Política y Espíritu* 1959c, 13-14). For the latter group the party was more than the figure or positions of Frei and should not choose its stands in terms of political or electoral expediency. The left wing, led by Silva and Chonchol, was even more explicit. Viewing Frei's non-Christian Democratic followers as conservatives looking for a more effective bulwark against threats to their privileged position, this group argued instead for alliance with the political left (*Política y Espíritu* 1959c, 14).

When the votes were counted, *freístas* won narrowly over "purists," with leftists finishing third. The Congress approved "closer association" with the Partido Nacional Popular (PANAPO), a group of ex-*ibañistas* that had supported Frei in 1958, and within a year the PDC formally absorbed the organization's leaders and membership.[35]

During this period, the Christian Democrats held to the middle of the road, opposing Alessandri and yet steering clear of the Marxist left, which was now united in the Frente de Acción Popular. Sensing disenchantment among those who had supported Alessandri in 1958, they waged the April 1961 parliamentary elections under the banner of "Christian Democracy or Communism." The party won twenty-three seats in the Chamber, four in the Senate, and 16 percent of the total vote, less than Frei had in 1958, but nearly double its own support in 1957.

Encouraged by these gains, *freístas* urged that the party's bid for the presidency in 1964 be made along the same lines. Purists and leftists objected, arguing that anticommunism was an inappropriate basis on which to build support. They joined forces to wrest leadership from *freístas* and reorient the party's positions and popular image in a more progressive direction. New president Renán Fuentealba directed Christian Democratic trade unionists to reaffiliate with the Marxist-dominated CUT, and party declarations began to speak of the need for "social revolution" and of a willingness to work with "other" revolutionary forces.

It is doubtful that Frei or his supporters would have gone along

[35] Among those joining the PDC at this time were Carlos Sívori, Julián Etcheverría, Mario Hamuy, and Luís Martín Mardones, all of whom became staunch *freístas* and were later elected to the Chamber of Deputies.

with such a move, but the issue was never posed frontally. In early 1963 the Socialist party broke off exploratory talks, unilaterally proclaimed Allende its candidate for 1964, and resumed its customary attacks on the Christian Democrats. Within days the Communists followed suit, prompting abandonment of the FRAP by the Partido Democrático Nacional (PADENA), another group of ex-*ibañistas* who pledged their support for whomever the PDC would nominate.[36]

The party's adoption of a strongly anticommunist reformism was both encouraged and blessed by the country's Catholic bishops. In pastoral letters issued in April and September 1962 they decried existing poverty and injustice and called for (and spelled out) strategies promoting economic growth and socioeconomic reforms. Several of their specific suggestions coincided with positions advocated at the time by the PDC. And lest electoral implications were not clear enough, they went on to condemn both Marxism and collaboration of any sort with any Marxist group.[37]

In effect, the bishops, many of whom were friendly (and at one time had studied) with leading Christian Democrats, espoused a Christian Democratic solution to the country's problems. Seemingly aware of the risks of partisan identification, they nonetheless moved the Church into political alignment with the PDC, enhancing its stature and political following among Chilean Catholics (Smith 1982, 110-111). Their endorsement strengthened the hand of *freístas* within party ranks. So did the results of the April 1963 municipal elections, from which the PDC emerged as the country's largest single force. In June the party nominated Frei and kicked off a campaign designed to attract a diverse, multiclass support base. Appealing to "all ... who are working for change within liberty," it proposed a "national and popular movement which, repudiating the false dilemma of capitalism or communism, is capable of uniting Chile for the solu-

[36] Among this new wave of *ibañistas* to move into the PDC were Jorge Lavendero, Rubén Hurtado, José Foncéa, and Luís Pareto. All four were elected to Congress in 1965 as Christian Democrats.

[37] See "El Deber Social y Político en la Hora Presente" in the Jesuit monthly *Mensaje* (1962a, 577-587). The party's decision to embrace the notion of revolution was facilitated by recent trends in Catholic social doctrine. Authoritative Catholic thought traditionally had opposed revolution on grounds that it was necessarily violent and destructive and thus worse than the evils it sought to cure. Recently, however, violence and revolution had been disentangled, with the former understood to be one of several means one might or might not use in the pursuit of the intrinsically worthy end of revolution (see *Mensaje* 1962b).

tion of her problems and the conquest of a better future" (*Política y Espíritu* 1963b, 58).

Frei initially called for administrative and political reforms, expanded public services, and a "more just" distribution of tax burdens and income. In the words of one Frei associate it was an updated version of his 1958 platform, one that looked to advances in modern technology to open the way to "unsuspected opportunities for material and cultural well-being."[38] In early 1964, following extensive internal consultations, the party issued its own more ambitious platform. Calling for a "revolution in liberty," it pledged economic development with and through social reform. Increased production would finance needed reforms and welfare programs, and these in turn would free up additional productive resources.

Despite these adjustments Frei's platform and campaign were objects of controversy within party ranks. Leftist elements were critical of his copper and agrarian reform proposals and of what they took to be conciliatory gestures to the right (in order to assure its support). In general, party leaders felt that the commitment to structural change should be more explicit and more prominent. In their literature, these aspects, and not the promise of growth and development, were emphasized. In the Third Declaration of Millahue, for example, the party pledged that the Frei government would

> put an end to the power of concentrated wealth, and to the privileges such power engenders in minority control of the means of production, the price of human labor, consumer goods, the banking structure, and all national resources. [*Política y Espíritu* 1964, 50-53]

Nonetheless, such statements were overshadowed by the more conciliatory stands and statements of the candidate, whose campaign retained its antileftist flavor. The special March 1964 election in Curicó was decisive in this regard. There the right-wing candidate was badly beaten by his FRAP opponent, underscoring the center-right coalition's loss of majority support. Shortly thereafter the coalition was dissolved and the center-right candidacy of Radical Julio Durán effectively withdrawn. With the

---

[38] The remark is Patricio Aylwin's (*Política y Espíritu* 1963a, 47). This early phase of Frei's campaign was based on the "blue book," a report that had been prepared by a committee of party technocrats associated with Frei.

field narrowed to Frei and Allende, Liberals and Conservatives quickly endorsed Frei. Along with the many "independents for Frei" committees they added considerable anti-Marxist flavor to his campaign.[39]

Frei won a solid victory, capturing 56 percent of the vote to Allende's 39 percent. He prevailed by substantial margins among traditionally conservative groups (e.g., women, rural provinces, the urban middle sectors, etc.) and held his own in leftist strongholds as well.[40] His victory marked only the third time since 1938 that a presidential candidate had won an absolute majority of the votes cast.

Again, survey data help to clarify the character of Frei's support. In August 1964 Hamuy polled 1,095 potential voters in the same three districts of Greater Santiago (Hamuy 1964). Like his 1958 survey, this one also differentiated among party members, supporters, and "independent" Frei supporters in terms of background and length of association, thus providing evidence of the changing composition and orientation of Christian Democracy as it made its bid for power. Because the sample was confined to the Santiago area and did not always elicit direct responses to the most relevant ideological and strategic questions it may be wise not to give it undue analytical weight or conclusiveness. But if it cannot establish why, it at least confirms that different sectors within the movement were thinking and moving in very different directions.[41]

The first thing to be noted is the continued broadening of Frei's electoral constituency. Table 2-7, which details the occupational statuses of those supporting the three presidential candidates

[39] Conservatives were quoted as pledging support for Frei "hasta las urnas," i.e., as far as the ballot boxes, implying they would oppose him beginning immediately after the elections. These committees were responsible for propaganda tying Allende to Moscow, to religious persecution in Cuba, etc. Testimony before the U.S. Senate Foreign Relations Committee was later to reveal that the millions of dollars spent in this way came from the Central Intelligence Agency.

[40] Using ecological analysis, Petras and Zeitlin conclude that Allende did better the larger the percentage of industrial (i.e., manufacturing, mining, and construction) workers living in the district (Petras and Zeitlin 1970, 21). For a more general analysis of the vote see Gil and Parrish 1965.

[41] The survey proved to be a fairly reliable predictor of actual electoral behavior. Although in the survey Frei received 68.5 percent of those expressing a preference, he received a slightly smaller percentage (60.9 percent) of the actual vote in these districts. In the 1964 election, 44 percent of Frei's total vote came from Santiago province, including the three districts covered by Hamuy's survey plus the smaller (and largely rural) fourth district.

(Durán's candidacy was revived on a *pro forma* basis several months before the election), shows a marked increase in white and blue collar support for Frei since 1958 (see Table 2-3). He won a majority of the votes in each sector (with figures of 68 percent and 59 percent respectively), and as is indicated in Table 2-7 almost two-thirds of his support came from blue and white collar workers.

In contrast with 1958 Frei's 1964 supporters were predominantly women (62.9 percent) and included the lion's share of those voting for the first time (75 percent). As in 1958 he enjoyed disproportionate support from the country's regularly practicing Catholics, both among the population as a whole and particularly within the working class (see Table 2-8). Frei was supported by 76 percent of all white collar Catholic voters and by 92 percent of those who regularly practiced their religion; among blue collar Catholics the corresponding figures were 61.2 percent and 76.9 percent. In general, Frei supporters were still largely

TABLE 2-7
Occupational Statuses of Prospective Voters
by Candidate Preference, August 1964

Candidate Preference	Managers, Owners	Professionals, Technicians, Small Businessmen	White Collar Workers	Blue Collar Workers	
Allende	3.5%	32.9%	25.7%	46.9%	n = 113
Durán	14.3	19.1	47.6	19.1	n = 21
Frei	5.0	31.2	31.9	31.9	n = 260

SOURCE: Hamuy 1964.
NOTE: $x^2 = 15.8$, p = .01

TABLE 2-8
Extent of Religious Practice of Prospective Catholic Voters
by Candidate Preference, August 1964

Candidate Preference	Seldom- Never	Irregular	Regular	
Allende	40.9%	46.5%	12.7%	n = 142
Durán	44.0	36.0	20.0	n = 25
Frei	24.4	44.4	31.2	n = 475
All Catholics	28.8	44.6	26.6	n = 642

SOURCE: Hamuy 1964.
NOTE: $x^2 = 27.3$, p = .000

centrist in their ideological sense of themselves but were more inclined than they had been in 1958 to identify with both the right (34.8 percent) and the left (18.3 percent), suggesting a certain polarization, at least at the nominal level.

The 1964 survey also probed the ideological and political views of potential voters. Like the 1958 survey, questions dealt with abstract propositions as well as concrete issues. In each case responses can be characterized as more or less progressive. Table 2-9 compares the responses to eight ideological questions of those supporting the three candidates. The first of these concerned ideological identification. The second asked whether or not the respondent thought social change was necessary. The third asked what was expected in the way of change. Here those indicating either reforms or social justice are taken to be more progressive than those mentioning general or specific economic improvements. The fourth question concerned whether communism was a "real danger" or simply a pretext for resisting social change. The fifth asked for one's views on the Cuban revolution and United States' efforts to undermine it. The sixth concerned whether or not the respondent believed that a few strong leaders could do more for the country than could laws and speeches. The seventh asked whether or not a person whose situation had not improved lacked sufficient force of will. The eighth asked whether or not, given human nature, there would always be war and conflict. As can be seen in Table 2-9, those supporting Frei tended to hold more conservative views on all but one of these issues.

Frei's triumph has been viewed by some as expressive of wide-

TABLE 2-9
Progressive Ideological Views of Prospective Voters
by Candidate Preference, August 1964

Candidate Preference	Ideological Identification	Social Change	Changes	Communism	U.S.-Cuba	Strong Leader	Force of Will	Conflict
Allende	59.3%	81.5%	5.7%	81.6%	87.4%	*2.0	*3.0	*2.9
Durán	29.7	68.3	5.0	23.1	53.9	*3.3	*2.8	*2.2
Frei	18.4	66.0	2.2	9.7	40.5	*2.6	*2.5	*2.6
x^2	279.4	18.6	27	31.2	126.5	32.6	23.6	10.6
p	.000	.004	.000	.000	.000	.000	.008	.38

SOURCE: Hamuy 1964.
NOTE: Values preceded by an asterisk (*) are measured on a scale of from 1 (strongly agree) to 5 (strongly disagree).

spread popular commitment to structural reform and change (Sigmund 1977, 34; Grayson 1968, 364-366; Gil and Parrish 1965, 49). In contrast, these data indicate relatively weak commitments of this sort on the part of those supporting his candidacy. On virtually all issues Frei's constituents lag behind both Allende and Durán supporters. In fact, the same survey suggests only minimal awareness of the reformist aspects of Frei's program, despite the prominence they were given in party and campaign literature. Only a small percentage of Frei's followers were able to identify him as advocating either social or agrarian reform (from 4 to 10.5 percent, and from 10 to 15 percent respectively).[42] Instead, conventional "bread-and-butter" concerns were at the heart of conceptions of and commitment to "change." Jobs, housing, educational opportunities, and inflation were far more important issues than the struggle between freedom and dictatorship or the new communitarian structures into which people would be organized.

On more immediately political and strategic questions similar relationships emerge. These are depicted in Table 2-10. The first question asked for one's assessment of an Alessandri government. The second probed the reasons for which the respondent supported his or her candidate. Here the more progressive responses mentioned the candidate's party or platform, the less progressive his religious beliefs and personality. The third and fourth questions concerned how one felt about alliances between the PDC and the right and left respectively.

As these data indicate, Frei supporters were anything but "progressive" in the context of Chilean politics at this juncture. They lagged badly behind Allende supporters on all issues and trailed those of Durán on two of the four immediate political issues and nine of the twelve issues overall. Durán, it should be noted, was closely associated with the Alessandri administration and with the Radical party's conservative wing.

The character of Frei's constituency was largely a function of eleventh-hour support from Liberals and Conservatives. Ideological conservatives normally averse to the middle of the road were drawn to Frei by the collapse of the ruling rightist coalition and by fear of Marxist revolution. In publicly backing Frei they

[42] It might be argued that urbanites would be less concerned with an issue like agrarian reform. Nonetheless, 71.4 percent of the Communist party members and 45.5 percent of the Socialist party members who were interviewed identified Allende as calling for agrarian reform.

TABLE 2-10
Progressive Political Views of Prospective Voters
by Candidate Preference, August 1964

Candidate Preference	Alessandri	Reasons	Alliance with FRAP	Alliance with Right
Allende	*2.9	76.8%	51.8%	68.3%
Durán	*2.3	64.1	24.3	44.1
Frei	*2.3	41.9	34.8	28.3
x^2	76.4	66.5	17.8	72.8
p	.000	.000	.000	.000

SOURCE: Hamuy 1964.
NOTE: Values preceded by an asterisk (*) are measured on a scale of from 1 (very good) to 5 (very bad).

brought their traditional constituencies with them. For right-wing economic and political elites Frei and the Christian Democrats were a "lesser-of-two-evils" option. For their middle-class and popular followers they were an "acceptable" and increasingly promising alternative around whom the traditional bread-and-butter hopes and expectations began to revolve.

For his part Frei claimed not to have sought or bargained for right-wing support. He argued, in fact, that those supporting him also endorsed his reform program and would help him to carry it out. The survey data indicate otherwise. As in 1958 there was no connection between attitudes (as opposed to mere candidate preference) and degree of religiosity,[43] but when Frei supporters are differentiated in terms of party status and length of association significant patterns again emerge. Table 2-11 compares ideological self-placement among the following five subgroups: *falangistas* (party members who had supported Frei in 1958 and anyone but Allende in 1952), Frei sympathizers (those identifying with the PDC who supported Frei in 1958), new members (party members who had not supported Frei in 1958), Alessandri sympathizers (those identifying with the PDC who supported Alessandri in 1958), and new voters (those supporting Frei in 1964 who had never voted before). Individual differences and the downward trend of leftist inclinations across the subgroups are

[43] The x^2 factors for relationships between extent of religious practice and the issues and attitudes in Tables 2-10 and 2-11 were significant at levels ranging from .32 to .96.

both significant, with recent converts and new voters decidedly more conservative.

These differences are paralleled in Table 2-12 by supporter attitudes on the same ideological issues already examined. As in previous tables, either the scale score or percentage of those giving the "progressive" response is indicated. If longer-standing members were, in fact, more progressive than recent arrivals, their scores should be consistently higher.

Statistically significant associations emerge in only two of the eight issues. *Falangistas* were more committed to social change and showed less enthusiasm for strong leadership. In three of the remaining five issues (U.S.-Cuban relations, the importance of will in overcoming adversity, and the perenniality of conflict) more recent Frei supporters were consistently less progressive, although not always in the same order nor to a statistically significant extent.

Patterns are also mixed with respect to more immediate political issues. *Falangistas* were significantly more negative in their assessments of the Alessandri government and tended to support Frei for his party ties or platform stands. The associations are also in the expected direction on the issues of allying with the Frente de Acción Popular and the right, but they are not strong enough to overcome the small number of cases under examination. Table 2-13 compares the attitudes of Frei supporters on these questions.

In addition to differences between longer-standing party members and more recent arrivals Hamuy's data suggest a steady

TABLE 2-11
Ideological Self-Placement of Christian Democrats
and Frei Supporters, August 1964

Subgroup	Left	Center	Right	
Falangistas	44.4%	55.6%	—	n = 9
Previous Frei				
supporters	22.9	65.7	36.8%	n = 32
New members	26.4	36.8	36.8	n = 23
Previous Alessandri				
supporters	10.8	60.2	28.9	n = 71
New voters	19.7	46.1	34.2	n = 73

SOURCE: Hamuy 1964.
NOTE: $x^2 = 22$, p = .004
$\quad$ tau b = $-.17$, p = .002

TABLE 2-12
Progressive Ideological Views of Christian Democrats
and Frei Supporters, August 1964

Subgroup	Social Change	Changes	Commu- nism	U.S.- Cuba	Strong Leader	Con- flict	Force of Will
Falangistas	88.9%	22.2%	100.0%	55.6%	*3.7	*1.9	*2.1
Previous Frei supporters	82.4	21.2	97.1	53.1	*2.6	*2.0	*2.6
New members	85.2	41.6	82.6	39.1	*2.3	*2.9	*2.6
Previous Alessandri supporters	68.3	19.7	91.3	35.6	*2.7	*2.5	*2.6
New voters	58.9	33.3	93.8	41.5	*2.3	*2.9	*2.5
	n = 242	n = 223	n = 226	n = 214	n = 239	n = 243	n = 245
	tau b = .18	x^2 = 12.1	x^2 = 5.2	x^2 = 12.9	x^2 = 32	x^2 = 19.3	x^2 = .16.5
	p = .000	p = .43	p = .26	p = .37	p = .04	p = .49	p = .68

SOURCE: Hamuy 1964.
NOTE: Values preceded by an asterisk (*) are measured on a scale from 1 (strongly agree) to 5 (strongly disagree).

TABLE 2-13
Progressive Political Views of Christian Democrats
and Frei Supporters, August 1964

Subgroup	Alessandri	Reasons	DC-FRAP	DC-Right
Falangistas	*3.0	88.9%	44.4%	55.6%
Previous Frei supporters	*2.5	60.6	12.9	32.3
New members	*2.4	44.4	34.8	29.2
Previous Alessandri supporters	*2.2	48.7	35.7	26.5
New voters	*2.3	23.0	28.2	27.9
n	239	234	204	200
tau b	−.11	.29	−.02	−.06
p	.02	.000	.37	.16

SOURCE: Hamuy 1964.
NOTE: Values preceded by an asterisk (*) are measured on a scale of from 1 (very good) to 5 (very bad).

radicalization among the older members, one which would parallel that taking place among the PDC's left leaders and militants. Consider the shifts, for example, in ideological self-placement among *falangistas* and party supporters between 1958 and 1964. If members, party supporters, and Frei supporters are taken together for 1958, and again for 1964, the Christian Democratic movement's sense of itself appears to remain stable. In 1958, 50.9 percent of the 108 surveyed (10 party members, 83 party supporters, and 15 Frei supporters) placed themselves in the political center, 32.4 percent on the right, and 16.6 percent on the left. Six years later, 52.5 percent of 215 surveyed (36 members, 106 party supporters, and 73 Frei supporters) placed themselves in the center, 27 percent on the right, and 20.5 percent on the left. If broken down, however, much of the movement leftward can be seen as confined to party members, while rightist sentiment remained strong among Frei supporters. Table 2-14 compares ideological self-placement of the three groups over the six-year period. The data are drawn from two distinct samples and are presented only as a very general indicator of possible trends among the subgroups.

Left-leaning attitudes are strongest among party members and were generally reflected in *falangista* views on the topical political and ideological issues. The strong rightist sentiment among Frei supporters is hardly surprising either, given the context of their incorporation into the political process. What is remarkable, perhaps, is the number of *freístas* (the most conservative segment of the most conservative electoral coalition) who consid-

TABLE 2-14
Ideological Self-Placement of Christian Democrats
and Frei Supporters, August 1958 and August 1964

Subgroup	Left	Center	Right	
Party members				
1958	30.0%	50.0%	20.0%	n = 10
1964	41.7	36.1	22.2	n = 41
Party supporters				
1958	19.3	49.4	31.3	n = 83
1964	15.1	61.3	23.6	n = 442
Frei supporters				
1958	9.2	63.0	27.8	n = 54
1964	17.8	42.9	34.0	n = 512

SOURCE: Hamuy 1964.

ered themselves "leftists." This was most probably due to ideological inflation, i.e., the weakening of terms and standards of political discourse, which came in part from the pervasiveness of reformist language and rhetoric and in part from voter identification with the views of political figures without adequate consideration or commitment.

Summary

The 1950s and early 1960s were years of spectacular growth and expansion for Chilean Christian Democracy. As it grew in political prominence, its social base broadened. Among its new members and supporters were workers, marginals, peasants, women who previously had not been active politically, and voters who had backed either Carlos Ibáñez or Jorge Alessandri in previous elections. With the broadening of its electoral base the party lost the elan and cohesiveness of its earlier days; the uncompromising and strongly ideological spirit of the Falange gave way to the more pragmatic style and positions of a catch-all party seeking to be many things to many different sectors.

This shift was closely associated with the political ascendancy of Eduardo Frei. "Purist" and radical critics opposed it but found it difficult to argue with the success that it engendered. On occasion they were able to muster majorities and prevail on certain issues. Frei gradually became a political phenomenon unto himself, however, able to define his views, and with them the PDC, largely as he saw fit. Under his influence the party became an alternative to the left, blending its call for "reforms" with assurances to bourgeois and petit bourgeois sectors. Frei promised to revitalize economic and political institutions and proposed "more rational" and "more disciplined" strategies and programs for bringing about growth that would provide for the needs and aspirations of all. Pledges of this sort propelled him into the presidency amid general optimism and high expectation.

There was, of course, the problem of the Chilean electorate's penchant for abandoning candidates to whom it had turned enthusiastically only a short while earlier. Frei's margin of victory had been substantial and his popularity was extremely high, but Aguirre Cerda and Ríos, and later Ibáñez and Alessandri, had been popular too and yet lost their followings and momentum by the mid-point of their respective administrations. Because the Christian Democrats appeared more dynamic, seemed to hold well-

77

defined views on the major issues of the day, and had apparently built their following on more solid ideological and organizational bases, however, many observers believed them to be different and thought they would be less susceptible to this phenomenon.

Such impressions reflect limited knowledge of Chilean Christian Democracy prior to the 1964 presidential campaign and little sense of the views of the supporters drawn to its ranks as a result of that campaign. On the one hand, the party had been divided since the late 1940s on the basic issues of identity, constituency, and policy. The majority wing, committed to providing an alternative to left- and right-wing distinctions, favored a broad coalition rallied around Frei, who sought to appeal to all classes and social forces. So-called "purists," in contrast, viewed the party as a smaller, more explicitly progressive vanguard force that would work with, but not absorb, others. A radical minority, finally, felt that existing class and political divisions were real and likely to endure and that the party should align itself with the left in bringing about a socialist society.

The PDC was thus anything but a united or coherent political force as it prepared to assume power. In the years prior to its assumption of governmental responsibilities this lack of cohesion had often worked to its advantage. Its left-wing elements gave it a certain credibility in "popular" and intellectual circles, while the developmentalist and anti-Marxist views of its more conservative mainstream appealed to women, small businessmen, status conscious professionals and white collar workers, and many blue collar workers and marginal elements traditionally supportive of conservative candidates and programs.[44] Once in power, however, the party would be denied the luxury of selectively, and not always consistently, responding to the initiatives of others. Instead, its own positions and policies would become the focal point of national politics, and it would have to learn to think and act with coherence and cohesiveness that it had not previously exhibited.

The ideological and political divisions among longer-standing leaders and militants were compounded by the rapid influx of new members and supporters between 1957 and 1964. During

[44] Among the seventy workers indicating a preference for president in Hamuy's 1958 survey, Allende polled 54.3 percent and Alessandri a surprisingly strong 24.3 percent. Among the fifty-six independent workers (tradesmen such as carpenters, plumbers, gas fitters, and the like) Alessandri polled 50 percent and Allende only 19.6 percent.

this period, the Christian Democratic party moved from relative obscurity to become the country's largest political force. Its electoral support increased more than tenfold, its registered membership more than fivefold. According to survey data, those drawn to the party during this period were significantly more conservative than longer-standing party members and militants. Many of the latter had experienced a species of radicalization and saw the Alessandri years as evidence of both the failure of orthodox capitalist development strategies and the need for structural reforms and not just economic growth. In contrast, newer members and supporters were concerned more with the material fruits of future growth and prosperity. Many were attracted by Frei's personal qualities, by his firm opposition to the Marxist left, or for reasons of political expediency as he and the Christian Democrats emerged as a dominant national force. In effect, they were not unlike the supporters of other movements and times in modern Chilean politics. They cared about jobs, the cost of living, and general economic conditions, not the ideological views or long-term agenda of the candidate or his party.

The PDC's various factions and constituencies were thus at odds over what they wanted and expected from the new Christian Democratic government. Cooperation and harmony among them would be difficult to obtain. The newer arrivals would give the pragmatically oriented Frei additional leverage in his dealings with the party; but while they had voted for "changes" and reforms there was no indication that they were willing to make the sacrifices needed if these things were to be achieved. Nor was there any reason to believe that they were less likely than previous Chilean constituencies to abandon their candidate and his party if and when they failed to fulfill campaign expectations and promises.

« 3 »

IN POWER

Expectation ran high as Frei assumed power. His "revolution in liberty" seemed a promising alternative to Marxist revolution and the conservative status quo. A new era of progress and stability in Chile was proclaimed, and Christian Democracy was hailed as the wave of Latin America's future.[1]

Frei and the Christian Democrats were the beneficiaries of rising demands and expectations that previous administrations had failed to meet. Following initial economic and political prosperity, however, they were engulfed by these same currents. Despite elaborately conceived investment and development programs they were unable to jar the economy loose from its longstanding stagnation. In addition, social and political polarization, which Frei and the party vowed to transcend, grew sharper, leading to widespread unrest and conflict and eroding their seemingly solid political base. Once-enthusiastic supporters defected to the right and left, looking for the same things but drawn in opposing directions. In finishing third to Allende and runner-up Jorge Alessandri in 1970 the Christian Democrats were overtaken by resurgent political rivals they had hoped to render obsolete.

To be sure, the Frei government could boast of significant accomplishments. It introduced agrarian reform to the countryside, expanded public services benefiting the poor, redistributed national income more equitably, and reversed the country's chronic balance of payments deficit, accumulating substantial foreign exchange reserves. On these and other counts it was one of the most successful Chilean governments ever. Nonetheless, it failed to fulfill its own objectives or the expectations of those initially supporting it. As with previous governments its once substantial support base dwindled steadily as time wore on. In retrospect the

[1] Radomiro Tómic, Frei's newly named ambassador to Washington and later the party's unsuccessful presidential candidate in 1970, is said to have predicted thirty years of unbroken Christian Democratic rule. For his part journalist Tad Szulc described the Christian Democratic victory as "the most significant political development in Latin America" since the rise of Castro, and possibly since the end of World War II. Szulc saw Frei as "the spokesman for an ideology which may well be the answer to the hemisphere's search for a new identity" (1967, 102).

obstacles to growth and reform in Chile appear to have been underrated and the character and constancy of Christian Democratic support equally overrated.

Frei's revolution in liberty has been analyzed in various tones and terms. For sympathetic observers like Paul Sigmund (1977, 124-127) Christian Democracy was a broad, genuinely popular, and more successful movement than critics and analysts have acknowledged. According to Sigmund, the Christian Democrats made important economic and political changes but were denied their political fruits because of opposition intransigence, resulting economic difficulties, and to a lesser extent their own ambition, miscalculations, and divisions (pp. 124-127).

Marxist critics, in contrast, see Christian Democracy as the instrument of a "progressive" bourgeoisie, whose project failed for both structural and political reasons. Petras (1969, 12-16 and 240) views it as a "new right" force filling the vacuum left by the collapse of Radicalism and the old (Liberal and Conservative) right. Its "corporatist" and "populist" factions were able to work together during 1965 and 1966, but vied with one another for control in 1967, and went their separate ways in 1968, as Frei and the corporatists assumed control with staunch support from a once hostile bourgeoisie.

Similarly, Stallings and Castells see the PDC as dominated by a "hegemonic" modern industrial bourgeoisie whose failed attempt at reform radicalizes its not insignificant working-class supporters. Stallings (1978, 62) depicts the party's internal struggle as one between bourgeois and petit bourgeois elements, with workers, peasants, and slum dwellers in secondary support roles. The dominant bourgeoisie, after forcing Frei to dilute and reverse his program, ultimately abandons the Christian Democrats, allowing more progressive petit bourgeois elements to take control during the administration's later stages.

Castells (1974, 377) terms the PDC a "populist party" at the service of a divided and not terribly enterprising bourgeoisie. He concedes that the "old oligarchy" could not see the Christian Democratic project as being in its interest and that in the end even the "modern industrial fraction" reacted defensively and irrationally. But it did so, he argues, only after Frei's reformist effort had failed and class struggle had begun to intensify (pp. 375-376).

These analysts offer different assessments of the performance, meaning, and long-term impact of the Frei years. They differ in their treatments of three interrelated issues: the party's relationship to the bourgeoisie; the nature and significance of its internal divisions; and the effect of the reformist experience on its working-class following. The pages that follow offer an analysis of the Frei government with an eye to these issues. Each is important for understanding the PDC itself and the fate of its Revolution in Liberty.

Frei's Program and Strategy

The Christian Democrats promised simultaneous prosperity and reform with full respect for the rights and freedoms of all, including those at whose expense the reforms would come. Although "structural change" had been a prominent campaign theme, Frei offered no reform agenda as such. Banking, factory management, and agrarian reforms were mentioned as objectives, but only the latter of these was ever discussed in programmatic terms. Greater emphasis was placed on raising living standards and on achieving certain investment, growth, and inflation rates rather than on redefining social structures or relationships.

For Frei and his advisors, however, growth and reform were seen as mutually dependent. Sustained development would be impossible unless the national market was expanded and the country's human resources more fully tapped. And yet if reforms were to endure and bear fruit they required a strong economic base. Accordingly, modernization of industry and the promotion of traditional and nontraditional exports were given high priority, but so too were immediate improvements in the lot of the poor, redistribution of national income, and agrarian and other reforms.[2]

Growth would come from private sector initiative, although publicly financed infrastructural and industrial projects were also contemplated. Access to credit would be restricted to those capable of assuring its productive use. The needed capital would come from increased private savings and investment and from public revenues derived from joint venture associations with the

---

[2] Frei's hopes for growth and reform were nourished by a faith in the potential of modern industrial technology. He saw technology as the key to increased productivity and thus to the elimination of the scarcity from which social conflict arose. With increased production, goods and services would be more equitably distributed without sacrificing particular interests or high levels of growth.

American copper companies. Inflation, which was seen as an obstacle to growth and as particularly burdensome to the poor, was also given high priority.

Politically, Frei broke with the country's longstanding tradition of coalition governments. He would base his government on the PDC alone and fill cabinet and other top administrative posts with either Christian Democrats or unaffiliated technocrats. Moreover, in public statements following the election, high-ranking party and government officials took the position that Christian Democracy was the sole expression of legitimate national interest and thus had a mandate for carrying out its program without deals or concessions.

Frei clearly hoped to turn his conjunctural electoral majority into a permanent political majority, thereby making such deals and concessions unnecessary. The upcoming congressional elections of March 1965 offered an inviting opportunity in this regard. If the PDC could retain and absorb those who had supported Frei in September, the new government would have sufficient legislative and broader political support to move quickly on its program, whatever the other parties were willing or not willing to do.

The strategy was ill-advised for several reasons. For one, it was not clear that all who had backed Frei in September supported his program or would wish him to have a parliamentary majority. Second, a majority of the seats in both houses of Congress was simply out of the party's reach. Control of the Chamber of Deputies was possible, as all 147 of its seats were at stake in the election. But only 20 of the 45 Senate seats were being contested, and with but 2 seats prior to the election the PDC could not win a majority even if it were to win all 20. Finally, the attempt to wrest followers from other parties was sure to cause anger, resentment, and retaliation from the parties themselves and from others close to them, whatever the results of the March elections.

This was the case, for example, with labor, investor, and entrepreneurial groups, each of which would be crucial to the success of Frei's program at one juncture or another. Some of them had ties with "traditional" political parties and were already alarmed by what they saw. Circumstances clearly called for concessionary negotiations with these groups, but Frei appealed directly to their constituencies, convinced that they were ripe for the taking and that they had no alternative but to support him.

However plausible they seemed in the wake of the September election, such judgments would prove mistaken. The administration's arrogant pretensions and style quickly cast it in the role of common enemy. This encouraged convergence among uncongenial forces who would prove to have more life and staying power than was ever imagined. In fact, the Christian Democrats badly misread the lessons of their political successes. They had come to power by mobilizing the unorganized and by constituting for conservatives a lesser-of-two-evils alternative. But they had not made inroads into organized labor or the business community, nor had they cut into hard-core right- or left-wing political loyalties. These remained intact and would be formidable obstacles to both economic and political success.

The Early Period

Frei's strategy worked well during 1965 and 1966. A combination of tax reforms, credit and investment programs, wage increases, and expanded social programs stimulated growth while bringing immediate improvement in the lot of the poor.

During the period, the government provided credits, loan guarantees, and subsidies to the private sector and invested directly on its own. Changes in the rules governing bank deposits and credits allowed it to influence credit allocation and better control the money supply. In addition, attractive price levels were offered to producers and retailers, although basic necessities (food, housing, and transportation) were subsidized in order to keep them within the reach of lower-income families. Finally, new tax regulations, including the country's first wealth and inheritance taxes, its first property tax assessment in thirty years, and improved collection procedures, had the effect of increasing government revenues, penalizing idle money, and redistributing income shares.[3]

As a result, the Gross National Product grew by 6.1 percent in 1965 and 9.2 percent in 1966, while inflation, as measured by the official cost of living index, was held to levels of 29 percent and 23 percent respectively. On the social side, considerable time and money were poured into education and public works projects and social assistance programs. By the end of 1966 significant

[3] On tax policies see Foxley, Ainant, and Arrellano 1979, 18-63. For figures on sharp increases in social expenditure for this period see Ffrench-Davis 1973, 332.

strides had been made in housing, school, and health facility construction, and income distribution had become significantly more equal.[4]

Monetary and structural measures were used to attack inflation. New investment, more discretionary credit allocation, and rationalized import procedures helped to absorb inflationary pressures by pushing up production and productivity levels. Price controls, wage guidelines, and general fiscal prudence (pegging government expenditures to available revenues) were also enforced.[5]

Frei hoped to raise the wages of low income earners without generating additional inflationary pressure. Accordingly, the exceptionally low-paid would get increases equal to or higher than the previous year's rise in the cost of living; all others would be given raises equal to the increase, if any, in their productivity during the same period. Pressure from organized labor produced wage hikes that exceeded guidelines in both categories, however. In fact, the increases were so substantial that they helped to raise the share of wages and salaries in the national income from 42 percent to 51 percent in just two years.[6]

While helping wage earners, many of whom were employed in the public sector, the increases undercut the fight against inflation. The administration had apparently foreseen this possibility but showed little interest in negotiating with the Marxist-dominated CUT. From the beginning of the Frei administration, in fact, the Christian Democrats did what they could to weaken the CUT, to promote rival union structures and organizations, and to otherwise counter what it assumed would be unremitting hostility from Communist and Socialist labor leaders. Typical of its

[4] The growth and inflation figures are taken from Edwards 1972, 18 and 30. Edwards questions the government's consumer price index and, using an alternative (García-Freyhoffer) index, places the inflation rates at 44 percent and 37 percent for these years.

[5] For a discussion of the Frei government's economic program see Molina 1972, 64-79.

[6] These figures were mentioned to me in several interviews with Christian Democratic officials. I have been unable to corroborate them with official data for this two-year period, but they appear consistent with other data for the Frei years. Molina (1972, 85) indicates, for example, that the percentage of national income going to wage labor rose from 47.9 percent in 1964 to 54.4 percent in 1968 before falling to 53.1 percent in 1969. Conversely, he points to a decline in the percentage going to entrepreneurs from 26.3 percent in 1964 to 21.6 percent in 1965 and to 20.6 percent in 1966.

many moves reflecting and yet perpetuating its difficulties with organized labor was the government's naming of management labor lawyer William Thayer Arteaga long an advocate of parallel unionism, as minister of labor.

The Christian Democrats did have a basis for their pessimism, however. Their experience with the CUT's Communist and Socialist leadership during the preceding ten years had been frustrating and disquieting. As a vocal minority whose delegate representation averaged around 15 percent at the various CUT congresses (Angell 1972, 218), they fought unending battles to gain secret ballot elections, recognition of their growing following among agricultural workers, and elimination of what they termed sectarian provisions of the organization's Declaration of Principles.

For their part Socialist and Communist unionists were extremely suspicious of Christian Democratic motives. In their view the defense of nonclass-based unionism or free unionization was a means of diluting worker militance and organizational strength. The Christian Democrats would usually lose such struggles and either walk out of the Congress or abstain from the final vote. On several occasions they actually resigned from the CUT and attempted to set up a rival confederation. In virtually all confrontations Christian Democratic workers and labor leaders were the most adamant in their mistrust and hostility toward the Socialists and Communists and had to be dragged back to the bargaining table when party leaders wished to make concessions or overtures to their Marxist counterparts.

Labor movement tensions and rivalries were heightened by Frei's victory. Half the Christian Democratic delegates to the 1965 Congress refused to attend, and those that did walked out before the final session. Beyond the normally divisive issues Christian Democratic workers were stung by harsh Marxist criticism of "their government." Concurrently they were being told by their own leaders that the FRAP would try to use the CUT to promote labor unrest in order to undermine Frei's program and enhance its political position. Faced with such a context Christian Democratic workers withdrew from the CUT and over the next three years attempted, without success, to form a viable rival confederation.[7]

---

[7] Angell (1972, 205-210) mentions three specific efforts: those to create the MUTCh (Movimiento Unido de Trabajadores de Chile) in 1965, the Comando de Trabajo later the same year, and the UTRACh (Unión de Trabajadores de Chile)

The Frei government's hostility toward organized labor contrasted sharply with its courting of *marginados* or urban slum dwellers.[8] During 1965 and 1966, considerable time and resources were devoted to Promoción Popular, a program encouraging self-help and political involvement among the urban poor. Financial, technical, and legal assistance was given to local groups, helping them to meet material needs while providing organizational experience and working relationships with government agencies and personnel.

Promoción Popular would create the functionally based, intermediate social organizations envisioned in Christian Democratic theory. More immediately, it would help to institutionalize support for the government among the "marginal" population. Unlike most industrial workers the *marginados* had not yet been captured by the Marxists, and their needs were more modest and easier to meet. Progress was hampered, however, by Promoción Popular's lack of legal status and adequate funding. Opposition groups feared political use of the new organizations and held up monies earmarked for them. As a result, the program was confined to a relatively modest scale through 1967 and discontinued at that point.

The advances achieved during 1965 and 1966 were helped along by increases in the world market price for copper and by the economy's idle industrial capacity at the time Frei assumed power.[9] They were also the result of decisions and initiatives taken unilaterally by the executive branch. Where legislative approval was needed, as in the case of copper and agrarian reform proposals, the government was less successful. Frei had hoped to avoid such problems by winning or piecing together progovernment majorities in the Senate and Chamber of Deputies, but despite the party's impressive 42 percent of the overall vote, he failed to do so. Christian Democrats did win 82 of the 147 Cham-

---

in 1968. Christian Democratic unionists returned to the CUT in 1968 when the party's union department was taken over by left-wing dissidents.

[8] The term was popularized by the Jesuit Institute DESAL. It referred to unemployed slum dwellers, underemployed or unskilled workers, and peasants, all of whom lived on the "margin" of national life. A representative sample of DESAL analysis is Centro de Estudios para el Desarrollo Social de America Latina 1965. For a critical study of the concept and DESAL's use of it see Perlman 1976.

[9] By July 1966 the price of copper had reached 70 cents per pound, nearly double what it had been when Frei took office. The increase amounted to an additional U.S. $350 million in revenues (assuming production of five hundred thousand tons).

ber seats (a working majority) but won only 12 of the 20 seats at stake in the Senate and could only count on the support of one or two additional senators, thereby falling short of the number required for effective control.[10]

In the case of the copper proposals congressional opposition prevented the new agreements from taking effect until mid-1967, thereby denying the government additional revenues with which to finance other projects. Under his "chileanization" program Frei hoped to obtain an interest in all major mines. Kennecott, whose Braden subsidiary operated the El Teniente mine, agreed to sell 51 percent of its stock in exchange for exploitation rights and special tax breaks. The other company, Anaconda, pledged to increase investment and production and to sell 25 percent ownership in the new Exótica mine but refused to relinquish stock in either the Chuquicamata or El Salvador mines, two of the country's three largest.

These agreements were challenged by critics on the left and right. Communists and Socialists objected to the financial terms and administrative arrangements, while National party (a fusion of the Liberal and Conservative parties) leaders opposed any exemption of the companies from the new restrictions on property rights contained in the pending agrarian reform legislation. Thanks to Radical party support the bill won initial Senate approval, but when this was later withdrawn passage came to depend on the Nationals, who in turn refused to consider the copper bill unless concessions and assurances were offered on agrarian reform. After a four-month stalemate compromise was reached on agrarian reform, and the copper agreements were enacted. They had emerged essentially intact, although valuable time and revenues had been lost.

Congressional opposition also delayed consideration and pas-

[10] The Chilean president's ample veto powers enabled him to alter to his own liking any bill coming from the Congress. Since his vetoes could only be overturned by a vote of two-thirds of the members of both houses, he could effectively legislate with a negative, one-third-plus-one minority. In order to prevent this, the opposition must refuse to initiate the legislative process by rejecting "the idea of legislating" in a particular area, for which a one-half-plus-one majority is needed. Frei's frequently reiterated determination to retain the original provisions of his policy proposals gave opposition forces further reason and rationale for employing a tactic they may have used anyway. Although seemingly obstructionist, this refusal to consider certain political issues was the only means at the disposal of the opposition for avoiding presidential domination.

sage of agrarian reform legislation. Frei did not submit his bill until November 1965 because he wanted to win approval of the copper agreements first and because the Christian Democrats themselves were divided on certain of its provisions. Then, before the bill could be considered, a constitutional amendment had to be passed permitting the expropriation of private property. This was the issue on which the right refused to legislate until Frei promised not to restore (by means of veto power) features to which it objected. And, of course, there were the further complications of the efforts of both left- and right-wing groups to modify specific sections. Frei was forced to make limited concessions to the right (Chonchol 1971), but once he did, in January 1967, fourteen months after its submission, the amendment was passed and the bill approved and signed in a matter of months.

Such maneuvering frustrated the government's legislative program but did not yet find echo in the population at large. During 1965 and 1966, most Chileans appeared relatively pleased with the Frei government. Workers and urban slum dwellers had more jobs, earned higher wages, had more things to buy, and enjoyed more extensive social and public services than ever before. Under such circumstances traditional left criticism was not as compelling as it might have been.[11]

The right also found it difficult to generate antigovernment sentiment. The landlords and idle rich affected by reforms to date were few and as yet inspired little sympathy among other elites, most of whom seemed uncertain as to what to expect from Frei over the long run. With increased consumer demand, on the other hand, most petit bourgeois types (e.g., shopkeepers, small farmers, small businessmen, professionals, etc.) seemed to be prospering and had little reason to resent or oppose Frei.

The government's problems at this stage were economic, not political. In his State of the Union message of 1966 Frei warned of dire consequences if government spending remained high and private savings and investment low. His development program had called for savings and investment rates of 20 percent of the GNP, most of which was to be covered by the private sector. He had hoped that new, readjustable interest savings programs, capital gains exemptions (from tax liability), and a rapidly ex-

[11] Real wages (in constant *escudo* values) increased by 13.9 percent, 10.8 percent, and 13.5 percent in 1965, 1966, and 1967 respectively (Ffrench-Davis 1973, 345).

panding national market would provide sufficient stimulus. They did not. Personal savings remained low, private investment as a percentage of GNP actually fell, and what new private investment there was went into modest growth areas like textiles, synthetic fibers, rubber, leather goods, and shoes. Over the six years of Frei's administration private investment would remain roughly constant but would constitute an increasingly smaller relative portion of overall investment (Ffrench-Davis 1973, 278).

This shortfall was offset by increased public investment and by the availability of idle industrial capacity, particularly in construction and related industries. Major government investment projects included the large copper mines, public works and education, and the petrochemical, steel, electronics, and cellulose industries. Thanks to the idle industrial capacity, increases in production were possible without substantial new investment. This condition would not endure, however, and new investment would be needed if growth rates were to be sustained.

The administration's social and economic objectives, compatible to this point, thus came into conflict. Frei responded by proposing a "truce" to opposition groups. He proposed limiting government expenditures and urged increased savings and investment from those in the private sector who had the necessary means. He had in mind cutbacks in funding for housing and public works, investment credit, and agrarian and social security reform programs. He apparently felt the need to define relative priorities between growth and further social change and came down in favor of the former.

The proposed "truce" failed to achieve its objectives. Socialists and Communists dismissed it as an ill-disguised "tranquilizer" intended to calm capital's nerves and ease the strain on its pocketbook; the right insisted that no real truce was possible unless and until Frei renounced his entire program. For their part business and industrial interests remained unwilling to invest their own money in expanded productive activities. When the government reduced credit, they cut back production and began using up existing stocks. As a result, per capita income for 1967 remained virtually stagnant, income itself grew by a scant 1.4 percent, and with production falling vis-à-vis demand inflationary pressures continued to build.[12]

[12] Aranda and Martínez (1970, 162) show that as a percentage of Gross Geographic Product private investment fell steadily from 7.8 percent to 4.7 percent between 1965 and 1968.

Analysts contending that Frei and the PDC represent the country's enlightened or modern bourgeoisie offer superficial and unconvincing explanations for this lack of investor support. Castells (1974, 356) simply disparages the class as timid and defensive, while Stallings (1978, 62) argues that despite its successful reversing of Frei's reformist policies it was somehow frightened off and "went back to the right" amidst increasing polarization between workers and the bourgeoisie (pp. 115-120). It is unlikely, however, that a dynamic industrial bourgeoisie would be so readily frightened off, or for that matter that such a timid force could control a party with as broad a support base as the PDC. If, on the other hand, the bourgeoisie is seen as either a recent convert or a reluctant supporter that lacked a better alternative, such actions are much more logical. But neither Stallings nor Castells consider such a possibility.

Instead, Stallings confines herself to detailing the bourgeois-Christian Democratic ties, i.e., the bourgeois backgrounds and interests of Frei's cabinet members and advisors, the committee and policy-making boards on which the bourgeoisie enjoyed direct representation, and Frei's support among leading entrepreneurial associations. As proof that these ties were put to productive use she points to a slowdown in Frei's reformist program beginning in 1966, the stability of bourgeois income shares within the industrial sector during the Frei years, and the prosperity enjoyed by the plastics, consumer durables, and chemical industries in particular (pp. 56-62).

There are several problems with Stallings's argument. In her discussion of Frei's advisors and ministers, for example, she provides no substantive information beyond their bourgeois roots or ties. One does not learn if they were major policy makers in their areas of interest or in what other sense they can be said to represent themselves or other capitalists. It matters little, apparently, that someone in the construction industry (the case with two ministers and several congressmen) might have little contact, sympathy, or credibility with people in the modern industrial sector, or that the policies pursued by the government fell far short of what both groups were demanding.

In fact, these Christian Democratic entrepreneurs were maverick or lone-wolf types. None had held office or positions of influence in any of the major entrepreneurial associations. Stalwart Christian Democrats like William Thayer, Edmundo Pérez Zúkovic, Sergio Ossa, Eric Campaña, Domingo Santa María,

Andrés Zaldívar, and Raul Deves were either successful businessmen themselves or lawyers with professional and personal ties to the business community. During the late 1950s and early 1960s, as members of the Union Social de Empresarios Cristianos (USEC), they won some entrepreneurial converts to the party and helped to raise money for its electoral campaigns and party publications. But they were far less successful in selling its reformist views to the dominant bourgeois elements, most of which continued to regard the Christian Democrats as naive romantics, if not dangerous subversives.[13]

As for the boards and committees on which the bourgeoisie was represented, these produced little in the way of Christian Democratic concessions or entrepreneurial satisfaction. The major business associations were the National Agricultural Society (Sociedad Nacional de Agricultura, or SNA), the Industrial Development Society (Sociedad de Fomento Fabril, or SOFOFA), and the Production and Commerce Confederation (Confederación de Producción y Comercio, or CPC). Although each included "social Christian" elements identified with Frei and the PDC, they were all dominated by forces whose ties were to the National party. In fact, a detailed study of the associations during this period indicates the emergence of a solid anti-Frei consensus at precisely the time that Stallings sees bourgeois domination of the party to be at its height.[14]

When USEC president Sergio Silva Bascuñán was chosen to head the CPC in late 1965, this was taken by some to reflect the emerging hegemony of pro-Christian Democratic elements. In fact, it was an admission by the traditionally oriented majority that it had neither access to nor influence with the Frei administration and that it had failed to extract any concessions from it. There were good reasons for this. Under Frei, policy-making posts were staffed largely by Christian Democratic or independent technocrats committed to reform and distinctly unsympathetic to the interests of the country's traditional landowners, indus-

[13] Frei's appointment of Christian Democratic businessman Raúl Deves as his personal liaison to the private sector, to which Stallings attaches great significance, was a departure from traditional political practice as it bypassed existing channels and relationships. Far from confirming the party's close ties with bourgeois circles, however, it constituted an admission of their inadequacy.

[14] David Cusack's unpublished dissertation (1970) is the most complete and insightful study of this subject. Much of the following discussion draws on his work.

trialists, and business people.[15] Where they could, they moved resolutely ahead with expropriation of land, expansion of health, educational, and housing facilities, tax and wage increases, price controls, and other moderately redistributive programs. Entrepreneurial groups took exception to these initiatives but were hampered by Frei's considerable popularity, by his government's seeming indifference to their concerns and criticisms, and by their their own lack of strategic and tactical consensus.

After an initial period of grumbling and complaining, private sector leaders opted for a change. People (like Silva Bascuñán) with ties to the PDC were pushed to the forefront in hopes of improving communication and countering or restraining the reformist thrust. At the same time the organizations began to strengthen their own bonds and relationships. Their efforts involved full-scale discussion and debate regarding growth, reform, the Frei administration, and the Christian Democratic party. In this discussion antiadministration forces enjoyed the upper hand and within a year (June 1966 to July 1967) further marginalized reformist and pro-Christian Democratic elements, fashioning a militant antigovernment consensus. In the process they bridged earlier divisions between small and large entrepreneurs and between industrial and agricultural interests.

Another difficulty with Stallings' argument is its failure to adequately define the terms hegemonic and dominant. For example, bourgeois hegemony might be taken to mean the imposition of party leaders committed to carrying out a bourgeois strategy and bourgeois policies. Or it could mean the setting of policy limits beyond which relatively autonomous party leaders are unable to go. Or finally that the bourgeoisie is one of several class forces whose support is of value to a party or government and therefore might be pursued through the offering of policy concessions. The degree of influence and beholdenness vary considerably here and carry very different implications for a party's autonomy and class character. Stallings seems to have in mind something along the lines of the first or second cases but is not explicit in this regard.

Nor, for that matter, does she attempt to assess the significance of the policy concessions that are made or offered, though

---

[15] These functionaries were by no means all leftists or radicals. In fact, many were apolitical, if not antipolitical, *técnicos* (technical personnel) opposed to any watering down of policy proposals for reasons of political expediency.

this would seem essential in any effort to prove domination. If the concessions were on major policy issues or platform planks and inconsistent with previous positions taken by the party the case for domination would be strong. But if they were not central and were offered within a general faithfulness to one's initial program the characterization would seem gratuitous.

When administration policy during 1966 to 1970 is examined in this light the "concessions" made to the bourgeoisie turn out to be relatively minor and hardly suggestive of bourgeois domination. Frei's proposed truce with the private sector, for example, was clearly an attempt to bargain for its support, but it was hardly a "caving in" or "descent to the right" (Stallings 1978, 108-115). In fact, state expenditures rose during the following year, despite his concerns and assurances. In addition, public sector wages for blue and white collar workers rose an average of 13 percent in real terms, expenditures for education, health, agrarian reform, and social security reform remained at preexisting levels, and only housing and public works projects were actually cut back (Ffrench-Davis 1973, 178-179 and 344-345).

Moreover, the administration went ahead with its tax reform program. During 1967, wealth tax rates increased, personal income and corporate profits taxes rose and became more progressive (by virtue of their "adjustability" vis-à-vis inflation), and several smaller taxes or tax increases would be introduced (Ffrench-Davis 1973, 179). During 1965 and 1966, these levies fell most heavily on higher-income earners, i.e., the very investors to whom the government was allegedly "caving in," and would continue doing so for the foreseeable future. Administration officials apparently remained convinced that the taxes were both necessary (to finance growth and social development programs) and fair and were unwilling to bargain them away.

For Stallings the ultimate "proof" of bourgeois dominance of the Frei government is in the stability of bourgeois income shares during the years 1964 to 1970. According to her figures, these held at the 53 percent mark in the all important industrial sectors and were increasingly concentrated in the chemical, plastics, and consumer durables industries where government support, and presumably Christian Democratic involvement, were substantial.

Even were this the complete picture one must question the assumption that those benefiting from the policies of an administration must be the dominant force within it. This might be the case over a period of twenty to twenty-five years, with various countervailing or mitigating factors balancing one another out. But in a single six-year period the distribution of rewards is affected by so many factors and forces that it says little about power and influence among the various classes.

Normally one assigns dominant power status to those able to dictate terms that are consistently favorable to their interests and detrimental, or at least less favorable, to those of their partners. This was not the case with the bourgeoisie under Frei. As previously seen, wage earners did well in terms of both wage increases and income shares during the first two years. Moreover, Stallings' figure of 53 percent refers to the industrial sector alone. She ignores the mining, agricultural, and commercial sectors where important reform projects were centered, although she concedes that overall bourgeois income shares fell from 36 percent to 32 percent during the same period. In fact, when other areas of the economy are included (Table 3-1), the bourgeoisie emerges as the principal victim of a distributive pattern favoring white and blue collar workers.

For Stallings the decline of overall bourgeois income shares merely underscores the privileged status and hegemonic role of modern industrial fraction. Unfortunately she does not identify these special interests, and thus it is difficult to know of whom she is speaking. Given the bourgeoisie's integrated character, however, the sudden drawing of sharp distinctions between modern and nonmodern sectors seems suspect. And simply to assume that the government's financing of and joint-venture involvement in projects in the modern industrial sector reflects the hegemonic status of the private interests with whom it is associated is at best gratuitous.

In this light Frei's policies would be better understood as stra-

TABLE 3-1
Participation of Population in National Income
by Class, 1960 to 1972

Social Class	1960	1964	1970	1972
Bourgeoisie	27%	36%	32%	27%
Petite bourgeoisie	22	16	15	12
White collar	29	28	32	36
Blue collar	22	20	21	25

SOURCE: Adapted from Stallings 1978, 56.

tegic responses to changing economic and political conditions (e.g., low levels of investment, larger than expected wage increases, rising rates of inflation, etc.) than as the result of a takeover by bourgeois forces. The first significant concessions to the private sector were offered in late 1966 and early 1967 in an effort to stimulate investment and growth, although existing tax impositions were retained, land continued to be expropriated, and the notion of a noncapitalist road to development became a major topic within party circles. And of course the concessions offered failed to generate investor confidence or support. Apparently they were not sufficiently appealing, and in any case more and more entrepreneurial elements were beginning to view a right-wing political renaissance with increasing interest and confidence. In fact, bourgeois forces truly came together as a class during this period, defining the Christian Democrats as their primary antagonists and not their preferred instrument or "other face."

Petras, Stallings, and Castells notwithstanding, the Christian Democrats were a multiclass force, whose dominant elements were petit bourgeois in character. During the Frei administration, the party's leadership, congressional delegation, and high-ranking bureaucratic personnel remained predominantly petit bourgeois.[16] Most were lawyers, educators, engineers, or economists without apparent additional income or interests. Some of the lawyers had personal or financial ties with their industrial, commercial, or banking clients, but most were either general practitioners or labor and administrative lawyers who did not. Most were products of comfortable middle- and upper-middle-class family backgrounds, whose fathers were professionals, moderately prosperous businessmen, or small landowners.

It is true that the greater part of these petit bourgeois types endorsed Frei's courting of the private sector. They did so for reasons and interests of their own, however, and not because they had wilted under the pressure or superior guile of bourgeois forces. Most valued their professional status. While committed to progress, greater equality, and social justice, few felt close to or trusted the working class and most favored an aristocracy of

[16] Of the party's 81 senators and deputies for whom data were available, 57 (70 percent) were from the petite bourgeoisie, 11 (12.7 percent) from the bourgeoisie, 9 (11.1 percent) were white collar workers, and 4 (4.9 percent) were blue collar workers. These figures are based on the author's calculations of data drawn from *Punto Final* 1967, 4-6; Lira Massi 1968a and 1968b; and various editions of *Diccionario Biográfico de Chile*.

talent and quality in which their own high place and influence were assured. A substantial number had taken advanced degrees, some abroad, in such fields as sociology, economics, and administration. Like Frei, many had enormous faith in technical knowledge and expertise. They were confident of their understanding of the country's problems and their party's solutions to these problems. In fact, their technocratic and ideological self-confidence made them less open and less vulnerable to bourgeois or other influences on or within the party. They saw other parties and forces as mired in superficial, politically self-interested approaches to problems, while labor and entrepreneurial groups were seen as self-interested, unimaginative, and overly bureaucratic forces with whom it was neither necessary nor appropriate to negotiate.

Internal Divisions

If general economic trends boded ill for the Christian Democrats so too did the emerging signs of divisions within PDC ranks. These had surfaced as early as July 1965 over the party's role in policy making and the pace of the Revolution in Liberty. Frei's proposed truce exacerbated the conflict and drew the party into an internal debate that would culminate in the secession of its left wing.

In mid-1965 the first voices of dissent were raised by left-wing Christian Democrats questioning the slow pace of reform, the administration's "catering" to private capital, and its hostility towards labor and the left. They were supported by younger party militants and by those unhappy with the party's limited role in policy making.[17]

[17] Dissension sharpened considerably in March 1966 with the tragic events at the El Salvador copper mine. Army troops breaking up a demonstration of striking miners left eight dead, including two women. The government had declared the strike "illegal" and blamed "leftist agitators" for the loss of lives and revenues (production was halted for seventy-seven days). Communists and Socialists countered, charging the government with the murder of innocent workers seeking justice. Within the PDC some defended and others condemned the government's actions. Left-leaning elements viewed El Salvador as an illustration of Frei's general insensitivity to workers and their needs, a judgment shared by the Jesuit monthly *Mensaje*, which termed the episode a taint on the government's revolutionary credentials (see "Huelgas y Disparos," in *Mensaje* 1966, 78-83). Frei loyalists bitterly resented these charges and accused critics of making common cause with those responsible for the tragedy.

A party plenum in April 1966 attempted to bring loyalist and dissenting factions together. While the administration was praised for its accomplishments to date, it was also urged that immediate action be taken on peasant unionization, agrarian reform, and worker participation in the management of firms in which they were employed. The conciliatory value of these resolutions was undercut by Frei's proposed truce the following month. Convinced that the pace of reform was already inadequate, progressive elements were further disheartened and the party's malaise deepened.

These developments prompted a decision to hold a party congress in late August, at which would be discussed such topics as the meaning of the Revolution in Liberty, its relation to the party's ideal "communitarian society," party-government relations, and the policies and programs to be undertaken during the next four years. Dissenters formed two groups: *rebeldes* (rebels) led by Senator Rafael Gumucio and Deputies Alberto Jerez, Julio Silva, and Vicente Sota, and *terceristas* (third forcers) led by Deputy Bosco Parra and the Agricultural Development Institute (INDAP) Vice-President Jacques Chonchol.[18] The two groups held similar theoretical views, although at the tactical level *terceristas* took a more conciliatory line toward the Frei government. The third faction represented was the *oficialistas* (progovernment people), i.e., those supporting Frei and the strategies and policies of his administration. All three groups were composed of predominantly petit bourgeois elements. The *rebeldes* were backed by more progressive Christian Democratic unionists, but *oficialistas* enjoyed majoritarian support across class lines.[19]

Final resolutions represented a compromise among the various factions. The more theoretical issues reflected *tercerista* and *re-*

[18] Chonchol is widely but wrongly associated with the *rebelde* faction, presumably because of his long and close association with leading *rebelde* Julio Silva Solar and because he left the party at the same time. For most of the Frei period, however, he shared the more conciliatory tactical perspectives of Bosco Parra and other *terceristas*. See, for example, the coverage of the Congress in *El Mercurio* (Santiago) during August 1966.

[19] Stallings is correct in pointing out that one-half of Frei's cabinet members were of bourgeois backgrounds. Of these, those who were party members were solidly in the *oficialista* camp. Furthermore, all 11 of the bourgeois members of Congress were *oficialistas* as well. Of the 13 representatives who were from working-class backgrounds, however, 9 (70 percent) were *oficialistas*, although most of them were white collar workers. Three of the 4 blue collar workers were *rebeldes*.

belde thinking, but specific policy matters and the statement on party-government relations were *oficialista* in character. On virtually all issues the margins were narrow, marking a leftward shift in party sentiment. Efforts were made to present a united exterior, but the working papers and accounts of debates leaked to the press revealed significant differences. Initially conceived as a means of resolving internal divisions and difficulties, the congress merely confirmed and accentuated them.

Internal dissension worsened with time, hurting the government in various ways. First, it tended to demoralize many activists and supporters. Left-right and party-government conflicts were supposed to be features of pre-1964 political life from which the PDC had claimed immunity. Evidence that this was not the case shook the party's self-image, undermined the morale of its members, and caused many to look more critically at both the party and the government.

Second, the divisions affected the implementation of policy. *Rebeldes* and *terceristas* held important positions in the bureaucracy, and policies designed with one set of criteria were often carried out by Christian Democrats of a different persuasion and thus in a totally different way. One example of this was the efforts of radicals in the Agrarian Reform Corporation (CORA) and INDAP. Frei chose to proceed cautiously on agrarian reform, not wishing to alarm those landlords working their lands efficiently. CORA officials occasionally authorized the transfer of properties not expropriable under existing law, however, while INDAP personnel devoted their time and energies to peasant organizing, invariably fostering demands for immediate concessions of land (Kaufman 1972, 102-103). Such activities heightened landowner suspicion that the administration would seize all lands despite assurances to the contrary, thereby discouraging their productive efforts and quickly leading to reductions in agricultural output. Similarly, because the government frequently would not accede to the demands for land that its own agencies had aroused and encouraged, it also alienated peasant support that might have been won or retained.

Finally, the party's internal differences tended to strengthen the intransigence of both Marxist and right-wing opposition forces, undermining the government's ability to win support for its policies on an issue-by-issue basis and generally weakening its political position. The criticisms of left-wing Christian Democrats lent greater force and authority to those of the Marxist left, even

99

as they confirmed right-wing suspicions that the PDC was in fact a radical political force. Conversely, as *oficialistas* responded to *rebeldes* and *terceristas*, the right was encouraged and the left's misgivings reenforced. The effect was to leave the party in a species of political no-man's land and to help shore up the appeal of polar ideological and political perspectives.

Decline and Rupture

Over the next two years problems and setbacks brought Frei's reformist experiment to a virtual standstill. Neither industry nor agriculture ever fully recovered from the recession of 1967. Government programs were either eliminated before they took effect or failed to bear the fruits expected of them. Support for the government and the PDC eroded steadily, as forces of the left and right reasserted themselves. Christian Democracy remained engulfed in dissension, and in May 1969 the better part of its left wing broke away. By mid-1969 the Revolution in Liberty was in shambles, the victim of mistakes, internal contradictions, and the political and economic constraints of Chilean society.

The municipal elections of 1967 were the first blow. As a rough indicator of administration support their implications were unflattering. The PDC won 35.6 percent of the vote, a drop of six percentage points from its March 1965 totals. Socialists and Communists were the principal beneficiaries of this decline, polling over 29 percent and recovering their pre-1964 levels of strength. The Radical party, under a new leftist orientation, jumped from 13 percent to 16 percent, while the right-wing National party advanced from 12.5 percent to 14.7 percent.

The Christian Democrats were thus victims of *el desgaste de poder* (the drain of power), the phenomenon whereby an incumbent administration loses its initially broad support not despite but because of its incumbency. The party retained its strength in rural and some mining areas but lost ground in the major urban centers, in low income districts, and among *marginados*. The latter chose not to vote (as suggested by the high rate of abstention in low income districts) or to support Socialists or Communists, whose support in these areas increased substantially (Francis and Lanning 1967).

Without survey data for the period one can only speculate as to the causes and meaning of this decline. The PDC's internal difficulties certainly hurt in ways and for reasons previously

100

suggested. Given the sequence of developments, moreover, it is also tempting to relate the alienation of *marginado* support to policy changes and deteriorating social and economic conditions. The recession set in, and the administration began to cut back as the novelty of initial benefits was wearing off and demands for further concessions were being voiced. With declining economic prospects, additional price increases, and cutbacks in some social programs, frustration and greater susceptibility to leftist appeal were probably inevitable among low-income groups.[20]

Party leaders acknowledged the loss of marginal and working-class support and set about to regain it by pursuing better relations with the left and with organized labor and by looking for ways to accelerate the Revolution in Liberty. When it met again in July, the PDC approved an initial draft of a "noncapitalist development program" and chose *rebeldes* and *terceristas* to lead the party in the months ahead. The moves were a direct challenge to Frei and his policies.[21]

The *vía no capitalista de desarrollo* was made public in August.[21] An expanded version of radical proposals to the party congress the previous year, its major concern was that the country's industrial development be carried out in ways that would undercut, not strengthen, its capitalist structures. The plan proposed a division of the economy into public, mixed, and private sectors. The latter would be barred from certain areas of production and limited in the profits it could earn but was otherwise free to function as it saw fit. The state would exercise direct and indirect controls to insure the public interest and to facilitate worker participation in decision making. Foreign investment would be limited to joint ventures in which significant technical or marketing benefits were provided and would be subject to the same restrictions as domestic capital. The report also urged a reversal of attitudes and policy toward organized labor, insisting that it be viewed as an ally and source of support for the Christian Democratic revolution, not as an enemy or rival (*Política y Es-*

[20] Unfortunately there are no survey data to substantiate such speculation. Had Goldrich, Pratt, and Schuller been able to interview slum dwellers in 1967, as in 1965, there might be some. But the exposé of Project Camelot in late 1965 made this impossible. See Goldrich, Pratt, and Schuller 1967.

[21] The program was formally entitled "Informe de la Comisión Político-Técnica" but was more commonly referred to as the Chonchol Plan, after Commission Chairman Jacques Chonchol. It is reprinted in *Política y Espíritu* 1967, 27-123.

píritu 1967, 118-119). *Oficialistas* attacked the report without success. For his part, Frei chose to ignore the proposals, apparently hoping that party leadership would revert to more congenial hands before too long.

Confrontation came in October over wage adjustment (*reajuste*) legislation. Finance Minister Molina proposed wage increases for 1968 equal to the rise in the cost of living during 1967 but offered only half of this in cash and the rest in five- and ten-year bonds.[22] The proposal was thus a forced savings plan, designed to supplement inadequate savings and investment by the private sector. It was attacked by just about everyone, including the new PDC leadership. To those on the right it smacked of socialism and collectivism, while to the left it was a heavy imposition on already overburdened workers. PDC leaders agreed to support it but only if lower-income workers were excluded, employers contributed their fair shares, and the funds were used for "noncapitalist" projects.

Administration officials rejected these suggestions. Concerned mainly with increasing savings and investment and reducing inflationary pressures, they felt that the modifications would undermine both objectives. The lines were thus drawn, with the administration standing alone against all. The right and left combined to block agreement to legislate on the subject, while the PDC pressed its views in meetings with Frei and his advisors and in statements to the press. For almost four months the controversy dominated national political life and was widely acknowledged to be a test of the administration's overall economic strategy. The intensity of feelings generated was tragically apparent on November 23, when twenty-three people were killed in clashes between security forces and demonstrators protesting the proposal.

The impasse with the PDC was broken in January 1968, when party leaders agreed to submit to a vote of confidence before the plenary council. Frei himself attended the sessions and twice addressed the assembly. His appeal at 2:30 A.M. of the final day was apparently decisive. Shortly thereafter a vote was taken and

---

[22] The bonds were colloquially referred to as *chiribonos*, implying close kinship with *chirimoyas*, the name for both the delicious Chilean pear apple and checks written without covering funds.

the directorate's position rejected by a 278 to 202 margin. *Rebelde* and *tercerista* leaders immediately resigned and were replaced by proadministration elements.

The proposal's passage was still uncertain, however. Frei now had a majority in the Chamber but was still in trouble in the Senate, where only a simple majority was needed to prevent legislating on the subject. The negative votes of Socialists, Communists, and Radicals fell one short of this majority, so it remained for the right-wing Nationals to seal the proposal's fate. When they did, forcing its withdrawal, Molina and several other cabinet officials resigned. The new finance minister, Raúl Sáez, later submitted a similar plan, but it was rejected as well, and Frei was forced to strike the forced savings provisions in order to obtain passage of a wage adjustment bill.

The administration never recovered from this defeat. Economically, its savings and investment program and its strategy of foregoing short-term consumption for long-term expansion and stability were rejected. Politically, it had been caught in a vice between hostile and uncompromising antagonists of the left and right. It had been stripped of its spirit and momentum. Over two years of Frei's term remained, and many important policy matters were still to be considered, but by early 1968 it was clear that the Christian Democratic Revolution in Liberty had died while in its infancy.

AGRARIAN REFORM

Another source of frustration was agrarian reform. Compared with previous efforts, Frei's was an impressive undertaking. His government expropriated more land, redistributed it to more people, and did more to improve rural living conditions than any in the country's history. Yet few policy initiatives left as much frustration or resentment in their wake. The program's fate underscores the limitations and liabilities of reformism in Chile.

Frei's program was aimed at improving rural living standards and increasing agricultural output and productivity. The government (as distinct from individual officials) intended no drastic restructuring of social or economic relations in the countryside. Instead it sought to moderate the existing concentration of land and resources.[23] Oversized and inefficiently worked lands would

[23] At the time three thousand landowners controlled between 70 and 80 percent of the arable land and most of the available water and credit.

be expropriated, but the "efficient producer who does not amass land, who produces and complies with the law" would not be threatened: rather he would be "aided as never before" (Frei 1964, 51). Reconciling popular aspirations for land with entrepreneurial demands for security and support would be a difficult task, but Frei's advisors insisted it could be done.

In terms of numbers the program went far beyond previous reform efforts, although its effects on social structure and production were a source of frustration or disappointment for all. The total amount of land expropriated over the six-year period was 3,200,000 hectares, of which 265,000 were irrigated. Of these, only 18 percent was of land exceeding the legal limit. The rest were either abandoned or inadequately worked properties or lands sold to CORA by their owners.

Through mid-1967 land was expropriated under existing legislation. Although modest in scope, this legislation was pushed to and beyond its limits by determined CORA and INDAP officials. Landowners, fearful that the terms of sale and/or expropriation would be less favorable under new legislation, were willing to settle with agrarian reform authorities even though they were not legally obliged to do so (Chonchol 1971, 291). During 1965 and 1966, slightly over one million hectares of land were expropriated. Of these, fewer than one hundred thousand were organized into *asentamientos*, the experimental cooperatives administered by CORA as an alternative to individually owned and worked land holdings.

The government's submission of its bill in November 1965 sparked a national debate among administration officials, dissenting Christian Democrats, and left- and right-wing opponents. The major issues concerned the amount of land a landowner could retain, the distribution and organization of expropriated properties, and the importance of production versus distribution goals.[24] Left-wing critics were willing to support the Frei bill as a step in the right direction, however, and it became

[24] The administration proposed a limit of eighty hectares and made the *asentamiento* an interim phenomenon whose members ultimately would assume individual ownership of smaller parcels. Right-wing groups insisted on a higher minimum, on individually owned family farms, and on modification of compensation provisions, appeal procedures, and other features. Socialists, Communists, and left-wing Christian Democrats urged lower limits and therefore more expropriation and collective forms of organization if more than a small number of peasants were to benefit.

law in mid-1967. The eighty-hectare limit was retained, except for particularly productive properties, and both individual and cooperative forms of ownership would be allowed.

Ironically, the pace of expropriations slackened under the newer, tougher law. In 1967 fewer than 300,000 hectares, roughly half the amount of the previous year, were expropriated, and of those only 50,000 were irrigated. The figures for 1968 were 657,000 and 44,700 respectively (ECLA 1970, 155). Even more disappointing was the lack of adequate production and credit facilities for new owners from 1967 on. While less dramatic than the expropriations these supplemental supports were essential if either the social or economic potential of reform were to be realized. Without them production levels would fall, and the new structures of operation almost certainly would fail to survive.

Several considerations dissuaded the government from doing more: the financial expense involved, the apparent costs in terms of agricultural production, and the effects on overall investor confidence. In terms of expense the cost per family settled and supported on expropriated land was roughly U.S. $10,000. Of this, the major portion, 73 percent, was for loans and credits; 17 percent went for the purchase of equipment and only 10 percent for the compensation of previous owners (p. 156). These costs convinced Frei's advisors that the original goal of one hundred thousand families was out of the question, particularly in view of current economic conditions. They were less concerned, it seems, with the disheartening and divisive effects that such cutbacks would have on the various sectors of the rural population.

The apparent effects of reform on food production was a second factor in the government's decision to decelerate. Agricultural production actually rose under Frei by an average of roughly 1.5 percent per year, and given the drought of 1967/1968, this was by no means a disgraceful figure. But these modest gains were clearly in spite of agrarian reform. Although the government could point to *asentamientos* on which production levels exceeded those under the previous owners, there were more cases in which the reverse was true (Kaufman 1972, 116). Moreover, many landlords, though not legally expropriable, felt threatened and planted fewer crops, invested less money, and generally proceeded with hesitation. Seventeen percent fewer hectares of wheat, oats, barley, corn, rice, beans, and potatoes were planted in 1969 than in 1964, for example, and actual production fell by 16.3 percent during the same period (Edwards 1972, 27).

A third factor was the administration's concern for improving relations with entrepreneurial elements. Many of these, while recognizing the need to "rationalize" agriculture, were troubled by events in the countryside. They were alarmed by the reformist zeal of CORA and INDAP officials and by the growing militance of newly formed peasant organizations, some of which occasionally seized lands not expropriable or not yet expropriable because of pending court appeals. In particular they were fearful that radical trends enveloping the countryside would affect their own agricultural holdings and/or their holdings in the commercial and industrial sectors. The reduced expropriation levels of 1967 and 1968 were designed to persuade them that they had nothing to fear in either regard.

In terms of the numbers affected the organization of peasant unions and the passage of wage and work place reforms had a greater impact on rural living conditions and social relations. Whereas in 1964 there were only eighteen agricultural worker unions with a membership of 1,800, by 1970, thanks to new legislation and energetic organizing efforts, there were 130,000 workers organized into three national confederations. Many of these workers earned higher wages, enjoyed better working conditions (a shorter workday), and were held up as a standard against which less fortunate rural inhabitants, small holders, tenant farmers, and other laborers compared their conditions. As such, they played an important role in stimulating discontent and unrest in rural areas.[25]

In fact, although it attempted to accommodate everyone, Frei's balanced approach to agrarian reform ended by alienating virtually all. The modest level and pace of expropriation prompted some landowners to form paramilitary organizations to resist and at the same time alienated peasant supporters whose demands and expectations had not been met. In effect Frei moved with sufficient resolution to enrage or alarm one side without satisfying the other. He managed to adversely influence food production without alleviating the unjust social conditions or relation-

[25] This phenomenon was reflected in shifting membership totals of the leading peasant confederations. As time wore on the Marxist Federación de Campesinos e Indígenas (Ranquil) and the INDAP sponsored El Triunfo Campesino (allied with the Christian Democratic left) grew larger, surpassing the government's Confederación Nacional de Campesinos (Libertad). In 1970 Triunfo had 46 percent, Ranquil 32 percent, and Libertad only 21 percent of all unionized workers. See Stoltz Chinchilla and Sternberg 1974, 120.

ships affecting most rural inhabitants. He awakened land hunger and general social consciousness but then failed to meet rising expectations. In agrarian reform as elsewhere the attempt to balance competing concerns and interests satisfied none.

ECONOMIC STAGNATION AND SOCIAL UNREST

The Chilean economy continued to stagnate during 1968 and 1969. The initial compatibility between growth and reform was never restored, and social assistance and reform projects remained subordinate to other priorities, first containment of inflation and later economic expansion. Under the circumstances the party's political standing continued to erode. The most significant desertions were among middle-sector groups, for whom continuing economic trends, increasing tax burdens, and political mobilization and violence were all matters of concern.

During 1968 and 1969, the economy languished despite record high copper prices and foreign exchange earnings. Gross Domestic Product grew at an annual rate of 2.8 percent, barely outpacing population growth, while the manufacturing and construction sectors were stunted by continuing low levels of private savings and investment. Efforts to win investor confidence led Frei to postpone some reforms and programs of immediate benefit to lower- and working-class groups, thus further alienating the left opposition and left-wing Christian Democrats. Had he succeeded in attracting investment, he might have had more resources to devote to such things later on. But as it was, he lost on both counts, sacrificing reforms and improvements and yet failing to get the investment he sought in doing so. From a mark of over 18 percent in 1965, Gross Domestic Savings fell to an average of less than 14 percent from 1967 to 1969. The bulk of this was of public origin, as private investment fell off sharply. Despite administration encouragement and inducements Chilean entrepreneurs financed their operations largely from depreciation allowances and profits, devoting little money to new investment or expansion of productive capacity.[26]

Stagnation hurt the administration politically with all groups. It affected employee income levels and the availability of public services. Its impact on middle-sector groups was aggravated by

---

[26] Between 1966 and 1968 an average of 55 percent of the Gross Domestic Capital Formation came from depreciation, 11 percent from deficits, and only 34 percent from savings (Ruddle and Odermann 1972, 350).

their increased tax burdens. White collar workers, shopkeepers, professionals, small businessmen, and civil servants were required to pay higher income and property taxes, to make additional social security contributions for their domestic or commercial employees, and to pay special excise and luxury taxes.[27] While hit less heavily than wealthier Chileans, they had fewer means with which to escape or endure additional impositions, and for a consumption-conscious group like Chile's middle sector the reduction of disposable income was not readily accepted and had important political repercussions.

Stagnation was accompanied by rising inflation and fueled an upsurge of strikes and general unrest. By 1968 the official inflation rate had climbed back to 27 percent, and that year virtually every major public employee group, including postal workers, National Health Service personnel, public school teachers, members of the armed forces, and judicial branch employees, went on strike or otherwise openly protested over wages and work benefits. These conditions, coupled with the slowing or shelving of reform projects, also gave rise to land and building seizures, demonstrations, and confrontations between protest groups and police. In some cases the farms, buildings, or vacant lots seized were claimed by those involved; in others, they were used as public fora from which to plead a cause. In either case discord and disruption seemed the order of the day, and the law and authority were flaunted regularly and with seeming impunity.[28]

[27] Under Frei income tax receipts jumped by more than 50 percent per year except during 1967 and 1968 when they rose by 30 percent and 26 percent respectively. Property tax receipts doubled in 1965 and rose again by 28 percent in 1967 and 1968, before tailing off in 1969 (Ruddle and Odermann 1972, 350). In addition, social security contributions made it difficult and in some cases impossible for middle-class families to retain their cherished domestic servants (*empleadas*) and thus were bitterly resented. Indirect taxes (which included exise, luxury, and sales taxes) increased at annual rates of 54 percent (1965), 47 percent (1966), 36 percent (1967), 48 percent (1968), 50 percent (1969), and 47 percent (1970). Among the things for which exise and luxury taxes were charged were automobiles, televisions, hotels, telephone service, air travel, and restaurants, all of which were attractive to middle-sector people. Unfortunately I do not know the breakdown between sales (essentially regressive) and excise and luxury (progressive) taxes, and despite the slight increase in the incidence of indirect vis-à-vis direct (income and property) taxes it is impossible to characterize the overall change in tax structure.

[28] Typical in this regard were the many *tomas* or seizures of universities, public buildings, vacant lots, health service offices, and even boy scout headquarters and primary schools.

Frei's response to the unrest was to replace popular Interior Minister Bernardo Leighton with Edmundo Pérez Zúkovic, who was known for his strong anticommunist and probusiness sentiments.[29] Pérez Zúkovic's ironhanded approach provoked further confrontation, perhaps because it virtually assured the protesting group media exposure. In any event the government was increasingly ineffective in dealing with the popular unrest and mobilization, causing some to look elsewhere for defense of their status and interests. Although with less to lose than wealthy industrialists and landlords, middle-sector Chileans were no less concerned at the thought of losing what they had and now had reason to join them in a common front.

With such developments Christian Democracy's electoral prospects remained poor, and the 1969 congressional elections witnessed the continued erosion of its support. As in 1967 both the left and right gained, although this time the right advanced further. The PDC polled less than 30 percent of the vote and won only 55 of 150 seats in the Chamber of Deputies. The FRAP parties combined for 31.2 percent (up from 29 percent), while the rightist Nationals jumped from 14.2 to 20 percent, electing 34 deputies. Abstention was high (26.8 percent), and again the PDC slipped more in urban areas than in the mining or agricultural provinces. In Valparaíso, Santiago, and Concepción the party's vote fell by over 35 percent, while those of the PN rose by over 200 percent (Grayson 1969b, 63-65).

Stagnation, rising inflation, burdensome taxation, and concern with growing unrest were all factors in the middle sector's disenchantment with Frei, and as such they were effectively exploited by the Nationals. Another factor was the PDC's internal divisions, which cast doubt on what Christian Democracy stood for and where it would go once Frei completed his term. Middle-sector groups that had been relatively secure under Frei but feared the party's left wing must have been disconcerted as they looked to 1970 and beyond.

Feeding from and further reenforcing these sentiments was the impending 1970 presidential candidacy of former president

[29] Pérez Zúkovic, who had been an early *falangista*, was a self-made and highly successful businessman (in construction). He was avowedly hostile to party "ideologues" and leftists. In 1965 he became minister of public works and was considered one of Frei's most trusted and influential advisors. He was assassinated in June 1971, apparently by a left-wing paramilitary group calling itself the *Vanguardia del Pueblo*.

Alessandri. For Chileans of diverse social strata, his name was synonymous with authority, integrity, and less complicated if not materially better times. To exploit his popularity the Nationals argued that support for them in 1969 was an endorsement of Alessandri's candidacy in 1970. This association helped to swell their totals, pulling in longstanding *alessandristas* and those adversely affected by Frei or alarmed at the prospect of a Christian Democratic government under someone other than Frei.

The election also had consequences for the PDC's internal life. *Rebelde*, *tercerista*, and *oficialista* candidates campaigned openly on separate platforms and appeals, although not even *oficialistas* would endorse the government's performance unqualifiedly. The results favored the *oficialistas*, who garnered 70 percent of the party's total vote and 43 of its 55 Chamber seats. *Rebeldes* and *terceristas* could point to substantial support, particularly in working-class areas and among young people, although it is impossible to know what amount of their support reflected conscious ideological affinity rather than other sources of appeal.[30]

Leftists and *oficialistas* blamed each other for the poor showing. The left bemoaned the party's unwillingness to choose sides in the increasingly polarized political struggle, while *oficialistas* blamed the left for contributing to the polarization and undermining efforts to move beyond it. These terms were carried over to discussions of the upcoming presidential election. *Oficialistas* urged adoption of a *camino propio* strategy, with the party going its "own way" in opposition to the left and right. The left wing countered with a call for Christian Democratic participation in a united "popular unity" coalition with the left.

These positions continued the party's longstanding internal cleavage. The left was still in a minority, although it drew support from those concerned with establishing a post-Frei political identity. Hoping to capture majority backing, it decided to force the issue, demanding the convening of a plenary council to decide the question of campaign strategy. *Oficialistas* agreed but called for new delegate elections that they subsequently dominated. A close vote was nonetheless likely as party president

---

[30] *Rebelde* candidates did well in both Concepción and in Santiago's third district, the latter which includes several large working-class *comunas*. At the time *rebelde* and *tercerista* candidates were estimated to have received roughly two hundred thousand votes. If half of these are added to the left's vote its percentage moves up from 32 to 36 percent, the level of support with which Allende would win the presidency the following year.

Fuentealba and presidential hopeful Radomiro Tómic endorsed the popular unity position. For their part Gumucio, Silva, Jerez, and Chonchol threatened to leave the party unless it agreed to join forces with the left.[31]

The meeting was held during the first week in May. For two days the issue was debated but on the third delegates chose the *camino propio* thesis by a 310 to 205 margin. Following the vote, Tómic was offered but declined the party's nomination, suggesting that someone willing to work within the framework adopted be chosen instead. The left was true to its word as well. On May 6 *rebeldes* Gumucio, Silva, Jerez, and *tercerista* Chonchol resigned from the PDC. They were joined by peasant, labor, and youth sector leaders and by a handful of provincial activists. Most *terceristas* put off a decision until they could assess the party's presidential platform, which was to be defined during the next several months.

In the meantime Tómic and others continued efforts to drum up Socialist and Communist support for a joint Christian Democratic-FRAP candidacy. Following repeated rebuffs, Tómic accepted the PDC nomination, voicing the illusory and self-indulgent hope that vigorous campaigning would generate support from the "popular" grass roots, if not the parties themselves. Neither this logic nor the progressive platform completed in August were able to lure back the *rebeldes*, although for the moment they did help to retain most *terceristas*.

Denouement

The period from mid-1969 through September 1970 was important for Chilean politics, however anticlimactic for the Frei administration. Frei's Revolution in Liberty had ground to a halt. Its initial support base was sundered and its outlook for the future bleak. At this juncture neither an economic revival nor major policy initiatives were likely.

Moreover, political attention shifted to the upcoming presidential election for which active campaigning was soon underway. As under previous governments nearing the end of their terms the election offered new hope to a frustrated electorate and helped

---

[31] At issue, they argued, was the seriousness of the PDC's commitment to revolutionary change inasmuch as this was impossible without the active collaboration of other revolutionary forces.

to consign the incumbent regime to caretaker status during its final year. It was not that there was little to do. Several important issues remained to be dealt with but none carried the drama or implications they might have had the government's fate not already been determined.

During 1969, tensions heightened and violence and unrest intensified. Clashes between protestors and police were daily occurrences. On the one hand, militant landowners organized and armed themselves to forcibly resist peasant seizures and duly authorized expropriations. On the other, the leftist MIR began sporadic urban and rural guerrilla operations, including a series of bank robberies.[32]

In October Chile was jolted by an army uprising (*el tacnazo*) that brought new uncertainty to the political process. Military units headed by Army General Roberto Viaux seized control of the Yungay and Tacna regiments, ostensibly to protest low pay and poor working conditions. Broader concerns and purposes were clearly involved, however, among them military uneasiness at the prospect of a victorious leftist candidacy in 1970. Following high-level negotiations, the rebels surrendered and their leaders were charged with and convicted of insubordination. Although silenced expeditiously, the incident cast the supposedly apolitical Chilean military in a new light. Viaux himself insisted that his objectives had been "non-political" but that he could have overthrown the government "had he wished to" (Olavarría Bravo 1971, 56). The insinuation was disturbing, and the possibility of military intervention became a factor in the political calculations of all sides from this point on. In fact, in the months that followed rumors of impending coups abounded, and on several occasions officers were actually arrested, although details of the alleged conspiracies were never made public.

During 1969, Frei resumed negotiations with the American copper companies, hoping to bring Anaconda's Chuquicamata and El Salvador mines under the agreement reached earlier with Kennecott. He first insisted on partial ownership and greater participation in profits, but during the discussions bills calling for outright nationalization were submitted to the Congress by opposition groups. This improved Frei's bargaining position and

[32] Labrousse puts the date of the MIR's founding as August 1965, with the coming together of groups led by former Socialists Miguel Enríquez and Bautista van Schouwen (Labrousse 1972, 140).

allowed (some would say obliged) him to raise his demands. Anaconda met those demands to avoid being nationalized, agreeing to sell 51 percent of each company immediately and the remainder once 60 percent of the initial block of stock had been paid for.

The other proposal occupying Frei's attention dealt with constitutional reform. This motion gave the president the power to dissolve the Congress and call new elections, reserved certain policy matters, including the *reajuste*, to the executive, and lowered the voting age from twenty-one to eighteen. Frei had proposed these things in early 1965 but failed to win support for them. He again submitted them in January 1969 and by December won approval on the condition that the bill would not go into effect until November 1970 (and thus be of no use to Frei himself).

The new year brought an upswing in the tempo of presidential politics. Popular Unity parties nominated Allende for the fourth time, and he immediately joined Alessandri and Tómic on the campaign trail.[33] For the next nine months the three shared the center ring in the national political arena.

The campaigns varied in tone and content. Alessandri campaigned less on issues than on personality and general political sympathies. As in the past he offered himself as one above politics and politicians, a wholesome Chilean alternative to the "foreign" ideologies of his Marxist and Christian Democratic opponents. He hoped for support from the resurgent National party, from Frei supporters unwilling to support another Christian Democrat, and from those voting for the first time. He promised good things to just about everyone. Progress, reform, and change were all possible but only if rooted in a reinvigorated economic base. This would require renewed support for and incentives to the private sector, restrictions on government spending (and therefore on social programs), and a reorientation of the agrarian and other reforms with an eye to improving production levels and overall investment climate.

From a political point of view Alessandri could assume the support of entrepreneurs and landowners. He was free, therefore, to focus his campaign on middle-sector groups, women, workers of various sorts, and the slum-dwelling poor. His prospects were

[33] The Popular Unity coalition consisted of the Socialist, Communist, Radical, Social Democratic, Independent Popular Action, and MAPU parties. MAPU (Movimiento para Acción Popular Unitario) was founded by left-wing Christian Democrats who had abandoned the party in May.

good. Many of these people had hoped for or expected more from Frei and were now looking beyond the Christian Democrats. They had supported Alessandri in previous years and might still find his paternalistic populist line appealing.

Allende's campaign was the obverse of Alessandri's. He also sought to appeal to those frustrated during the Frei years but focused primarily on lower or "popular" classes as well as middle-sector groups. His speeches emphasized the plight of the poor, the elderly, workers, and slum-dwelling marginals, and he promised to aid them by transforming, not reenforcing, existing economic structures. More specifically, he would raise working-class incomes and living standards immediately, workers would begin participating in factory management, monopolies would be eliminated, the agrarian reform accelerated, and economic policies governed by considerations of social, not corporate, interests. Allende made clear that his would be a government of and for the Chilean masses, although he assured professionals, small businessmen, and other middle-sector groups that they had nothing to fear from it.

Both Alessandri and Allende had natural socioeconomic constituencies. Neither had difficulty deciding how to orient his campaign. Tómic did. His largest potential store of votes were the Christian Democrats, although many of these were Frei partisans, not ideologically committed militants. Moreover, in retaining those disillusioned under Frei, he would have to choose to whom he would give the greater priority: those who thought Frei had gone too far or those who thought he had done too little.

He chose the latter, more it would seem for reasons of personal preference than sober political calculus.[34] He attacked foreign capital and promised an intensification of agrarian reform, nationalization of the banks, worker participation in factory ownership and management, and a series of political reforms. He also stressed the need to stabilize and revitalize the economy and warned that this required sacrifices from all.

Unfortunately, it proved difficult to maintain Christian Democratic support while reaching out to the left. In effect, Tómic had to out-promise Allende and at the same time sell himself as a moderate and a real alternative to (and defense against) Marx-

[34] Tómic made the wrong choice, at least in terms of numbers, although Sigmund (1977, 108) is probably correct in arguing that he could not have held on to all of Frei's 1964 supporters even if he had chosen to associate himself more closely with Frei.

ist revolution. The polarization developing since 1967 made this virtually impossible.

Frei took almost no part in the campaign. He confined his public appearances to the inauguration of projects initiated or completed by his government. In keeping with Chilean tradition, he made no endorsement and played no active role, although he was believed by some to favor Alessandri.

Election returns gave a plurality of votes to Allende, who won 36.2 percent of the total. Alessandri was a close second at 34.9 percent, while Tómic finished third with 27.8 percent. The Popular Unity and Christian Democratic totals were remarkably similar to those of the 1969 congressional elections, while Alessandri improved considerably on the Partido Nacional's showing.

The election was not a plebiscite on the Frei administration. Indeed, had Frei been the candidate the Christian Democrats would have done much better.[35] Still, it was clear that he had lost ground and had failed to establish an effective alternative to the left and right. Although an appealing alternative in the bipolar campaign of 1964, his balanced middle-of-the-road approach failed to solve the country's problems or satisfy its expectations. In the three-cornered competition of 1970, over 70 percent of the electorate preferred proposals and perspectives of the traditional left and right.

Public Opinion and the Frei Years

Analysts of the 1970 election agree that Tómic's candidacy, and hence a second Christian Democratic administration, were undermined by social and political polarization during the Frei years. Allende is credited with solidifying his support among the working class, as evidenced by his strong showing in Santiago, Concepción, and the copper-mining north. Alessandri, on the other hand, is generally conceded the bulk of upper- and middle-class votes and a substantial portion of those who previously supported Frei.[36]

These generalizations are based on ecological analyses of electoral data and suffer from weaknesses characteristic of that

[35] It is not clear, however, that if he had been eligible to run Frei would have won reelection in a three-way race. A fair amount of the generally favorable sentiment toward him may have reflected the fact that he was *not* a candidate.

[36] See, for example, Sigmund 1977, Stallings 1978, Morris 1973, and Francis 1971.

method. Principal among these is the highly questionable assumption that most voters in a given electoral district vote in a
manner presumed rational for residents of such a district. Fortunately Professor Hamuy returned in August 1970 to the same
Santiago districts surveyed in 1958 and 1964 and provides a firmer
basis for characterizing the thinking of likely voters.[37] His 1970
survey did not probe political and ideological attitudes as extensively as did previous surveys, but it does permit the questioning
of several widely held assumptions about this juncture in Chilean politics. Two such assumptions are: 1) that 1964 to 1970
were years of intense social polarization, producing a convergence of class and political divisions, and 2) that chief among
those moving leftwards were Christian Democratic workers radicalized by the reformist experience (Stallings 1978; Castells 1974).

One of the more important phenomena to emerge from Hamuy's survey is the broad support that both Alessandri and Tómic
received from Chilean workers. Although Allende drew the bulk
of his support from workers (62.6 percent), more blue and white
collar workers actually supported either Tómic or Alessandri.
Table 3-2 details the occupational situations of those supporting
each candidate.[38] As will be argued below, the potential for class

[37] Hamuy's August 1970 survey was Research Project No. 37 of his Centro de
Opinión Pública. Although it underestimated the support that would emerge for
Allende and overestimated that for Alessandri (it projected Alessandri as narrowly winning over Allende in these districts, when in fact he would trail him
32.7 percent to 39.3 percent), in other respects it was an accurate predictor of
voting behavior, having correctly anticipated Tómic's 27.8 percent showing. In
my research I have not had access to the study itself but to a portion of it repro-
duced by the Jesuit Centro Belarmino in its survey of attitudes on the Church
and priesthood the following year (Centro Belarmino 1971). Hamuy gave Centro
researchers the cards and sample of his 1970 survey, allowing them to conduct
follow-up interviews dealing with religious matters with as many respondents of
the original sample as could be contacted. Six hundred twenty-nine of the seven
hundred thirty original respondents were reinterviewed. Their answers to questions concerning religion were superimposed on certain columns, eliminating some,
but preserving most, of the 1970 data. Original data for those who could not be
contacted were set aside, in effect reducing the size of the sample. I have not
used the data gathered in 1971, but inasmuch as the 1970 data in which I am
interested are only available in partial form I refer to them as Centro Belarmino
1971. The data's relative accuracy in predicting subsequent electoral behavior
suggests that the survey instrument's content remains "valid," even though the
sample size and composition were effectively altered. For additional discussion
of these matters see the Appendix.

[38] These "class" categories are developed from the somewhat broader occupational categories used by Hamuy. The category of white collar workers corre-

consciousness inherent in one's class situation may not be realized because of contravening ideological and institutional political factors.

Another interesting characteristic emerging from the data is the division of practicing Catholics between Alessandri and Tómic. While in previous years the Christian Democrats had been major beneficiaries of the Catholic vote, in 1970 practicing Catholics split their preferences between Alessandri and Tómic, giving slightly greater support to the former and a respectable amount to Allende as well.[39]

Tómic and the Christian Democrats clearly lost the election by failing to retain a sufficient portion of those supporting Frei in 1964. Among the 1964 Frei supporters interviewed by Hamuy, Alessandri won 45.3 percent of the preferences and Allende siphoned off 12.4 percent. Tómic could retain only 42.3 percent. These figures can be read to suggest that while Frei had not moved quickly or far enough for some the vast majority of his

TABLE 3-2
Occupational Statuses of Prospective Voters
by Candidate Preference, August 1970

Candidate Preference	Managers, Owners	Professionals Technicians	White Collar Workers	Blue Collar Workers	Service Workers	
Alessandri	9.9%	11.0%	31.9%	35.2%	12.1%	$n = 91$
Tómic	1.4	17.6	36.5	35.1	9.5	$n = 74$
Allende	4.3	8.5	20.2	55.3	11.7	$n = 94$

SOURCE: Centro Belarmino 1971.
NOTE: $x^2 = 19$, $p = .01$

sponds to his category of employees, some of whom (e.g., high-ranking civil servants) might be more accurately characterized as professionals or technical workers. Among the blue collar workers (his term *obrero*), on the other hand, were both skilled and unskilled industrial workers (of whom some worked in large factories and others in small shops) and independent workers. Clearly people in very different productive roles and relationships are being lumped together. Unfortunately, there is no way to break each group down, and the terms, however inadequate, will have to stand.

[39] According to Centro Belarmino 1971, practicing Catholics gave disproportionate support to the Christian Democrats. Of all Catholic respondents, 27.9 percent expressed affinity for the PDC, but among those who considered themselves "practicing" Catholics the figure was 40 percent. Conversely, although leftist parties received the support of 22.8 percent of the larger group, they were backed by 40 percent of those who considered themselves "lax" Catholics. The x^2 factor of 19.3 is significant at .004.

117

original constituency thought he had gone too far (and switched to the more conservative Alessandri) or were generally satisfied (and stayed with Tómic).

Interestingly enough, many former *freístas* did not think of themselves as having changed politically. The ideological terms in which they classified themselves were strikingly similar to those used by Frei supporters six years earlier (see Table 3-3).

Significant changes do take place, however, among longer-standing Frei supporters, i.e., those who had backed him in 1958 as well. As Table 3-4 indicates, in the 1964 survey they were moving leftwards, but by 1970 many were leaning in the opposite direction.

In contrast with trends during its rise to power, the years in power thus had a conservatizing effect on longer-standing members and supporters. These self-assigned labels hold different meanings for those using them, of course, and could be derivative of nonideological sentiments, e.g., support for or opposition to personalities associated with the labels. Accordingly, it might be helpful to look at other characteristics of those who supported Frei in 1964.

TABLE 3-3
Ideological Self-Placement of 1964 Frei Supporters
August 1964 and August 1970

Position	1964 Supporters in 1964	1964 Supporters in 1970
Right	32.0%	36.9%
Center	49.6	42.5
Left	18.4	20.6
n	434	233

SOURCES: Hamuy 1964 and Centro Belarmino 1971.

TABLE 3-4
Ideological Self-Placement of 1958 Frei Supporters
August 1958, August 1964, and August 1970

Position	1958 Supporters in 1958	1958 Supporters in 1964	1958 Supporters in 1970
Right	27.8%	6.8%	31.6%
Center	63.0	59.3	52.6
Left	9.3	33.9	15.8
n	54	59	38

SOURCES: Hamuy 1958, Hamuy 1964, and Centro Belarmino 1971.

Although differing from those continuing to support the Christian Democrats, those switching to Alessandri and Allende were not as distinct as one might have expected. In terms of occupational status, for example, those switching to Allende included proportionately more blue collar workers, but far greater numbers of workers (blue and white collar) either remained with Tómic or went to Alessandri. Table 3-5 relates the occupational statuses and class preferences of those supporting Frei in 1964.

These data suggest that those abandoning the Christian Democrats in 1970 came from all class strata and that far more blue and white collar workers were switching to Alessandri than to Allende. Such workers may not have been among the country's best organized, most conscious, or politically most active working-class elements. Few of them belonged to a union (only 4.7 percent of those supporting Frei in 1964, for example), and most may have worked in small shops at relatively unskilled tasks. But they do constitute a cross-section of the working-class population in the country's largest industrial area and as such belie claims of increased class differentiation and polarization. Indeed, quite the reverse trend appears to have been taking shape.

Also of note are the relationships between electoral preferences and perceptions of personal economic circumstances, change therein, and the general condition of the country. Table 3-6 provides a breakdown in percentage terms. Not surprisingly, those staying with Tómic viewed themselves and the country more positively, although the similarity in perception of *allendistas* and *alessandristas* is certainly striking in view of Alessandri's association with a middle- and upper-class support base.

TABLE 3-5
Occupational Statuses of 1964 Frei Supporters
by Candidate Preference, August 1970

Candidate Preference	Managers, Entre- preneurs	Professionals, Technicians, Small Businessmen	White Collar Workers	Blue Collar Workers	Service Workers
Allende	10.0%	—	11.9%	13.6%	18.2%
Tómic	10.0	69.2%	52.4	38.6	45.5
Alessandri	80.0	30.8	35.7	47.7	36.4
n	10	13	42	44	11

SOURCE: Centro Belarmino 1971.
NOTE: $x^2 = 11.8$, $p = .157$

119

A final matter worth noting were the assessments made by each group of Frei's performance in office. Here the same general trend appears: those supporting Tómic give Frei higher marks, those shifting to Alessandri and Allende lower. In no case, however, are the marks terribly low. On a scale of 1 to 6 (excellent to very bad), the average rating given by Tómic supporters was 2.6, that of *alessandristas* 3.4, and that of *allendistas* 3.8.[40]

Among respondents who had previously backed Frei there is thus a shift to the left by a small number of predominantly working-class types apparently radicalized during the Frei years and to the right by more than three times as many predominantly working-class voters. Such findings cast serious doubt on claims that the Frei years produced a hardening of class lines or a polarization of social or class forces.

Reenforcing these doubts is the lack of evidence that Frei supporters moving to the left held hopes, expectations, or views that differed from those moving rightward or remaining loyal. The three groups identified the same areas of need and appeared to have similar aspirations for themselves and the country. Presented with a list of five problem areas (agrarian reform, more jobs, greater educational opportunities, elimination of housing shortages, and reduction in cost of living increases), respondents were asked which they considered the most important. Although the list is not exhaustive, nor is it clear what one might have had in mind in choosing one over the others, agrarian reform had been a symbol for structural change in Chilean politics for years, even for the urban population, and thus it afforded an opportunity to indicate support for such change and not just for

TABLE 3-6
Economic Perceptions of 1964 Frei Supporters
by Candidate Preference, August 1970

Candidate Preference	Difficulty or Hardship	Personal Situation Worse	Country Condition Bad
Allende	68.8%	34.4%	39.3%
Tómic	49.5	13.7	15.6
Alessandri	55.2	37.6	39.3
	$x^2 = 6.9$	tau b $= .18$	$x^2 = 26.5$
	p $= .32$	p $= .001$	p $= .000$

SOURCE: Centro Belarmino 1971.

[40] The x^2 factor of -161.9 is significant at .000.

personal economic betterment. The pattern of responses is given below in Table 3-7.

Here the distribution of concerns (as measured by the x^2 factor) appears significant, although the most notable variation was the concern for agrarian reform of a small number of those supporting Tómic. In fact, most supporters of the three candidates exhibited a remarkable uniformity of viewpoint across the board (as measured by the tau b factor), one characterized by the absence of the concern for structural change. Their presidential preferences thus do not appear to be ideological and would seem to be of a more limited partisan or political nature, i.e., for a candidate or political tradition.

The ability of each candidate to retain longer-standing supporters lends additional strength to this impression. Allende, for example, did well among first-time voters (39.4 percent compared to 35.5 percent for Alessandri and 25.1 percent for Tómic) but did best of all (81.4 percent) among those who had backed him in earlier campaigns. Similarly, Alessandri's strong showing was based largely on his recapture of previous supporters, including most of those endorsing Frei in 1964. Table 3-8 compares retention levels for the three candidates.

All three candidates kept at least 60 percent of those supporting them or their party's candidate in 1958. Tómic's strong showing among Frei's 1958 backers (69.4 percent), his poor showing among Frei's 1964 supporters (42.3 percent), and Alessandri's stronger showing among the latter (45.4 percent) confirm the view that much of Frei's 1964 constituency included right-wing voters lacking a viable alternative at that point. In each of the three cases support reflected the strength of a political identity

TABLE 3-7
Priority Concerns of 1964 Frei Supporters
by Candidate Preference, August 1970

Candidate Preference	Agrarian Reform	More Jobs	Educational Opportunities	Housing Shortages	Inflation	
Allende	—	31.3%	12.5%	—	56.3%	n = 32
Tómic	7.4%	30.6	15.8	3.7%	42.2	n = 108
Alessandri	—	34.5	12.9	2.6	50.0	n = 116

SOURCE: Centro Belarmino 1971.
NOTE: $x^2 = 14.1$, p = .08
      tau b = .022, p = .349

TABLE 3-8
Previous Voting Behavior of Prospective Voters
by Candidate Preference, August 1970

Candidate Preference	1958 Allende	1958 Frei	1958 Alessandri	1964 Allende	1964 Frei
Allende	87.5%	2.8%	11.8%	80.0%	11.3%
Tómic	7.8	69.4	26.4	5.4	42.3
Alessandri	4.7	27.8	61.2	12.5	45.4
n	64	36	121	112	258

SOURCE: Centro Belarmino 1971.
NOTE: 1958 figures: $x^2 = 154$, $p = .000$
      1964 figures: $x^2 = 185$, $p = .000$

or self-image built up over time among followers of a party or personality. With that identity may come a predisposition conditioning assessments of current conditions and events in favor of one's candidate or party and at the expense of others.

The notion that politics was moving in an increasingly polarized or radicalized direction is further undermined when one compares the backgrounds and attitudes of longer-standing and newly recruited supporters of the three candidates. As Table 3-9 indicates, those supporting Allende for the first time in 1970 were less, not more, working class in character than those who had supported him previously. When seen over time, the Allende constituency, although expanding and holding its working-class supporters, grew less predominantly working class in character. Tómic and Alessandri supporters, on the other hand, were growing more, not less, working class in character.

There is also evidence that the views of more recent arrivals were somewhat less radical in the case of *allendistas* and more radical in the case of *tómicistas*. Of the older Allende supporters 98.2 percent considered themselves "leftists," while the figure drops to 93 percent in the case of those who supported him in 1964, and to 84.8 percent for new voters. Among Tómic supporters the corresponding figures were 12 percent, 23.6 percent, and 25 percent, although the percentage of those considering themselves rightists also tended to be higher among the more recently affiliated.[41]

Assessments of the Frei government's performance reinforce these trends. Although no discernible pattern holds among Alessandri supporters, the longer-standing Christian Democrats held

[41] The x^2 factor of 332.5 is significant at .000.

122

TABLE 3-9
Occupational Statuses of Allende, Tómic, and Alessandri
Supporters by Length of Affiliation, August 1970

Candidate Preference	Managers, Owners	Professionals, Technicians, Small Businessmen	White Collar Workers	Blue Collar Workers	Service Workers	
Tómic						
Frei						
58 and 64	—	30.0%	30.0%	30.0%	10.0%	n = 10
Frei 1964	2.3%	13.6	43.2	31.8	9.1	n = 44
New						
supporter	—	20.0	25.0	45.0	10.0	n = 20
Alessandri						
Alessandri						
1958	17.2	13.8	24.1	37.9	6.9	n = 29
Frei						
58 and 64	60.0	—	40.0	—	—	n = 5
New						
supporter	3.3	20.0	30.0	26.7	20.0	n = 30
Allende						
Allende						
58 and 64	3.3	10.0	10.0	66.7	10.0	n = 30
Allende 1964	—	—	18.2	77.3	4.6	n = 22
New						
supporter	7.3	12.2	26.8	36.6	17.1	n = 41
n	14	31	63	97	26	

SOURCE: Centro Belarmino 1971.
NOTE: $x^2 = 73.2$, p = .000

TABLE 3-10
Assessment of Frei Government by Candidate Preference
by Length of Affiliation, August 1970

Tómic Supporters			Alessandri Supporters			Allende Supporters		
Frei 1958	Frei 1964	New voters	Alessandri 1958	Frei 1964	New voters	Allende 1958	Allende 1964	New voters
2.2	2.7	2.9	3.4	3.8	3.5	4.2	3.9	3.4

SOURCE: Centro Belarmino 1971.
NOTES: Numbers represent a scale of from 1 (excellent) to 6 (very poor).
tau b = .42, p = .000

more favorable views, while old-line *allendistas* were more critical than recent arrivals. More recently recruited Tómic supporters were more critical of Frei, more recently recruited Allende supporters less (seeTable 3-10).

These patterns suggest more the influence of partisan formation and identity than of class consciousness and polarization. Those who had supported a candidate in previous campaigns were decidedly more favorable to his cause, more positive toward his party's efforts and accomplishments, and more likely to be critical of his rivals.

Summary

The Frei years, which began with hope and expectation, ended in frustration, disappointment, and division for the Christian Democrats. Frei and his party fell short of their growth and reform objectives and were shunted to the side as right- and left-wing forces reasserted their hold on Chilean voters.

Bitter as it was to face, their failure was by no means total. Their government's accomplishments were many; its record among the best in the country's history. If it failed to reactivate Chile's stagnant economy, its long-term investments in public works and education and in the copper, petrochemical, steel, electronics, and cellulose industries would bear fruit in the years to come.[42] If it failed to meet its goal of providing land to one hundred thousand peasant families, it did provide it to over twenty-eight thousand and set in motion the mobilization of peasant workers that would transform social relations in the countryside. Finally, if the Frei government failed to prevent the resurgence of left-wing and right-wing options in Chilean politics, it did consolidate the PDC's once insignificant support at between 25 and 30 percent of the national electorate, making it the country's largest single political force.

Unfortunately the Christian Democrats were unwilling to pull either the right or the left into their orbit and unable to outflank them. In retrospect it is remarkable that they did as well as they did, given the obstacles and liabilities with which they had to deal. Three such factors of particular importance were: the absence of even minimal working relations with organized labor and the left; the disinclination of the private sector to invest or expand productive capabilities; and the presence within party ranks of deeply rooted ideological and strategic divisions.

Conflict between Christian Democracy and the left was the product of mutual mistrust and hostility. Most Socialists were disdainful of Frei and the PDC from the beginning, while Com-

---

[42] See Molina 1972, 84.

munists, although expressing more positive sentiments, were nonetheless more interested in luring away progressive elements than in cooperating with the administration as such.[43] As for the Christian Democrats some called for talks and proposed other initiatives but never had the backing of both party and government, or of Frei himself. In fact, neither Frei nor the Christian Democratic mainstream had any interest in working with organized labor or the Marxist parties. To do so would be to grant that the left was a fact of life with which one had to live and compromise, and that was not a concession they were politically or ideologically prepared to make.

With neither partner interested in working with the other, and with each harboring designs on at least part of the other's constituency, the prospects for civil relations, much less collaboration, were slim. So too, therefore, were those for labor keeping its demands within the bounds of the government's antiinflationary or general development programs.

Problematic relationships also impeded government efforts to win the confidence and support of the country's financial and industrial bourgeoisie. With his initial electoral momentum and impressive economic start Frei refused to consider the concessions demanded by the right during 1965 and 1966. He was convinced that his reformist package was both reasonable and attractive and that there was no need to compromise. Later, with the private sector failing to respond, he proposed some changes and agreed to consider others. But these were too little and too late. By mid-1967 entrepreneurial forces had begun to coalesce and appeared to have concluded that even the government's modest agrarian reform was a threat to all and that there could be no compromise short of an abandonment of the government's entire program.

A third factor, that of growing internal dissension, compounded problems in each of the above regards and caused others as well. The developing polarization within the party encouraged both left and right opposition groups to fear the worst of the party and government as a whole and yet to hold out hopes of winning over more congenial segments and thus persist in their opposition stances.

In pulling these various strands together the 1970 survey data

[43] For a discussion of Communist and Socialist attitudes toward Frei and the Christian Democrats see Cerda 1971, 165-179.

should be kept in mind. The Christian Democratic years may have been a legitimate test of a reformist development strategy and may have been Chile's "last best hope" for an alternative to socialist revolution. Indeed, many Christian Democratic leaders and activists understood their enterprise in these terms just as, no doubt, many Socialists, Communists, and left-wing Christian Democrats explicitly rejected reformism and opted for a more revolutionary posture. But Hamuy's data strongly suggest that these were the views of a minority and that the "average" Chilean voter continued to think in fairly conventional bread-and-butter terms.

If polarization took place during and as a result of the Frei years, it appears to have been of a partisan political, not broader social or ideological, sort. Both Tómic and Alessandri retained considerable appeal among both white and blue collar workers, and those workers drawn more recently to the left were less radical in their views than longer-standing Allende supporters. It should also be stressed that those supporting a candidate need not have identified with either his ideology or his platform. Affective identification with a candidate, party, or movement has long been a prominent feature of Chilean politics, and almost certainly was in 1970 as well.

The various divisions among Chilean workers and the lack of support for the Christian Democrats among the bourgeoisie point up the need to look at "class" in more than simply situational or occupational terms. Those sharing the same relationship to the means of production did not therefore have or develop a common sense of their objective interests as a class. They remained divided or became more so because of cross-cutting ideological and institutional political orientations and loyalties.

During the Frei years, these factors tended to divide Christian Democratic and Marxist workers at their work places, creating conflictive productive relationships and precluding the development of class solidarity among them. They also appear to have made the country's leading bourgeois interests irrevocably distrustful of the Christian Democrats, whatever assurances or concessions were offered. The result of this for Frei was that the appeal of the Christian Democratic Revolution in Liberty remained confined to the large but isolated and ultimately nonviable political center.

If these enduring divisions spelled doom for Frei, however, they augured no better for the incoming Allende government. Chris-

tian Democrats and Marxists remained bitter rivals, and despite
Tómic's progressive platform the prospects for a viable center-
left alliance remained poor. There was no evidence, for example,
that Chileans other than Marxists had rejected Frei's "reformism," or that many were aware or supportive of the calls for
socialist transformation coming from either Allende or Tómic.
The data rather suggest that what mattered to all but the hard-
core ideological left were housing, jobs, the cost of living, and so
on. The concerns of most Chileans in these various respects remained to be satisfied, and Allende's success would likely depend
on his ability to provide such things in adequate amounts and
at reasonable prices. In undertaking this, however, he appeared
to face the same divisions and constraints that the more broadly
supported Christian Democrats encountered before him.

« 4 »

UNDER ALLENDE

In early April 1971 former Christian Democratic Deputy Pedro Felipe Ramírez warned his party colleagues of grave consequences unless they helped Allende's Popular Unity government carry out its program.

> From even before the election we have been saying that the failure of the Allende government would lead Chileans to times as bitter as those through which the Uruguayan people have lived in recent years, under a repressive and dictatorial government, with an economy in collapse, and in a state of generalized violence. All possibility of change, even from the standpoint of building a socialism of the sort advocated by Christian Democracy, would be postponed for many years. There is no Christian Democratic "alternative" at the present time because there is no "alternative" [other than Allende] for the country. [*Política y Espíritu* 1971a, 15]

Ramírez and other progressive Christian Democrats had pushed for cooperative relations with Allende's government from the outset of his presidency. Their concerns were shared and their efforts applauded by Allende himself and by others within the Popular Unity coalition. Attempts were made to reach agreements in June and September 1971 and again in March and June 1972. All failed, however, and relations between the two sides grew steadily worse. As 1971 unfolded, the PDC's initially constructive opposition gave way to denunciations of "totalitarian designs" and to almost daily confrontations between Christian Democratic and Popular Unity workers, students, civil servants, and peasants. During 1972, as economic and social conditions began to deteriorate, strikes, lockouts, building seizures, protest marches, and mass demonstrations by opposing groups became the regular fare of political life. The congressional elections of March 1973 left government and opposition forces at an impasse, further heightening tensions and prompting rumors and visions of an ultimate reckoning. This came with the military coup of September 11, which brought to power the very dictatorship of which Ramírez had warned.

Allende's fall has been the object of considerable controversy. Observers initially debated the role of external forces in destabilizing the Chilean economy. Attention later shifted to internal phenomena and to relations between Christian Democratic and Popular Unity forces. Allende's electoral support remained considerable during 1972 and 1973 but was less and less a match for the growing unity and intensity of those aligned against him. Had the PDC supported Allende, his government might have accomplished its goals. Had the Christian Democrats not moved or been pushed rightwards, Allende's support would have been sufficient to prevent his government's collapse. But neither was to be, and with the PDC joining the right in a series of anti-UP fronts in the Congress and in shops, factories, schools, farm lands, and streets throughout the country, Allende's fate was sealed.

Scholars and participants analyzing UP-PDC relations have stressed the internal divisions on both sides, the fact that neither fully controlled its component parts, and the steadily diminishing prospects for collaboration as each became engulfed in broader mistrusts and antagonisms. They disagree, however, as to whether a meaningful accommodation was ever possible, and whether either side truly wanted it.

For some (Altamirano 1977; Castells 1974; Stallings 1978), the PDC was a bourgeois political force committed to the existing order and to displacing Allende regardless of what he proposed or did; for others (Arriagada 1974; Sigmund 1977), the UP's totalitarian designs and methods drove a reluctant PDC into the arms of forces with whom it shared only a commitment to democratic institutions. Still others (Garretón and Moulián 1979; Garcés 1976; Roxborough 1976 and 1979; Valenzuela 1978) emphasize the interrelatedness of class and political factors, depicting a dynamic of polarization that was fed by mistrust, short-sightedness, and partisan self-interest on both sides.[1]

[1] Garretón and Moulián are Chilean sociologists and former Christian Democrats who left the party in 1969 to form MAPU. When it split in 1972, they aligned with the more reformist (MAPU-Gazmuri) of the two wings to emerge. Their analysis of the Allende years and of Chilean politics generally has been extremely influential within both Marxist and Christian Democratic circles in recent years.

Unfortunately, only the briefest summary of Garcés, Roxborough, and Valenzuela will be possible here. According to Garcés, a Spanish political scientist and personal advisor to Allende, Allende was repeatedly overruled and ultimately undermined by more militant allies and supporters. Garcés himself viewed a break with the PDC as inevitable in the long run but believed that the party

Perhaps the most searching of these multidimensional analyses is that of Garretón and Moulián. They see the party's opposition to Allende as part of an effort to keep its political identity and following intact. Although they consider the influence of bourgeois interests to be dominant, they insist that the party's other factions had reasons of their own for wishing to maintain its independent reformist posture and traditional electoral following. The fact that most Christian Democrats nonetheless moved steadily to the right they attribute to the dynamics of electoral politics, the hyperradicalism and sectarianism of leftist groups, and the receptivity of the PDC's largely middle-class following to the populistic and fascist appeals of right-wing forces (Garretón and Moulián 1979, 188).

---

would have accepted much of Allende's program if it had been implemented in a more conventionally institutional manner. The problem, he believes, was that both Communists and Socialists opposed dealing with the PDC as such, seeking instead to win away the party's progressive leadership and popular following. And this, according to Garcés, reenforced party unity, strengthened the hand of conservative elements, and encouraged premature collaboration with the Partido Nacional (Garcés 1976, 204, 212-214, and 222).

Roxborough argues that the Allende government could have saved itself from overthrow "by controlling its own supporters, modifying its program, [and] reaching some sort of agreement with the Christian Democrats" but that it did not and yet failed to arm itself either (1979, 157). He also thinks that economic difficulties arising in late 1971 made it impossible for Allende to retain the support of (i.e., to continue to "buy off") middle-sector groups (1976, 201) and that UP strategists underestimated the ease with which petit bourgeois forces could be mobilized in defense of "bourgeois" political institutions and practices (1979, 201-202).

Finally, Valenzuela (1978) believes that Allende's fall was the culmination of a breakdown of accommodation politics that had begun with the rise of the PDC as a centrist movement interested in supplanting right and left rather than in easing the conflict between them (1978, 35-39). From that point on political success came to be seen by virtually all forces as coming at the political and socioeconomic expense of others. In this context Allende was crippled from the outset by a widespread lack of confidence in either the rules of the game or those playing it. Similarly, the many moderates within both the UP and the PDC who genuinely sought a *modus vivendi* were forced to work at a virtually insurmountable disadvantage vis-à-vis more intransigent elements (p.49). Thus, he argues, though many Christian Democrats shared the broad goals of the Allende administration, as members and leaders of an opposing political party they were more concerned with their integrity and interests as a centrist political force (pp. 71-72). In the final analysis, however, he blames both sides for failing to see beyond the shorter-term considerations of party harmony and partisan advantage to the common stake that all had in both preserving the democratic order and averting a brutally repressive military dictatorship (p. 107).

My treatment of UP-PDC relations under Allende resembles that of Garretón and Moulián. Like theirs, it is couched within an analytical perspective emphasizing the ideological and strategic considerations that defined the options from among which classes and class fractions were obliged to choose. In particular, it sees these considerations as limiting the ability of social forces to strike bargains, make concessions, and otherwise meet political challenges.

Although I share their general orientation, however, Garretón and Moulián can be challenged, refined, or elaborated on a number of points. Among these are the PDC's class character, its initial disposition toward Allende's government, the evolution of its popular following, and relations between its leaders, activists, and general supporters or sympathizers.[2]

In the following discussion I will explore five propositions concerning Christian Democracy during the Allende years. The first is that the party's working-class base actually expanded but grew increasingly anti-UP and anti-Allende with the passage of time. Second, I argue that the party's hostility to Allende and the parties supporting him was primarily political in origin and basic character. Third, I hold that the party's dominant force remained its petit bourgeois sector, whose class interests were largely social and political. My fourth contention is that its working-class base supported but in no way forced the party's move to the right during 1972 and 1973. And finally, I argue that social disintegration and trauma during the final six months of the Allende government were so profound and widespread that they would affect political convictions and sentiments for years to come.

Initial Alignments and Attitudes

Those who have studied UP-PDC relations under Allende have noted the presence of conciliatory and confrontational elements in both camps. Unfortunately, they have generally misrepresented the character of the forces involved, the issues on which they differed, and the reasons for those differences. As they did earlier in dealing with the Frei period, most Marxists see the

[2] Garretón and Moulián regard the party's class character as complex and contradictory (1979, 188-189). They stress its multiclass (i.e., "popular," working-class, middle strata, or capas, and modernizing bourgeois) following and argue that at given moments each of these has decisively influenced party positions and actions.

Christian Democrats in one-dimensional class terms. For Alta-mirano, for example, they were simply the "other [i.e., reformist] side" of the bourgeoisie, and a breakdown of relations was there-fore inevitable. Party progressives were at best naive and mis-placed and in any case incapable of challenging the dominant *freístas*, whose neocapitalist and anti-Marxist views reflected the party's predominantly bourgeois and petit bourgeois character (Altamirano 1977, 89-90).

Stallings, who stresses the party's links to the modern indus-trial bourgeoisie, views its opposition to Allende entirely in these terms. She sees "bourgeois" *freístas* displacing more conciliatory petit bourgeois elements and successfully coopting various "al-lied" and "supporting" classes and class fractions. Apparently the lone exception to this was Christian Democratic workers, whom she sees siding with the left as the class struggle grew clearer and more intense (Stallings 1978, 63).

Although generally more flexible than more conventional Marxist analysts, Garretón and Moulián, Roxborough, and Garcés also consider the PDC to be a predominantly bourgeois force. Rupture with it was therefore inevitable at some point even un-der the best of circumstances.[3]

Material presented in Chapter 3 contradicts these analyses. There I showed the PDC to be a petit bourgeois force whose fol-lowing included a small and relatively marginal segment of the bourgeoisie. As will become clear in the following pages, more-over, the party's dominant petit bourgeois and allied class frac-tions had class and nonclass reasons of their own for opposing Allende, which were, for the most part, a function of conflicting strategic and political orientations. With some Christian Demo-cratic workers these conflicts would weaken and disappear in the face of emerging class consciousness and solidarity, but in many more instances they would grow stronger, further inhibiting such development.

If charges of bourgeois domination are questionable, so too are

---

[3] Valenzuela views the party's class character and its impact as more open questions. Although he concedes that bourgeois elements manipulated worker and peasant resentments in their own class interests, he does not think that their control of the party was either total or necessary (1978, 71-72). Garcés, on the other hand, while believing that a break with the party was inevitable, contin-ually characterizes it as a coalition of petit bourgeois and popular forces with only minor, although occasionally forceful, representation of bourgeois interests as such (Garcés 1976, 213-214).

the claims of those (Arriagada 1974; Sigmund 1977) who contend that the Christian Democrats were willing to collaborate in the building of a socialist society but were prevented from doing so by Marxist sectarianism and totalitarianism. There were elements within the party of whom this was true, but they were outflanked and ultimately overcome by far more numerous Christian Democrats for whom a UP-led revolutionary process was unacceptable from the beginning.

During the Allende period, the PDC contained three distinct groups. Two of them, Christian Leftists and *freístas*, were holdovers from the Frei period. A third consisted of those who had resisted alignments of any sort. Christian Leftists were former *terceristas* and *rebeldes* who stayed on when their colleagues bolted ranks in May 1969. Their principal following was among Christian Democratic students, although they had some support in labor, female, and peasant circles and among young *técnicos* as well. They were determined to make one last attempt at alliance with the left. A major vehicle for their efforts was the Tómic campaign, in which Bosco Parra, Luís Maira, Pedro Felipe Ramírez, and other Christian Leftists played important roles. Although polls indicated that a more positive identification with Frei would have produced greater electoral dividends, Christian Leftists were responsible for the campaign's radical policy stands and general antirightist flavor.

As in their *oficialistas* days, the *freístas* included former cabinet ministers, most of the party's congressional delegation, and the better part of its provincial and departmental leadership. All either shared Frei's anti-Marxist, developmentalist, and broader strategic views or were willing to defer to them. Their ouster from power notwithstanding, they were determined to remain a "progressive" alternative to Marxist revolution and hoped to revive the center-right alliance that had brought Frei to power in 1964.[4]

---

[4] With the Christian Democrats out of power, the term *oficialista* became less appropriate than *freísta*, although those to whom it applied were no more nor less intensely pro-Frei. *Oficialistas* saw the Frei years as fundamentally successful and a model for future Christian Democratic regimes. In their view Tómic's repudiation of Frei's record, his disdain of anti-Marxist votes, and his pursuit of leftist backing, which he should not have sought and could not win, were politically suicidal. Further, they believed Communists and Socialists to be ill-disguised totalitarians whose commitment to a peaceful democratic road to socialism was at best tactical. They saw them as arch rivals, not potential allies, in the struggle to build a new social order.

The third group included such party notables as Tómic himself, Renán Fuentealba, Benjamín Prado, Bernardo Leighton, and Narciso Irueta. Although they did not consider themselves a "group" in the sense that the others did, the term "social democratic" best describes the ideological and strategic views they shared.[5] Politically, they were liberal democrats and civil libertarians. Socioeconomically, they were moderate anticapitalists, ever seeking the painless, noncoercive reform of economic structures. They were disappointed that Frei's government had not accomplished more in the way of structural change and sought to make the party less closely identified with him. They had backed Tómic enthusiastically, but when Allende won a plurality they urged conditional support of his government, insisting on certain guarantees concerning its methods and objectives. While conceding the risks and difficulties involved, they believed that no real social transformation would be possible unless the Christian Democrats could work with organized labor and the left.

These divisions within the party were rooted in political rather than class factors. Although bourgeois elements did identify with the *freísta* wing, they were hardly its controlling force, or much less the party's as a whole. During the Allende years, the party's parliamentary delegation retained the largely petit bourgeois character (76 percent) it exhibited under Frei. Most were *freístas* (55 percent), although the Christian Left and social democratic factions had a respectable representation (16 and 29 percent respectively) as well. The organization's militant activists remained overwhelmingly petit bourgeois and were also spread fairly evenly among the three groups. As under Frei, the union department was divided between progressive and more traditional anticommunist elements.[6]

The party's support base, although substantially smaller than in 1964, remained broad and included a proportionally larger working-class component. Although Stallings (1978, 54) cites survey data indicating a predominance of white collar support

[5] I do not mean to associate these "social democrats" with Social Democratic parties in Chile or elsewhere. Not only were they loyal Christian Democrats but in most (though not all) cases they were believing Catholics who readily defended the rightful influence and prerogatives of the Church in social matters.

[6] Sources for the 1970 to 1973 period are given in Chapter 3, note 16. Most of the party's more radical trade unionists abandoned its ranks in 1969 and became active (and increasingly radicalized) in MAPU. For a brief but informative treatment of conservative Christian Democratic labor leaders, see Angell 1972, 185-186.

(48.9 pecent), she breaks respondents down in terms of presidential preferences and not party affiliations. Moreover, she apparently had access to occupational job category data (for which people were described as professionals, small businessmen, skilled and unskilled blue collar workers, white collar workers, independent workers, etc.). I have had to work with sectorial data (office workers, salesmen, artisans and general workers, transportation workers, domestic workers, etc.), and therefore can neither challenge nor verify her conclusions. Using this data, converting the sectorial categories to occupational ones, and looking at party affiliation and not candidate preference, however, a very different picture emerges.[7] As indicated in Table 4-1 Christian Democratic supporters tended to be less blue collar than their UP counterparts but were hardly the white collar force described by Stallings.

[7] With my sample and job category scheme, Tómic supporters break down into 1.4 percent managers and owners, 17.6 percent professionals, 36.5 percent office workers, clerks, salesmen, etc., and 44.6 percent independent, industrial, and domestic workers. Christian Democratic supporters, on the other hand, break down into 13.7 percent professionals, 38.7 percent office workers, clerks, salesmen, etc., and 48.5 percent independent, industrial, and domestic workers. I have stressed party rather than Tómic supporters as I believe they provide a more reliable basis for anticipating Christian Democratic responses to the Allende government. Beyond this, however, our different readings of Hamuy's data are largely due to the reduced size and altered character of the sample to which I had access (see Chapter 3, note 37). Thus, for example, Stallings indicates an n of 88 Tómic supporters, while I am working with ns of 74 Tómic supporters and 67 PDC supporters. An n of 14 fewer Tómic supporters would seem about right, given that the Centro Belarmino sample contained 100 fewer respondents overall. Moreover, it is quite possible that the occupational scheme data used by Stallings were among those knocked out by Centro Belarmino researchers in 1971. What is less clear, however, is whether the different ns and/or categories with which we were working fully account for our divergent judgments regarding white and blue collar status of the party's support base. I have talked with Professor Stallings in an effort to resolve this, but she no longer has access to the original 1970 data.

There are problems with both job category schemes. Occupational categories often fail to adequately distinguish professionals, small businessmen, and white collar workers, while sectorial categories lump together industrial and independent workers. In the interests of comparability not only with Stallings but with other Hamuy surveys as well, it seems best to convert the sectorial category data to which I have had access into occupational category form. I have done this by consulting Hamuy's 1972 and 1973 surveys in which both classification systems are employed and mathematical conversion is therefore possible. Using these surveys, I derived "average" distribution ratios for categories in the two schemes and from these constructed the occupational category breakdown presented in Table 4-1.

TABLE 4-1
Party Preferences by Occupational Status, August 1970

Preferred Party(ies)	Managers, Owners	Professionals, Technicians	White Collar Workers	Blue Collar Workers	
Popular Unity	1.3%	16.4%	23.3%	58.9%	n = 42
Christian Democratic	—	30.3	27.3	42.4	n = 66
National	—	37.5	34.3	28.1	n = 73

SOURCE: Centro Belarmino 1971.

This working-class base was not a very progressive one, however, a fact boding ill for PDC-UP relations. Some Christian Democratic sympathizers (14.1 percent) were actually planning to support Alessandri, and most of those sticking with Tómic (60.8 percent) expressed greater opposition to Allende than to Alessandri. Moreover, although most considered themselves to be "centrists," 30 percent described themselves as belonging on the right. On both issues, moreover, blue and white collar Christian Democrats did not differ appreciably from other party supporters.[8]

The period between the September 4 election and Allende's confirmation by Congress in late October was tumultuous. Rumors and warnings of conspiracies, secret deals, preventive and preemptive coups, and even civil war were daily fare. Within the PDC anxiety and conflict ran high. Christian Democrats could be found on opposing sides on several issues and were part of almost every rumored cabal. Recriminations between the various factions were frequent and intense.

With Allende receiving the largest number of votes of the three candidates, Christian Leftists and some social democrats, including Tómic himself, immediately acknowledged his "moral" claims to the presidency. Although they would have preferred Tómic, they were committed to "popular unity" and democratic social-

[8] When class status and attitudes of Christian Democratic supporters are related, no significant associations appear in either ideological self-placement (p = .65) or opposition to other candidacies (p = .84). It is possible, of course, that the broadly popular base was being deceived or manipulated by bourgeois and petit bourgeois forces. As will be argued below, however, the party's petit bourgeois leaders remained in control and came to oppose Allende in defense of their own interests. The bourgeoisie, on the other hand, never trusted the PDC and continued to support parties and movements of the traditional right.

ism and thus looked forward to Allende's government with enthusiasm. The fact that the PDC would play a secondary role in a government led by its longstanding rivals was not of great concern to them.

Other social democrats were less sanguine at the prospects of an Allende government. They were skeptical of both Communists and Socialists and worried about the influence of moderate elements in these parties. Nonetheless, they opposed any a priori rejection of Allende. That would amount, they argued, to a disenfranchisement of the left; it would imply, in effect, that democracy was fine as long as one side never won. Accordingly, even more wary social democrats preferred to believe, or at least to hope, that UP moderates would prevail over more radical elements, thereby affording a basis for PDC-UP collaboration.

Freístas, finally, shared none of these beliefs or sentiments and actively pursued alternatives to Allende. One proposal, which was also supported by party labor leaders, called for confirming second-place finisher Jorge Alessandri, who would then resign, setting up a new election in which Frei would be free to run.[9] This was voted down at a National Council meeting in early October, as party leaders opted for a more conciliatory position. A week before the kidnapping and murder of Army Chief of Staff René Schnieder the party voted 271 to 191 to accept Allende's pledge to honor a series of privately negotiated constitutional guarantees, the so-called Statute of Guarantees, and to support his confirmation in the Congress. Fearful of exacerbating tensions and possibly dividing the party, *freístas* chose not to press matters and accepted the will of the majority. They would not have minded breaking with the Christian Left but could not afford to alienate the more numerous social democrats.

The party's decision to confirm Allende represented the hopes of ascendant progressive elements. Neither their hopes nor their ascendancy were certain to endure, however attitudes, alignments, and relationships would evolve in response to a variety of forces and factors, several of which augured poorly for PDC-UP relations.

One of these was Frei, who strongly opposed rapprochement with the left, and whose prestige and influence were still considerable in Christian Democratic and broader political circles. A

---

[9] "Departamento Sindical del PDC Rechaza Apoyo a Salvador Allende," *El Mercurio* (Santiago), October 3, 1970, p. 25.

second factor was the anti-Marxist sentiments of the party's popular base, heightened as they had been during both the Frei administration and the recent presidential campaign. A third force was also political in character: the inclination of Christian Democratic workers, peasants, students, and *pobladores* to exploit the shortcomings of the regime in power in their own immediate political interest. For many, forceful opposition would be an irresistible way of winning or regaining power in their union or neighborhood association. In fact, it would be as difficult for Christian Democratic activists to persevere in either partial or constructive opposition to Allende as it had been for FRAP leaders to oppose Frei from 1964 to 1970.

A final obstacle to accommodation was lack of interest on the part of the UP. Few Popular Unity leaders shared Allende's interest in working with the Christian Democrats. Most had gone along, some grudgingly, with the Statute of Guarantees but opposed continuing to negotiate once Allende took office, believing that further concessions or agreements would be unnecessary or unduly costly.

Allende himself, a faction of his Socialist party, and most Radicals favored rapprochement, confident that if negotiations were judiciously handled most Christian Democrats would support important portions of the UP program. But Communist and Socialist party officials were much less confident and/or interested. During the first eighteen months of Allende's presidency, the Communists spoke in more conciliatory tones but remained opposed to accommodation with the PDC as such. Although solicitous of party "progressives," they persistently sought to discredit Frei and those aligned with him. In this way they hoped to force a definition and division of Christian Democratic ranks that would pull "popular" elements to the left as it pushed others to the right.[10]

Most Socialists also favored a confrontational strategy, believing that only a reformist movement could save Chilean capitalism and that parties like the PDC were therefore wily class ene-

---

[10] In 1968 Communist party Secretary Luís Corvalán wrote: "We wish to prevent reactionary forces from continuing in power, be it through a return to power by the traditional right or the retention of power by the Christian Democratic right. That is all. And for that reason we cannot accept an understanding with the entire PDC, or better said, with all Christian Democrats, since among them are not only people who want social change, but also those who wish to bring it to a halt" (*Ercilla* 1968, 12).

mies, not promising allies. They directed their attacks less at the "old right" than at the Christian Democrats, hoping to accelerate a coming to class consciousness among the party's peasant and working-class supporters.[11]

In fact, the divisions within each camp made collaboration virtually impossible from the beginning. Both Allende and progressive Christian Democrats were caught in dilemmas from which there was no escape. Neither could prevail within his own camp without alienating powerful partners; and neither could hold his own if abandoned by those partners. Without the Socialists, Allende and the Communists would have been dominated by the PDC, just as without their Frei wing, Christian Democrats would have been overrun by the UP. Thus, neither could force the issue, and each had to defer to harder-line forces, hoping for a change of heart once options and stakes became clearer. By the time they did, the deterioration of relations was well underway and could not be arrested.

The discussion that follows traces the three stages through which UP-Christian Democratic relations passed during Allende's presidency. The first, that of relatively constructive opposition, ran through mid-September 1971. The second, from September 1971 to March 1973, featured open, though still constitutional, warfare at both institutional and mass mobilization levels. The third covered the period following the March 1973 elections in which extralegal options were actively pursued.

Constructive Opposition

As the UP assumed power, it remained at odds over how to proceed. For Allende the important thing was to prevent the formation of a center-right alliance, which meant maintaining open and constructive relations with the reformist PDC. Communist and Socialist party leaders, on the other hand, sought to force

[11] As newly elected Socialist party Secretary General Carlos Altamirano put it in January 1971, "At the present time, the bourgeoisie is grouped around the Christian Democrats, and secondarily around the PN and the DR. The so-called left of the DC with its continuation in that party and its indecision, is serving as a shield for the right and the reactionary sectors which participate in the great conspiracy against the government of comrade Salvador Allende and the workers. Only a policy of profound transformations and growing acceleration of the revolutionary process will force a definition on groups of Christian Democratic workers" (see Jobet 1971, 2: 173).

the party to the right, winning over its progressive leadership and constituency. This fundamental divergency was never resolved. To the confusion of supporters and the despair or delight of opponents, the UP pursued both strategies simultaneously during its entire period in power. During the first year, important Christian Democratic converts were won but at the expense of the will and capacity of far greater numbers to resist the pull from the right.

In terms of policy issues UP-PDC relations were initially good. The party's social democratic leaders were content to let Allende govern, offering "critical" support for his budget and wage adjustment proposals for 1971 and for the constitutional amendment nationalizing the copper industry. In responding to Allende's first budget proposal, for example, the Christian Democrats thought its U.S. $4 billion deficit inflationary and urged elimination of "unnecessary" expenditures. But in the end they left it essentially intact, adding provisions for civil service job security and cutting only the discretionary use of unspent health funds, additional administrative and maintenance funds for the Ministry of Economics and the Postal Department, and unlimited publicity funds for the executive branch. These changes were acceptable to the government, and in later commenting on the budget's final approval Budget Director Arellano indicated the government's satisfaction with the form in which it had emerged from Congress.[12]

Allende's wage adjustment proposals were only slightly more controversial. The PDC criticized proposed arrangements for "normalizing" delinquent tax accounts as overly indulgent but accepted the tax reductions and either agreed to the new taxes or suggested functional equivalents,[13] most of which would fall on the shoulders of the very bourgeois interests with which its critics associated the party. The lone proposal to which it objected throughout called for a 15 percent wealth tax on firms (as opposed to individuals) whose net worth exceeded an amount twenty-five times the minimum wage. The protest was made on grounds that the tax would affect small- and medium-sized en-

[12] *El Mercurio* 1971a, 17.

[13] The Christian Democrats agreed to additional inheritance taxes, increased income taxes for the self-employed, a surcharge of 15 percent on the taxes of firms with assets exceeding 400,000 *escudos* (approximately U.S. $31,000), and increased taxes on import certificates, vehicle licenses, and vehicle transfers.

terprises with as little as U.S. $1,600 in assets and not the large firms that were ostensibly its object.[14]

Christian Democrats also supported the constitutional amendment nationalizing the country's copper mines. The party asked only that small- and medium-sized mine owners be assured of concession rights following nationalization, that the retirement benefits of mine employees and workers be preserved, and that the debts of the joint venture companies created under Frei be honored. Here, again, objections were minor, and the government's proposal emerged essentially intact. Allende accepted the PDC's amendments, and one high-ranking UP official reportedly thanked party leaders for helping to improve the quality of the bill.

The issue most sharply dividing Christian Democrats and the Allende government was bank reform. UP plans called for outright nationalization, some employee participation, but ultimate government control, particularly over credit and loan policy. It was the method of nationalization, not nationalization as such, that was at issue, however. The PDC preferred ownership and administration by employees and depositors to direct state ownership and control but was willing to give the UP its way. Party leaders agreed "to legislate" on the subject, in effect assuring the UP of its preferred version if a bill were sent to Congress.[15] But while it promised to submit a bill shortly, the government proceeded to offer generous terms to shareholders willing to sell immediately. In addition, it assumed control of a number of banks in which financial difficulties or serious irregularities had been discovered. By September 1971 it achieved effective control of the banking structure, thereby making special legislation unnecessary. Although they had employed similar tactics with their agrarian reform, Christian Democrats charged that the govern-

[14] Some analysts claim that the Christian Democrats not only opposed additional taxes on the bourgeoisie but were determined to leave the budget and wage adjustment bills underfinanced, thereby forcing the UP into inflationary deficit spending (Boorstein 1977, 116-117; Zammit 1973, 85-86). In thus arguing, however, they either confine themselves to the 1972 and 1973 proposals (by which time the political situation had changed markedly) or simply misrepresent those for 1971, as when they point to proposals rejected by the Christian Democrats without indicating their modest place in the overall scheme or to the measures agreed to in their place. If such things are taken into account, it becomes clear that the party gave the government most of what it had asked for.

[15] "DeCe Promete Apoyar Idea de Legislar sobre Estatización Bancaria," *El Mercurio* 1971b, p. 19.

ment was pressuring stockholders and attempting to circumvent the Congress. They had hoped that congressional debate of the issue might bring out the virtues of their "communitarian" approach and were angered that they would now be denied the opportunity.

Although there were other areas in which the party opposed government initiatives,[16] it could still claim to have provided "critical" support for UP policies. The significance of that support was overshadowed, however, by the harsher sounds and emotions of partisan electoral and political maneuvering, a struggle that inflated more than it reflected policy differences but had a greater impact on larger numbers of people.

Political relations began poorly in part because of the April 1971 municipal elections, which offered the UP an early opportunity to exploit its presidential incumbency and to prove that it had the support of a majority or near majority of the country's voters. Unfortunately, they also provided an occasion and/or excuse for stoking the fires of old rivalries and antagonisms. In doing so they distracted attention from policy issues on which agreement was either substantial or eminently possible. As a result, people on both sides were forced into confrontational stances and were caught in a conflict dynamic from which escape would be difficult.

To rapidly increase its electoral support the UP had to move ahead with its program to build a record of accomplishment of which to boast during the campaign. This meant deciding which parts of the program to send to Congress (where concessions and delays were likely) and which to decree by means of newly discovered administrative powers. With nationalization of banks and industries Allende opted for the administrative path. He knew the Christian Democrats would object but could not afford drawn out discussions or debate. He could only hope that the risky venture would yield proportionate dividends, that dialogue with the PDC would be possible following the elections, and that the UP would be strong enough to win a plebiscite (and therefore a new congressional majority) in the event that it was not (Garcés 1976, 227).

---

[16] Allende's proposal of a capitalization fund to finance new, publicly owned industries was one on which the PDC made some concessions but refused to make others, and no agreement to legislate on the matter was ever achieved. The nationalization of industries and agrarian reform were two others. They are discussed below.

Christian Democrats responded forcefully, some with relish, others to protect a political base from which to later negotiate a more cooperative relationship. Given the electoral context, however, both groups had to arouse sentiments likely to have an impact at the time, whatever their effect on longer-term relations. For some, this meant raising the specter of Marxist totalitarianism or otherwise appealing to anti-Communist sentiment. For others, it meant blaming the UP for a recession that had actually begun under Frei. Not to be outdone, the left countered by linking Frei and the Christian Democrats to various reactionary, proimperialist, and fascist forces and designs. These various charges and epithets had been part of the political struggle for years but were particularly destructive at this formative stage in an experiment whose success required the overcoming of traditional molds and antagonisms.

Popular Unity parties made a strong showing in the April elections, while Christian Democratic support fell slightly in relation to Tómic's vote the preceding September.[17] At a meeting later in the month the party reaffirmed its policy of "constructive opposition" promising to support initiatives "truly in the popular interest." Party leaders did not think this was the case with either the nationalization of textile firms or the agrarian reform, however, and they vigorously opposed UP moves in both areas. During May and June, the government took over eight of the country's leading textile firms. Owned by powerful but not widely admired immigrant families, several were known for their irregular and/or illegal managerial or financial practices, while others were paralyzed by striking workers whose wage demands they refused to meet. The firms thus appeared to be fitting targets of expropriation, and yet the Christian Democrats opposed the takeovers. Claiming to accept the nationalization of strategic or unusually dominant industries, they directed their censure at the use of emergency decree powers, criticizing the government's interpretation of long dormant constitutional provisions and what they saw as an attempt to escape congressional scrutiny and ju-

[17] The Popular Unity parties outpolled their combined opponents by a narrow margin. President Allende's Socialists received 22.8 percent of the total vote, although the Christian Democrats remained the country's largest single party with 26.3 percent. Given the coattail effect normally exerted by recently elected Chilean presidents, PDC leaders had cause for at least modest satisfaction. Rightist forces fell short (20.0 percent) of the vote garnered by Alessandri the previous September (34.9 percent).

risdiction. Pledging to consider each case on its merits, they insisted that nationalization proposals be submitted to the Congress, with the boundaries of the various sectors (public, private, and mixed), the criteria for expropriation, and the structure of worker participation and management all determined in advance.

Until the textile takeovers, expropriations had been carried out sporadically and on a limited basis. Allende assured the Christian Democrats that he would be submitting enabling legislation at some point but kept putting it off.[18] The takeovers suggested that nationalization would be stepped up but not in the manner urged by the PDC. This was particularly troublesome to progressive social democrats, many of whom began to suspect the UP of playing a "double game," one in which Allende's role was to provide a veneer of moderation for a movement whose nature and objectives were anything but moderate (*Ercilla* 1971, 8).

Skepticism was even more apparent among Christian Democratic workers, most of whom opposed the intervention, requisition, or buying out of the banks or industries in which they worked.[19] The Christian Democrats were not simply *apatronados*, or boss-dominated "company men." Their attitudes, which reflected deeply rooted ideological and institutional political divisions among Chilean workers, were formed during the 1950s and 1960s, a period in which the party defined its mission in largely anti-Marxist and anticommunist terms. From early on, therefore, Christian Democratic workers struggled with Communist and Socialist rivals in neighborhoods, at work places, and within labor organizations. Over the years intense and not entirely gratuitous feelings of mistrust, resentment, and antagonism built up on both sides. These feelings were often played on by others standing to gain from a divided workers' movement,

[18] Opinion within UP ranks was divided on the question. Economics Minister Pedro Vúskovic and others argued that there would be less economic and political opposition if there were no patterns or guidelines for nationalization; others held that the reverse was true, i.e., that it was precisely the uncertainty of things that would fuel growing anxiety and resistance (Garcés 1976, 225).

[19] Not untypical were the Christian Democratic workers at the Sumar textile plant whose connivance with its former owners (in handing out anti-UP and antitakeover literature) won them the enmity of their fellow workers. This action was cited as one of the reasons for their dismissal from the firm later in the year.

but the basic perceptions and fears were real and there from the beginning.

Developments at both the factory and neighborhood levels reenforced these feelings of mistrust and fear during Allende's first year. Christian Democratic workers were visibly uneasy at the thought of economic and social power concentrated in the hands of political forces with which they had struggled bitterly for years. They also suspected, plausibly enough, that public or state ownership might lead to a subordination of their immediate economic interests to broader government plans or priorities, of which they were already highly skeptical. And finally, Christian Democratic workers resented the decreeing of takeovers following upon strikes or other economic difficulties contrived by UP workers or the government itself.

In this context, it was less nationalization than its potential for political abuse that they feared. Partisan political affiliations and concerns thus mediated and often overrode those of material class situation. Christian Democratic and Marxist workers saw one another as adversaries and obstacles, not allies or fellow victims, and they tended to interpret each other's actions in the most threatening light possible. In fact, these divisions went beyond the ideological or political consciousness of workers sharing a place in the productive process. They actually permeated that process, cutting across structurally rooted interests and forming new and largely antagonistic class situations and experiences.

A second area of controversy was agrarian reform, in particular the new organizational units (Centros de Producción and Centros de Reforma Agraria, or CERAs) to be established on expropriated lands.[20] These structures were designed to increase the number of direct beneficiaries of land reform and to raise labor intensity within the agricultural sector as a whole.[21] They offered hope to the hundreds of thousands of migrant farmers, sharecroppers, and salaried farm laborers who were still without land, although they were less appealing to tenant farmers and others who had benefited, or stood to benefit, under previous pol-

[20] The former were large state farms to be established on a limited basis; the latter were intermediate-sized units encompassing several *asentamientos* and incorporating all persons living within that area.

[21] A revealing expression of government thinking and priorities in the area of agrarian reform is Jacques Chonchol 1971, 255-321. A comparison of the Frei and Allende reforms is provided in Stephan de Vylder 1976, 170-207, and John Strasma 1975.

icy provisions. In general, Marxist peasant unions affiliated with the Ranquil organization supported the CERAs, while the peasant, *asentado*, and small farmer groups associated with the Christian Democrats opposed them.

Although a number of party leaders and *técnicos* recognized the need for broader units of land use and ownership, the party itself resolved to oppose both the CERAs and the Centros de Producción. Apparently the needs of agriculture and of the broader rural population were less compelling than the concern for accommodating the party's increasingly restive peasant following and thereby shoring up its political standing and leverage. Accordingly, it made agrarian reform a major focus of criticism for the duration of Allende's term. As early as February 1971 people like former CORA head Rafael Moreno began denouncing the new agricultural units as unworkable, repressive, and typical examples of dogmatic collectivism. In their place, as the basic social and productive unit of Chilean agriculture, they urged extension of the limited membership *asentamientos* introduced under Frei.

In early June the first serious conversations concerning possible Christian Democratic-Popular Unity rapprochement took place (Garcés 1976, 207). Tentative agreement was reached on joint UP-PDC support of a left-wing Christian Democrat in a special congressional election in July. It was undermined, however, by the strong opposition of less conciliatory elements on both sides. As a result of this, the PDC ran a conservative medical doctor, who narrowly defeated his UP opponent with the help of tacitly promised right-wing support.

This first instance of center-right collaboration was a major victory for the conservative *freísta* faction, reflecting and further intensifying polarizing trends in the country as a whole. Within the PDC it pointed up the advantages of appealing to independent and right-wing elements, and in July and August Christian Democratic candidates won seats on the executive boards of the Electric Company, railway workers, copper mine workers, and Banco del Estado unions, thanks to independent and right-wing support. The new willingness to work with the right also provoked the secession of the party's radical Left Christian wing, including seven congressmen, the leadership of the party's youth branch, and a number of younger technocrats.[22] At first this ap-

[22] The congressmen included Luís Maira, Pedro Videla, Fernando Buzeta, Pedro Urra, Jaime Concha, Osvaldo Gianini, and Alejandro Jaramillo. Excongressmen

peared to be a victory for UP forces bent on attacking and discrediting the PDC as a whole, but it was soon clear that working-class and popular-sector converts were few in number and that their leaving would actually strengthen the hand of party conservatives.

In effect, the departure of the Christian Left weakened the will and ability of the social democratic faction to oppose the party's drift rightwards. Nonetheless, when Allende approached them in mid-September with another offer of compromise, they again went along. Following lengthy discussions, the party's social democratic leadership agreed to abstain on a vote to censure one of Allende's ministers in exchange for assurances that a) no additional firms be intervened or requisitioned; b) legislation providing for all future nationalizations be submitted to the Congress; and c) thirty-eight workers (of whom thirty-five were Christian Democrats) recently fired from their jobs at a nationalized textile plant be reinstated.[23]

With the agreement the censure motion failed, and hope settled over an agitated political arena. Not all were pleased, however. On one side, more conservative Christian Democrats questioned the utility and propriety of negotiations generally, although they did not attack the agreement as such. On the other, Socialist and Communist party leaders criticized both the concessions made and the very notion of dialogue with the PDC. In fact, obstructionist elements helped to undermine the atmosphere of trust and good will on which the agreement's fulfillment depended. Communist and Socialist party newspapers chose this delicate moment to launch an attack on the alleged financial improprieties of people closely associated with Frei. Frei responded in kind, accusing the Communists and Socialists of typ-

included Bosco Parra and Pedro Felipe Ramírez. Santiago Rojas, Alvaro Barros, and Jorge Leiva were typical of the many younger Christian Democrats who held technical positions in the public sector and were active in their employee unions. Upon leaving the PDC the Christian Leftists sought to join ranks with the ex-Christian Democrats who had formed MAPU in 1969, thereby constituting a united Christian Left movement. They succeeded in attracting Jacques Chonchol, Julio Silva Solar, Alberto Jerez, and Rafael Agustín Gumucio, each of whom was unhappy with the increasingly Marxist-Leninist orientation of MAPU activists, but most *mapucistas* apparently thought it best to continue operating independently and free of religious labels.

[23] The trouble at the Sumar plant from which the Christian Democratic workers had been expelled was typical of the problems Allende often faced in this regard. The leaders of the plant union were Communist party militants, and Communist leaders bitterly resented Allende's undermining of their position.

ically Stalinist efforts to destroy their adversaries through libelous character assassination. Christian Democrats of all shades quickly rallied around Frei, vowing to resist what they took to be an attempt to divide their ranks.

Allende tried to dissociate himself from these attacks and assured the PDC of his continuing commitment to improved relations. But his conciliatory efforts were undercut by developments on other fronts. For one thing, his government had just vetoed legislation authorizing the creation of a new national television network, programming for which would have come from Santiago's anti-UP Channel 13. For another, it had recently assigned the party's radio (Balmaceda) a new broadcast frequency, giving its old one to the Central Unica de Trabajadores. Finally, it was also maneuvering to buy up controlling shares in the country's principal producer of newsprint, Alessandri's Compañía Manufacturera de Papeles y Cartones. These moves caused many Christian Democrats to question the government's commitment to open debate and pluralism. Equally troubling was their timing, coming as they did even as Allende himself was making claims and offering assurances of a conciliatory nature.

There were two ways for Christian Democrats to interpret the situation. One was that Allende was not to be taken seriously, i.e., he was trying to allay fears and buy time any way he could. The other was that although conceivably sincere he was unable to deliver (or unwilling to pay the price for delivering) on his promises. After ten months in which Allende's assurances had failed to alter the course of government policy, however, his intentions were increasingly beside the point. Both *freístas* and social democrats were convinced, it seems, that the UP would continue much as it had to date unless the party stiffened its resistance.

The agreement's collapse thus led to a hardening of Christian Democratic opposition and signalled the beginning of a new stage in UP-PDC relations in which the party sought to block further UP advances by all available constitutional means. The shift marked the ascendancy of the party's conservative *freísta* faction.

It would be a mistake, however, to see this as a displacement of petit bourgeois elements by those tied to the bourgeoisie. As was shown at the outset of this chapter, the party's social democratic and *freísta* factions were both petit bourgeois in character.[24] They were threatened by UP initiatives for reasons and interests of a political nature typical of that group. Their concerns were not the wealth and power of others but the stability of the country's social order and political institutions in which they played leading and relatively comfortable roles. Although committed to progress, greater equality, and "social justice" as general propositions, most actually favored an aristocracy of quality and talent in which their own high place and influence were assured. Few really trusted or felt close to the working class, and most viewed the possible emergence of a mass movement capable of running society without their assistance or direction with alarm if not utter horror.

Thus the differences between the social democratic and *freísta* factions were ideological and strategic. Each was determined to defend its relatively privileged social and political positions. They simply disagreed on how this should be done and with whom the party should align in attempting to do so. Allende failed to honor promises and assurances required by the more progressive social democrats and thus had undermined their leadership and forced them to cede to the pressure of harder-line elements.

A majority of Christian Democratic workers strongly supported the strengthening of opposition to Allende. In fact, a number of otherwise progressive trade unionists initially identified with the Christian Left or social democratic factions had grown steadily more hostile to the UP during the course of 1971.[25] A few trade union leaders had abandoned the party with the Christian Leftists the previous month, but if anything this left anti-UP workers both stronger and more determined than ever.

Constitutional Opposition

Beginning in late September, Christian Democratic opposition intensified. Concluding that the government was not interested in "constructive" opposition, the PDC resolved to gird itself for confrontation. This meant taking the political offensive by mobilizing its members and sympathizers and by working more

---

[24] See page 134.

[25] As early as April, for example, progessive labor leader Samuel Astorga, head of the party's labor union department at the time, was saying: "We must stop the political action of the collectivist parties in the trade union base itself" (*Política y Espíritu* 1971b, 10).

closely with other opposition forces.[26] It also meant approaching political issues less on their merits than with an eye to blocking the government on all possible fronts. During this period, public support for the party would grow, particularly among blue collar workers and apparently in response to this harder-line stance. Deteriorating economic conditions beginning in late 1971 were also a factor in these trends. The PDC remained the dominant force within opposition ranks, although as politics grew more confrontational its nuanced views and measured responses were less appealing to certain groups.

Despite the breakdown of his agreement with the PDC Allende sent the Congress a bill laying down guidelines for the future nationalization of industries. It called for transferring firms with assets of more than fourteen million *escudos* to either the social (public) or mixed sector. Firms with fewer assets would be immune to expropriation. Under these terms only 150 of the country's more than 35,000 industrial firms would be taken, although the impact on production, employment opportunities, and advertizing revenues would be substantial. The 150 firms were later reduced to 91, and again to 74, in an effort to temper Christian Democratic and private sector opposition (Espinosa and Zimbalist 1978, 48-49).

The Christian Democrats countered with a rival proposal known as the Hamilton-Fuentealba bill, which was drafted as a constitutional amendment in order to make it more difficult for Allende to use his veto powers. Calling for case-by-case congressional approval of all transfers, it restricted the use of administrative decrees for the purposes of expropriation and established guidelines for worker participation and/or self-management in all reconstituted firms. The restrictions were drafted in such a way as to require the return to their original owners of many of the firms already taken over (Espinosa and Zimbalist 1978, 48). Thanks to National party support it moved quickly through committee, although the government's bill remained under more or less active consideration as well.

In defending their plan, Christian Democrats claimed to offer "a socialism with full and authentic worker participation." At best, however, the bill entailed a democratization of existing

[26] According to an authoritative editorialist in *Política y Espíritu*, the time had come to "overcome the limits of a purely parliamentary opposition, carrying the struggle to the base, to the streets, to effective protest and pressure against the abuses of the government and its parties" (*Política y Espíritu* 1971c, 13).

structures and relationships, one in which workers, managers, and capitalists would have a voice in the shape and decisions of their firm by majority rule. In the social and political context of the time it was clearly a means of blocking further implementation of the UP's socialist program and rolling back those initiatives already taken. As such it just as clearly represented a hardening of position. Earlier in the year the Christian Democrats had been willing to go along with Allende's nationalization plans on the condition that they be submitted to the Congress for discussion and debate. Clearly they had hoped, although they could not guarantee, that such discussion and debate would yield some concessions. Now they insisted that these concessions be included in the legislation itself, thereby signalling their unwillingness to rely on mere "assurances" or open-ended negotiations. Again, however, their efforts were less a defense of bourgeois economic interests (i.e., those of the owners of the affected firms) than of their own petit bourgeois stakes and influence in the political process, which they now believed to be under increasingly direct and strenuous attack by their traditional Marxist rivals.[27]

This determination to resist the government and its initiatives was also apparent in the party's support of the December "march of the empty pots," and in its response to Allende's wage adjustment proposals for 1972, its support of the impeachment of Interior Minister Jose Tohá in early January, and its alliance with the right in two important election campaigns later that month.

The party supported the march on the strong recommendation of its women's department. It had been organized by right-wing groups but managed to attract over one hundred thousand people, thereby revealing a growing reservoir of anti-UP and anti-government sentiment. Fights broke out between pro- and anti-UP groups, and many of the latter complained of rough and discriminatory treatment by police.

With these confrontations the issue of scarcity gave way to those of alleged repression and disregard for the rights of assembly and dissent. These became the basis of impeachment pro-

[27] One of the bill's authors, party president and leading social democrat Renán Fuentealba, had long been one of the party's most progressive figures. The other, Senator Juan Hamilton, was a wealthy corporate lawyer and leading *freísta* with ties to the bourgeoisie. But even though the party's small bourgeois faction identified overwhelmingly with the Frei faction, they were hardly its controlling force, much less the party's as a whole.

ceedings against Interior Minister Jose Tohá. Tohá was close to Allende, a voice of moderation among UP officials, and respected and trusted by most Christian Democrats. That the PDC went after him underscores the extent to which relations had deteriorated at this point. The National party was quick to endorse the move, and in early January, after extensive Senate debate, Tohá was formally censured and forced to resign, although he was immediately reappointed minister of defense and thereby kept his cabinet status.

Conflict also arose over the government's 1972 wage adjustment proposals. Unlike its response the previous year, the PDC denied the government the revenues it sought. According to one source, it voted to provide only 57 percent of what Allende had requested and insisted on indirect (largely sales) taxes rather than the income and property taxes he asked for (Stallings 1978, 203).

Finally, Christian Democrats again joined with Nationals to defeat government candidates in two important by-elections. In a Senate race in O'Higgins and Colchagua provinces, agrarian reform critic Rafael Moreno waged a vigorous anti-UP campaign with right-wing support. He won a narrow victory (52 to 46 percent) in a district that although it included the El Teniente copper mine had never been a leftist stronghold. In the other race, for a seat in the Chamber of Deputies from nearby Linares, party leaders allowed members to informally support the National party's Sergio Díaz, who won by a 58 to 41 percent margin.

These challenges and setbacks had a sobering impact on Communist party leaders. While they had expected PDC-right-wing collaboration, they had not bargained on its being enthusiastically supported by Christian Democratic workers, peasants, and *pobladores*, i.e., the very elements they had hoped to win over to the UP. Moreover, the fact that these sectors failed to respond positively to the improved wage levels and living standards achieved under Allende,[28] and instead closed ranks with middle- and upper-class merchants, professionals, and landowners, gave Communist party leaders considerable pause.

In this connection future prospects were a source of even greater concern. In early 1972 all indicators pointed to substantial eco-

[28] During 1971, Gross Domestic Product had risen by over 8 percent, industrial production by 12 percent, and domestic consumption by 13 percent, while unemployment had been cut by more than half and inflation had been held to 22 percent.

152

nomic difficulty ahead and to the virtual impossibility of main-taining the favorable conditions of the first year.[29] This could spell political disaster. At the least it would make retention or expansion of popular support more difficult, and it might well enhance the political capital of the traditional right. Accord-ingly, the Communists thought it best to alter the current course and urged that rapprochement with the PDC be sought. Allende welcomed the suggestion with open arms, and between March and June changes in personnel and policy were made in order to project a more moderate image. In addition, further expansion of the public sector was put off, and concessions and assurances were offered to key middle-sector groups. Finally, and most im-portantly, a compromise agreement would be sought on the terms of future nationalizations.

Time for achieving this was running out. The Hamilton-Fuen-tealba amendment had passed both houses of Congress in Feb-ruary, although it was vetoed immediately by Allende. In doing so he argued that a congressional override would require a two-thirds majority. The Christian Democrats claimed that only a simple majority was needed and were about to form such a ma-jority with the right when Allende proposed a "dialogue" to ex-plore the possibilities for compromise.

Discussions were held in March and again in June. They went well on both occasions, and promising agreements were reached, only to be disavowed by party leaders. The breakdown in March was the work of Socialists and led to the resignation of Allende's chief negotiator.[30] In June matters were again on the verge of resolution, when a shift in the Christian Democratic position led to a break-off of talks and a showdown in the Senate, the result of which would be a major constitutional crisis. Each side blamed the other for the failure. Popular Unity partisans charged Frei

[29] By late 1971 the money supply was outrunning production increases by a considerable margin, investment was off sharply, previously idle industrial ca-pacity was all but exhausted, and foreign exchange reserves were dwindling fast (due to sharp cutbacks in external credit). Under these circumstances neither present nor future demand could be met, and very substantial scarcity and infla-tion were virtually inevitable.

[30] Allende's minister of justice, Samuel Fuenzalida, had been handling the ne-gotiations for the UP. When Allende rejected the terms that Fuenzalida had worked out, he resigned claiming that he had been repudiated for doing precisely what he had been instructed to do. His party, the Left Radical party, or PIR, broke from the government over the incident and joined the opposition shortly thereafter.

with sabotaging virtually complete agreement on a) the firms to be dropped from the list of those to be expropriated (including four previously nationalized banks and the controversial Compañía Manufacturera de Papeles y Cartones), and b) the forms of worker participation to be adopted. PDC spokesmen denied this, insisting that important details had not yet been worked out, although they did concede that agreement in principle had been achieved and that the UP had made important concessions.[31]

In fact, the Christian Democrats rejected terms they had insisted on and bemoaned not getting the year before. The decision to do so seemed political or strategic in nature: many Christian Democratic leaders were not sure they could trust Allende to stand by an agreement once a crisis had passed; others simply wondered if reconciliation was in the party's interest. First there were indications that the harder line taken since September had won it increased popular support and would continue to do so as economic and social conditions worsened. Second, many of the party's peasant, blue and white collar worker, and petit bourgeois sympathizers had grown steadily more hostile toward Allende and might have been troubled if not alienated by any bridging of the gap at this point.

In this latter connection it is doubtful that either side could have carried out an agreement. Ultimately the presence and power of intransigents in both camps, and not the fact that talks were broken off or the ante raised by one or the other, precluded their coming together. Had formal agreement been reached, implementation would have come, or not, on a case-by-case basis, subject to the suspicions and preemptive actions of dissenting elements on both sides. By June 1972 these were such as to rule out conciliatory agreements of virtually any sort.

In backing off the PDC took an important and conceivably fateful step. This latest and best chance for compromise had generated considerable interest and expectation over an extended period of time. Another opportunity was not likely to arise before the March 1973 congressional elections. The decision to hold out and to build toward those elections was based in part on judgments that UP popular support had peaked and was falling and

[31] Newspapers (*El Mercurio* and *Clarín*) and news magazines (*Ercilla*) at the time carried fairly full accounts of the negotiations. Arriagada (1974, 184-190) also provides excerpts from letters exchanged by Fuentealba and Education Minister Jorge Tapia Videla, who later represented the UP in the talks.

that its own support was and would continue rising. Were the elections to confirm this, the party could deal with Allende from a position of greater strength. And if opposition forces captured the two-thirds majority of seats needed to impeach him, the PDC could conceivably return to power before 1976.

Survey data of this period lent some credence to these optimistic projections. In April Hamuy examined the same three Santiago districts. His data indicate that support for UP parties had dropped slightly since the municipal elections the previous year. Moreover, UP gains over 1970 appeared to have come at the expense of right-wing and independent forces and not the PDC, which also advanced, albeit less spectacularly. Table 4-2 indicates changes in party preferences (membership and/or identification) since August 1970.

The Christian Democrats were thus holding their own, even advancing modestly, despite the dramatic upsurge in UP support. Significantly, much of this strength was due to increased appeal among blue collar workers. Table 4-3 indicates changes in party support among blue collar workers between 1970 and 1972.[32] As these are not panel data, one cannot assume that the respondents were in fact the same people, but the patterns are sharply delineated enough to constitute a reliable indication of trends.

The increase in PDC support among workers suggests, though it does not prove, that the UP's gains came from independent or relatively apolitical workers who had previously supported Alessandri. In any case, PDC members and sympathizers continued

TABLE 4-2
Party Preferences, August 1970 and April 1972

Preferred Party(ies)	1970	1972	% Change
Popular Unity	23.7%	45.4%	+91.6%
Christian Democratic	24.4	25.7	+5.3
National	12.7	8.1	−36.2
Other, Independent	39.2	20.9	−46.7
n	615	842	

SOURCES: Centro Belarmino 1971 and Hamuy 1972.

[32] Unless specifically noted, the blue collar workers referred to in this and all future tables include industrial and independent workers, but not domestic servants or workers, among whom the PDC had a disproportionally large following.

TABLE 4-3
Party Preferences of Blue Collar Workers,
August 1970 and April 1972

Preferred Party(ies)	1970	1972	% Change
Popular Unity	43.7%	59.1%	+35.0%
Christian Democratic	18.2	21.4	+17.6
National, Democratic Radical	11.6	4.7	−59.5
Other, Independent	35.5	14.8	−58.3
n	110	257	

SOURCES: Centro Belarmino 1971 and Hamuy 1972.

TABLE 4-4
Ideological Self-Placement, August 1970 and April 1972

Position	All Respondents			Christian Democrats		
	1970	1972	% Change	1970	1972	% Change
Left	41.0%	54.4%	+32.6%	16.2%	8.2%	−50.6%
Center	31.2	28.9	−7.4	53.8	68.6	+27.5
Right	27.8	16.7	−39.9	30.0	23.2	−22.6
n	510	790		130	207	

SOURCES: Centro Belarmino 1971 and Hamuy 1972.

to be drawn largely, as in 1970, from blue and white collar strata.[33] This predominantly working-class base was significantly more conservative, however, despite the general shift leftwards on the part of the electorate as a whole. Both trends emerge clearly from Hamuy's data. Table 4-4 compares changes in ideological self-placement among all respondents to those among Christian Democratic party members and supporters between 1970 and 1972. Again the figures do not have the strength of panel data but do offer an indication of general trends.

The survey did not probe one's length of affiliation with the party, and it is therefore unclear whether the Christian Democrats leaving the left, moving to the center, or staying on the right were those of longer or more recent standing. Rightist sentiment was stronger and leftist sentiment weaker, however, among

[33] In 1970 the breakdown of party followers was 42.4 percent blue collar, 27.3 percent white collar, and 30.3 percent petite bourgeoisie. In 1972 the figures were 34 percent blue collar, 33 percent white collar, and 30 percent petite bourgeoisie.

blue collar workers and among supporters as opposed to actual party members. While 24.3 percent of the party's supporters identified with the right and only 6.1 percent with the left, the corresponding figures for party members were 16 and 20 percent.[34] Blue collar sentiment more closely resembled that of the party's following as a whole and was shifting along the same lines as can be seen in Table 4-5.

These patterns and changes contradict claims of radicalization among Christian Democratic workers. They also provide only the scantest support for those (Arriagada 1974; Sigmund 1977) who argue that Christian Democratic leaders were being pulled to the right by an increasingly militant anti-UP popular base. There was movement rightwards on the part of working-class members and supporters but hardly of earth-shattering proportions. The vast majority of those identifying with the party remained decidedly centrist in their self-perceptions, despite polarizing trends within the population as a whole. And since party leaders had themselves moved to the right in recent months there is no reason to doubt that they were still capable of defining the political orientation and agenda of the party faithful.

The Christian Democrats also improved their standing and influence within the labor movement. In late May the CUT held its first open election of federation officers. Previously leaders were chosen at national congresses whose delegates were given weighted voting rights in accord with their party's estimated following among unionized workers. Christian Democrats were given 14.4 percent of the delegates to the Fifth Congress in November 1968 and roughly 20 percent at the Sixth Congress in December 1971. Their upward surge continued in the May 1972 elections, in which party candidates won 26.3 percent of the votes cast,

TABLE 4-5
Ideological Self-Placement of
Blue Collar Christian Democrats,
August 1970 and April 1972

Position	1970	1972	% Change
Left	11.8%	5.7%	−51.7%
Center	58.8	69.8	+18.7
Right	29.4	24.5	−16.7

SOURCES: Centro Belarmino 1971 and Hamuy 1972.

[34] The x^2 factor is 6.2 and is significant at .044.

finishing in a virtual tie for second place with the Socialists (26.4 percent) and not far back from the winning Communists (30.9 percent). In addition, they topped both rivals in highly industrialized Santiago province.

Although some analysts (Stallings 1978, 63) have seen the elections as a resounding victory for the UP, they actually reflected a decline in its support, even allowing for distinctions between white and blue collar workers. In fact, had Christian Democratic affiliated peasant unions been permitted to vote, it is likely that party totals would have exceeded those of Communist candidates. At the time PDC officials argued that their candidates actually had won the elections but had been denied their victory because of an arbitrary extension of the voting period and a doctoring of official tallies. There was, in fact, considerable confusion on both counts, but these charges seem nonetheless implausible. Zapata (1976, 59n) notes that vigilance was exceptionally close at all stages and that the reasons given for the extended voting and delayed tallying were understandable given that this was the first such election ever held. Moreover, if one looks at the running totals issued by the parties during the eight-day period, UP totals (as claimed by the Communists and Socialists) remain at roughly the same percentage levels throughout, while those kept by the PDC showed that its portion of the vote actually declined with each tally, suggesting that the problems, if any, were not in this area.

If these political successes weakened Christian Democratic interest in reconciliation, so too did the indications of continuing economic deterioration. March, April, and May saw the deepening of supply problems and the beginnings of widespread *colas*, or lines. Most people had money but nothing on which to spend it. Supply problems reflected and in turn intensified inflationary pressures. Price increases in recent months were twice those of the previous year, and something had to be done. Early in June Communist Deputy Orlando Millas replaced Pedro Vúskovic as the principal architect of government policy. Under Millas the pace of nationalization slackened, and price hikes for basic consumption items were authorized in order to encourage production while limiting demand. Ironically, these "corrective" measures made it possible for the PDC to press bread-and-butter issues among both workers and marginals. It did so vigorously, although it sought to keep anti-UP activities and initiatives within legal and constitutional channels lest they be taken over by right-wing groups. As social and political tensions continued to build during 1972, this became more and more difficult to do. A most expressive case in point was the national *paro*, or work stoppage, of October and November.

The strike began on Wednesday, October 12, with the independent truckers association protesting plans to establish a government trucking line in a distant southern province. It spread quickly to merchant groups, professional guilds, some employee unions, student groups, peasant associations, and organizations of slum dwellers.[35] Although surprised by the speed with which the *paro* was joined by other sectors, the PDC readily endorsed it, denouncing the UP's "provocative designs" on the trucking industry and expressing its solidarity with the truckers and their "just demands." Anxious to confront the government on any issue that might generate broad interest and support, the PDC had more defensive concerns as well. Some party leaders wished to avoid repudiating Christian Democratic activists and supporters who were drawn into the strike through one or another of the various "middle-class" associations. Others urged joining in order to head off actions or developments that might produce anarchy and/or armed confrontations.

Blue collar Christian Democrats were noticeably absent from opposition ranks, however. Their leaders cited pending contract negotiations and argued that since worker interests were "not directly involved," they would remain neutral (*Ercilla* 1973a, 10). In fact, however, many Christian Democrats were supporting the efforts of their fellow workers (most of whom were Marxists) to keep the country's factories open and producing. A number of industrialists had shut down their plants in solidarity with striking *gremios* and in order to place additional pressure on the government. In response, workers of various political stripes, concerned for their jobs and also with making a show of strength, assumed control of their work places and kept most of them operating at full capacity for the duration of the strike.

Tensions mounted daily for almost a month but were broken in early November by Allende's appointment of three high-ranking military officers to cabinet posts. Their incorporation in the government effectively broke the strike. It immediately confined

---

[35] These organizations were among the petit bourgeois associations (*gremios*) that had emerged the previous year as independent anti-UP forces. Their primary concern was with their own economic interests, but massive publicity and the use of liberal slogans won them the support of other groups.

the conflict to physically and psychologically tolerable bounds, forced the opposition to accept the terms of resolution that Allende had offered at the beginning, and allowed attention to be refocused on the March elections.

Another Hamuy survey, taken just prior to these elections, revealed important shifts in attitudes and preferences since April 1972. It projected unchanged backing for government parties and increased support for the PDC and, to a lesser extent, the PN.[36] The broad questions it posed permit the drawing of a relatively complete picture of political attitudes and dynamics. Table 4-6 compares the distribution of party preferences in early 1973 with that for 1970 and 1972, revealing a sharp increase in Christian Democratic support.

The PDC's advance was spread evenly across class lines but was particularly impressive with blue collar workers, among whom its support jumped from 20.5 to 35 percent. As in 1972 these blue collar workers were largely (94.8 percent) unorganized, although they included about the same proportion (26.2 percent) of skilled, as opposed to unskilled, workers as the overall sample.[37] Its fol-

TABLE 4-6
Party Affiliation (members and supporters),
August 1970, April 1972, and February 1973

Preferred Party(ies)	1970	1972	1973	% Change 72-73
Popular Unity	23.7%	45.4%	45.4%	—
Christian Democratic	24.4	25.7	38.7	+ 35.5%
National, Democratic Radical	12.7	8.1	11.0	+ 17.2
Other, Independent	39.2	20.9	5.0	− 30.0
n	615	842	526	

SOURCES: Centro Belarmino 1971, Hamuy 1972, and Hamuy 1973.

[36] The new survey was the Centro de Opinión Pública's *Research Project No. 45*, February 1973, hereafter referred to as Hamuy 1973. For an indication of the survey's accuracy in predicting subsequent electoral behavior, see note 42.

[37] The increased blue collar support was not simply the result of the higher incidence of blue collar workers in the 1973 sample. In 1972 blue collar workers (excluding domestic workers) made up 29.9 percent of all respondents but only 23.9 percent of the party's supporters. In 1973 blue collar workers comprised 48.3 percent of all respondents and 49.1 percent of the party's supporters. The UP continued to command the support of 51.6 percent of all blue collar workers,

lowing among white collar workers and the petite bourgeoisie remained solid (36.4 and 42.1 percent respectively).

Equally significant were the patterns of ideological self-placement. Among the sample as a whole, leftist sentiment was down (by 13.4 percent) but remained strong (47 percent). On the other hand, centrist sentiment remained virtually the same (at 29.2 percent) and rightist sentiment rose a dramatic 41.9 percent (to 23.7 percent). The inroads made by rightist sentiment were particularly apparent among Christian Democrats. As can be seen in Table 4-7, a centrist orientation still prevailed, but both rightist and leftist inclinations were on the rise. Again, as these are not panel data the differences in leftist sentiment may not be significant, but surely those in rightist attitudes are. Moreover, virtually identical trends emerge whether all or only blue collar Christian Democrats are considered.[38]

TABLE 4-7

Ideological Self-Placement of Christian Democratic
Members and Supporters, April 1972 and February 1973

Position	All Christian Democrats			Blue Collar Christian Democrats		
	1972	1973	% Change	1972	1973	% Change
Right	23.2%	34.8%	+50.0%	24.5%	39.3%	+60.4%
Center	68.6	54.8	−20.1	69.8	51.4	−26.4
Left	8.2	10.4	+26.8	5.7	9.4	+64.9
	207	230		53	107	

SOURCES: Hamuy 1972 and Hamuy 1973.

down somewhat from its 58 percent showing of 1972. Christian Democratic support was particularly strong among workers who were practicing Catholics. Among all practicing Catholics the PDC again captured a disproportionate number, though not to the extent of earlier years. While winning 42.5 percent of all Catholic votes, it won 49 percent of those of practicing Catholics; Popular Unity parties, on the other hand, won 44 percent of the overall Catholic vote and 39 percent of those of practicing Catholics. The most convenient measure of the extent to which a party receives a disproportionate share of the votes from any particular subgroup is the difference (plus or minus) between its percentage following among the sample as a whole and that among the subgroup. In 1970 UP's differential was a minus 18 percentage points, in 1972 a minus 6 points, and in 1973 a minus 5 points.

[38] Again, the blue collar workers referred to here exclude domestic workers. In both years this group tended to be more progressive than regular blue collar workers. Of the sixteen interviewed in 1972, 25 percent described themselves as leftists, 50 percent as centrists, and 25 percent as rightists. In 1973 among the nine interviewed these figures were 12.5 percent, 62.5 percent, and 25 percent.

Neither survey provides any indication of previous political affiliations or preferences, so it is not clear who is moving in what direction. Since the percentage of its working-class followers belonging to unions fell from 7.2 to 5.2 percent between 1972 and 1973, however, most of the PDC's new, more conservative blue collar followers were probably nonunion workers. Many of these, after supporting Alessandri, were picked up by Allende and had since become disillusioned. On the other hand, the much smaller number of Christian Democrats (blue collar workers and others) who appeared to be moving leftwards most likely consisted of longer-standing supporters radicalized by the October-November strike or sympathetic to the general direction of government policy, although not to the UP parties themselves.

Hamuy's 1973 survey probed attitudes on a host of other topics and helps to identify the forces and pressures afoot during this period. His data depict a Christian Democratic party pulled in different directions by a variety of forces and considerations. Among the more crucial questions posed were those dealing with socialism, the proper role of the PDC, the causes of scarcity and speculation, the extent and causes of insecurity, and finally Allende, his government, its major deficiencies or excesses, and its principal accomplishments. As with previous surveys, it is possible to identify progressive as opposed to conservative responses. As can be seen in Table 4-8, the patterns differed sharply across party lines.[39]

On each of these issues the attitudes of Christian Democrats was remarkably similar to those of right-wing respondents. The vast majority opposed the establishment of a socialist society, favored a policy of limited opposition (as in 1971) or uncompromising opposition (together with the right) to the Allende government, and held generally negative views on the government's economic performance, although on this issue their judgments would seem less severe than might have been anticipated.

A key to what was happening to the party was the different

[39] The table indicates the percentage of respondents indicating a favorable attitude toward Chile's becoming a socialist country (socialism), support for PDC collaboration with the Allende government with or without cabinet participation (CD role), the judgment that the opposition bears responsibility for scarcity and speculation (causes scarcity and causes speculation respectively), a generally favorable evaluation of the Allende government, the impression that the country's economic situation had improved under it, and the belief that consumer goods were more readily available than was the case a year earlier.

TABLE 4-8
Progressive Ideological and Political Views of Prospective Voters
by Party Preference, February 1973

Preferred Party(ies)	Social- ism	Christian Democratic Role	Cause of Scarcity	Allende Govern- ment	Cause of Specu- lation	Economic Situa- tion	Availa- bility of Goods
Popular Unity	88.4%	78.6%	84.2%	*2.9	86.1%	94.6%	16.7%
Christian Democratic	21.9	26.2	30.3	*4.8	25.9	51.0	2.1
Right (PN or DR)	17.7	12.5	22.2	*5.3	14.8	43.5	1.5
Other, Independent	62.1	34.5	48.3	*4.4	41.4	67.7	6.7
x^2	258	203	175	410	247	238	79
p	.000	.000	.000	.000	.000	.000	.000

SOURCE: Hamuy 1973.
NOTE: Numbers preceded by an asterisk (*) are measured on a scale of from 1 (excellent) to 6 (very bad).

impacts of institutional political and class ties. These can be measured by looking at member and supporter attitudes in terms of occupational (i.e., class situational) categories. The first finding to be noted is that there were no significant differences in attitudes between members and supporters taken as wholes. Only with respect to socialism and ideological self-placement were responses even noticeably different (in each case party members held "more progressive" or "leftist" views), and even these were not statistically significant.[40] This suggests little disparity, at least as of February 1973, between members, who were likely to have been in direct contact with party leaders and materials, and more remote supporters who might have been more susceptible to other influences.

Among both members and supporters, however, attitudes varied substantially along class lines, although not consistently and not in the direction that untempered class analysis might have predicted. Table 4-9 indicates the percentage of party members responding progressively on six of the ideological and political issues included in Table 4-8, with significant patterns emerging on four of the six issues.

[40] On the issues of socialism and ideological self-placement, the x^2s were significant at levels of .11 and .26. On the role of the PDC, the causes of scarcity, the causes of speculation, and the Allende government, the x^2s were significant at .65, .53, .31, and .86.

163

TABLE 4-9
Progressive Ideological and Political Views of Christian Democratic Party Members
by Occupational Status, February 1973

Occupational Status	Ideological Identification	Socialism	Christian Democratic Role	Cause of Scarcity	Allende Government	Cause of Speculation
Professionals, technicians	33.0%	100.0%	33.0%	—	*5.3	—
Small businessmen	—	100.0	—	—	*5.0	—
White collar workers	22.2	44.4	50.0	20.0%	*4.5	22.2%
Skilled workers	—	—	50.0	75.0	*4.5	25.0
Workers	—	—	—	—	*5.5	—
	n = 21	n = 21	n = 22	n = 18	n = 22	n = 21
	tau b = .33	x^2 = 11.6	tau b = − .23	tau b = − .32	tau b = .01	tau b = .02
	p = .045	p = .021	p = .097	p = .072	p = .474	p = .456

SOURCE: Hamuy 1973.

Among party members those in working-class situations (skilled and unskilled workers) were significantly less "progressive" on questions of formal political definition (ideological identification and socialism) and yet less hostile to Allende on the issues of scarcity and the proper role for the PDC. Among party supporters, on the other hand, there are no significant patterns with respect to the formal issues, but on the more concrete political questions, workers (particularly skilled workers) were notably more progressive, as can be seen in Table 4-10.

Working-class supporters of the PDC were hardly pro-Allende. They strongly opposed socialism and, although predominantly centrist, leaned more to the right than the left.[41] But at this point they were hardly the militant, anti-UP base that was dragging a reluctant party rightward, either (Sigmund 1977; Arriagada 1974). They were not about to bolt PDC ranks for the left, as Communists and Socialists had hoped, but they were less critical of Allende and more inclined to blame others for the country's difficulties than the seemingly more progressive petit bourgeois Christian Democrats. In addition, they were less committed to the party's current oppositionist stance and more receptive to some sort of collaboration with Allende. Thus, it would seem that

[41] The percentage of skilled and unskilled workers identifying with the right was 29.3 and 56.1 percent respectively.

164

TABLE 4-10

Progressive Ideological and Political Views of Christian Democratic Supporters by Occupational Status, February 1973

Occupational Status	Ideological Identification	Socialism	Christian Democratic Role	Cause of Scarcity	Allende Government	Cause of Speculation
Managers, entrepreneurs	—	—	—	—	*6.0	—
Professionals, technicians	—	40.0%	—	10.0%	*5.3	—
Small businessmen	8.9%	21.4	25.0%	17.5	*4.8	30.8%
White collar workers	11.4	28.9	18.6	19.1	*5.0	16.7
Skilled workers	10.3	18.6	36.8	40.8	*4.6	27.8
Workers	9.8	10.3	22.5	50.0	*4.8	46.2
Domestic workers	12.5	11.1	33.0	25.0	*4.3	12.5
	n=207	n=205	n=193	n=188	n=213	n=193
	x^2=15.7	x^2=7.6	tau b=−.13	tau b=−.22	tau b=−.13	tau b=−.13
	p=.208	p=.26	p=.010	p=.000	p=.008	p=.015

SOURCE: Hamuy 1973.

NOTE: Numbers preceded by an asterisk (*) are measured on a scale of from 1 (excellent) to 6 (very bad).

the party's working-class members and supporters were being pulled in conflicting directions. Their productive experiences and their sense of their own and their neighbors' socioeconomic conditions, if not positive, were hardly catastrophic. Significantly, it was among the skilled workers in each group that these attitudes were most clearly marked, a fact suggesting the impact of a structurally based class dynamic. And yet these very workers were among the most inclined to the right and most hostile to socialism. They were not voting their pocketbooks but were being pulled in the opposing direction by partisan political conceptions and relationships.

Hamuy's preelectoral survey proved a generally valid predictor of actual electoral behavior. In the March 4 congressional elections opposition parties garnered 54.5 percent of the vote, while those supporting the government captured 43.7 percent. The Christian Democrats led all parties with 28.5 percent of the vote, followed by the National (21.2 percent), Socialist (18.4 percent), Communist (15.9 percent), and Radical (3.7 percent) parties.[42] These results were a moral victory for Allende and the UP. Even the most optimistic preelection projections showed them getting about 35 percent of the vote. Moreover, it was the first time in modern Chilean history that a government had received greater popular support in a mid-term election than when it had initially come to power.[43]

But in another sense the victory was pyrrhic, for it ushered in the third and final stage of UP-PDC relations, that of the open and unremitting struggle which would culminate in Allende's overthrow. With the elections the UP held 63 of the 150 seats in the Chamber of Deputies and 20 of the 50 seats in the Senate. The 20 Senate seats were more than the one-third plus one needed to block Allende's impeachment but otherwise did not materially improve the government's political position. Allende's lack of a legislative majority, and of any prospect of winning a plebiscite, would continue to frustrate his efforts to deal with economic and social problems.

The institutional political arena thus held little hope for either side, and so the locus of political and class struggle shifted to the country's streets, highways, factories, neighborhoods, and *gremial* and popular organizations. This was not an entirely new development. Mobilization politics had been part of Chilean politics since late 1971 but had remained instrumental or supplementary to institutional political processes: i.e., marches, demonstrations, strikes, lockouts, and building seizures were used by all sides to galvanize loyalties and/or make shows of strength from which to operate or bargain institutionally. With the March elections a stalemate was reached. Neither side was willing to concede nor expected the other to either. Each in its way began to think in terms of extrainstitutional and extralegal strategies and solutions. The government's strong electoral showing thus

[42] Although accurately predicting totals for the two rival political blocs, the the survey exaggerated support for the PDC and understated that for the National party. Apparently the latter was successful in capturing much of the independent (or undecided) vote and doubled the support attributed to it by the survey. If one looks at results from the first three districts of Santiago province (those from which Hamuy's survey was taken), however, the discrepancy was much less. The PDC polled 32 percent, 29.3 percent, and 29 percent respectively; the PN 22 percent, 16 percent, and 24 percent. See *El Mercurio* 1973, 11.

[43] The parties originally supporting Aguirre Cerda's government between 1938 and 1940 increased their portion of the vote in the congressional elections of 1941, but by this time their coalition had been dissolved, and some of them had ceased to support the government.

won it an institutional reprieve but opened up a new phase of struggle in which socialism, democracy, and ultimately institutionality itself would be casualties.

Total Opposition

Between March and September anti-UP sentiment among Christian Democrats intensified dramatically. Economic conditions continued to deteriorate and, with the institutional impasse unaltered by the elections, violent confrontations between opposing bands became almost daily occurrences. Lines of division hardened as fears and suspicions on both sides led to preemptive actions, heightened tensions, and ever more widely spread ill-will and despair.

Sensing that time was of the essence, Allende moved quickly on several fronts. Two days after the elections the government released its proposed educational reform, the Escuela Nacional Unificada, or ENU. The proposal's secular orientation, its insistence on uniform content for public and private schools, and its aim of facilitating the "construction of a new socialist society," prompted denunciations from the right, the PDC, the normally conciliatory Catholic hierarchy, and more ominously the military. Following a month of public debate and agitation, the proposal was withdrawn to be revised and submitted again at a later date.

On March 27, Allende took another forceful step, asking for the resignation of his civil-military cabinet. Its replacement by a new civilian cabinet brought an end to the political holding period in effect since November and signalled the resumption of partisan politics.[44] One of the first results of this move was the decision to begin expropriating land holdings less than the eighty-hectare limit stipulated by existing agrarian reform law. Another was Allende's rejection of a comptroller general ruling that forty-three of the firms requisitioned during 1971 and 1972 had been seized illegally and should be returned to their former owners.[45]

---

[44] The cabinet had served since the October-November *paro* both to bring the strike to an end and to assure peaceful and proper elections in March. During its six-month tenure, the government's general program was virtually placed on hold and efforts were made not to involve military ministers in politically compromising matters.

[45] By virtue of his *decreto de insistencia* the president can legitimately reject

167

The PDC answered these initiatives with challenges of its own. On April 25 it reactivated the constitutional crisis by formally overriding Allende's veto of the Hamilton-Fuentealba amendment.[46] In doing so it set in motion what one journalist called "a time bomb that would be difficult to disarm." Christian Democrats carried their struggle to other levels. They would now "fight fire with fire," answering Allende and the UP with their own demonstrations, building seizures, and other extralegal actions, and confronting the government on all possible fronts and issues.

New party president Patricio Aylwin, who was elected in May, personified this more confrontational posture. He pledged that the party's social base would "answer each abuse, violation of rights or arbitrary action," contending that

> in two-and-a-half years of government we learn once again that the Marxists only understand the language of power. In their march toward their political objectives, neither solemn commitments, nor constitutions, nor laws matter. Marxists only understand when another force opposes them. [*Ercilla* 1973a, 9]

Although party leaders wished to break the government's hand and were willing to oppose its initiatives regardless of their merit and however consistent with previous party positions, the fact was that neither Allende nor the PDC was in a position to "choose" their strategic posture at this point. Each was being pressured and preempted not by their remote support bases but by increasingly militant rank-and-file elements, among whom activism and antagonism had stepped up following the elections. Each side was forced to endorse strikes and defend building assaults and seizures by their respective militants whether or not they believed such moves appropriate. Neither wanted to lose the support of these forces nor appeared capable of stopping or controlling them had they wanted to.

Allende was hemmed in and preempted by the *cordones in-*

---

any judgment by the courts or the comptroller general with a decree signed by all members of his cabinet. This he did on April 16, once the new, all civilian cabinet had been formed.

[46] Although the party had discontinued negotiations with the UP on this subject in mid-1972, it took no action at the time, preferring to wait for the outcome of the March 1973 congressional elections. When these did not produce the hoped for "impeachment" majority, it went back to the constitutional question at the crucial juncture at which it had been left.

dustriales and the *comandos comunales*,[47] while the PDC was often outflanked by working-class, peasant, small farmer, merchant, and professional members and supporters who had joined autonomous and increasingly assertive opposition groups.[48]

Conflict between opposing forces became virtually institutionalized and led to the physical and emotional exhaustion of both protagonists and onlookers. Tear gas explosions, water tank incidents, burning barricades, and incidents of violent sabotage were daily occurrences. Twenty-minute bus rides became journeys of several hours as streets were repeatedly blocked off and traffic disrupted. Those reporting for work were often sent home because of strikes, lockouts, and building seizures. Fears and anxieties reached such levels that many ceased to care about the issues involved or with whom responsibility lay. They simply wanted an end to an unbearable situation.

The dynamics of this period were also affected by the increasingly evident anti-Allende sentiment of the armed services. Whether by design or not, news of uneasiness within military and police ranks began to filter into the political arena. In the case of the national police (the *carabineros*) this uneasiness was heightened by an almost daily responsibility for containing antigovernment activities with which most of its officers were in sympathy.

The possibility of a military move on the government had never been far from view since the Tacnazo of 1969. Following the March elections, however, it began to affect the strategic calculations of both sides, generally strengthening the determination and leverage of more intransigent elements. Within the PDC, for example,

[47] The *cordones* were the factory-based organizations of workers that emerged in the industrial areas (literally "belts") around Santiago during the 1972 *paro*. The *comandos* were broader organizations bringing together workers, *pobladores*, students, and others at the wider residential district level. Under the leadership of militant Socialists the *cordones* outflanked and gradually preempted party and government-controlled labor organizations. They instigated numerous factory seizures, generally ignored Allende's calls for patience, order, and due process, and played an increasingly prominent role in political activities beyond their own industries. On a number of occasions they forced the government to take over firms it had not wanted, or had promised not to take, and refused to give up others it had promised to return.

[48] From March on these groups were less and less receptive to the efforts of party leaders to diffuse conflict or reach understandings with the government. A particularly noteworthy case of this was the strike by copper mine workers at El Teniente.

harder-line leaders urged strengthening of the party's oppositionist credentials for the period of political maneuvering that
would presumably follow a military overthrow. *Freístas* in particular harbored hopes of Frei's somehow succeeding Allende, and
military intervention offered a new, though admittedly riskier,
variation on that theme. To prepare for such an eventuality party
leaders adopted an even harder line, lest there be any doubt of
its hostility toward Allende.

Within the UP, military uneasiness prompted Socialists, Left
Christians, and some *mapucistas* to begin preparing for armed
struggle. Weapons were acquired, paramilitary training introduced, and political work begun among both officers and enlisted
personnel in all three services, using *cordon* and *comando* structures.

This intensification of social and political struggle remained
complex and occasionally contradictory. Lines of division were
never entirely clear, nor was any person or group ever completely dominant on either side. A case in point was the strike
by El Teniente mine workers and employees in mid-April. On
the urging of their Socialist *and* Christian Democratic union
leaders miners struck for wage increases larger than those offered by Allende's hard-pressed government.[49] At issue was
whether mine workers were entitled to both the special monthly
wage adjustment they had received during 1972 and the most
recent cost of living increase, for which all workers were eligible.
The government insisted on deducting the monthly adjustment
already received from the overall increase, thereby denying double payment to already relatively privileged workers. Mine
workers, Socialist and Christian Democratic alike, countered that
the general bill should not affect legitimate entitlements earned
through previous struggle.

For both opposition and at least some progovernment forces
the issue was not material benefits alone but worker autonomy
as well. The Christian Democrats were concerned with the government's overly centralized and sectarian character, the Socialists with its reformist illusions and its willingness to temporize

[49] Although some authors have sought to dismiss the strike as the work of
largely Christian Democratic employee (administrative) unions, many Christian
Democrats were actually miners, while the Socialists, whose ranks included both
miners and administrative employees as well, were even more adamant in supporting the strike. The El Teniente strike is discussed in detail by Zapata (1976,
62-66).

with bourgeois opponents. Shocked to find themselves on the same side of an important conflict, Socialist and Christian Democratic workers nonetheless persisted in their struggle. The strike lasted for eleven weeks despite efforts by both CUT labor officials and some PDC leaders to diffuse and end it. It took a heavy toll in lost copper revenues and further agitated troubled political waters. The miners and their peasant supporters demonstrated in neighboring Rancagua and Santiago, and their leaders were detained and arrested following clashes with police. The strike was finally settled in early July, with workers getting the additional money in the guise of productivity bonuses.

The party's support of the strikers and their demands was strongly opposed by part of the social democratic faction. Tómic, Leighton, and other leaders thought the demands exorbitant and feared that the strike would dangerously exacerbate political tensions. But to press the issue at this point would have meant taking on increasingly aroused rank-and-file groups, i.e., the party's slum-dwelling, peasant and small farmer, student, and organized professional activists. Some of these had been hostile to the UP from early on, while others had joined the militant opposition only in the wake of the March elections. Both, however, were now determined to push Allende to the wall, and under the circumstances opposing them was something for which the dispirited social democrats were neither psychologically nor organizationally prepared.

Freístas and other once-hopeful but subsequently chastened social democrats preferred to believe, or at least argue, that the most immediate danger was of Marxist-Leninist dictatorship, not civil war or fascist counterrevolution. They did what they could to endorse and sustain anti-UP initiatives and movements. Many had come to see military intervention as both likely and a "patriotic and indispensable solution" to the country's crisis provided that democratic traditions were preserved and power quickly reentrusted to responsible civilian hands.

The likelihood of a takeover became apparent with the abortive coup (the so-called *tancazo*) of June 29, which had broad support from leading military elements but failed because premature disclosure led several key unit commanders to withdraw their support. Easily crushed by loyalist Army Commander Carlos Prats, the attempt nonetheless underscored the breadth and intensity of anti-Allende feeling within military ranks. Apparently the only questions that remained unresolved were how Prats

171

would be eased out and exactly when and with whose direct involvement the coup would come.[50]

Sensing this, PDC and right-wing groups kept their pressure up and sought to place themselves in as advantageous a position as possible for when "the time came." With more progressive social democratic elements dissenting, the party endorsed a disruptive and openly seditious revival of the previous year's truckers' strike and approved attacks on worker organizations associated with the government.

Amidst these developments came last-ditch but fruitless efforts at a UP-PDC dialogue, which was denounced by most Christian Democratic activists for whom now even talks with Allende were anathema. The fears aroused by the discussions were unwarranted. Among the issues considered were several that had divided the two forces for most of Allende's term: the scope and methods of future nationalizations and the disposition of those already undertaken. Also under discussion was the disarming of paramilitary groups and possible military involvement in a new Allende cabinet. As on previous occasions agreement was achieved on several points, thanks to concessions from Allende. But on others the president held back, contending that he could not compromise without provoking violent reaction from within his own camp.[51]

These were, in fact, the constraints within which Allende was operating. An adversary concerned with averting civil war or military intervention might have respected them and tried to work around them. On the other hand, it had been Allende's inability to control and/or speak for his followers that had brought things to their present crisis proportions and would render any agreement that might be reached meaningless in the days and weeks to come. In fact, at this stage neither side's leadership was in sufficient command of its forces to assure the fulfillment of any agreement that might be reached.

Negotiations soon collapsed, and the countdown continued. On August 22 General Prats resigned his positions as army commander and chairman of the joint chiefs of staff, culminating a gradual realignment within the military favoring procoup forces.

[50] *Ercilla*'s early July (1973b) edition carried a remarkably candid discussion of the entire operation and its various possible implications.

[51] The possibility that Allende was merely using this type of argument to afford himself greater leeway had bothered the Christian Democrats from the beginning of his term.

On September 2 Christian Democrats joined Nationals in issuing a sense of the Congress resolution claiming that the Allende government had lost its legitimate authority over the country's citizens. The resolution constituted an open if indirect invitation to the military to step in, which it did in decisive fashion on the morning of Tuesday, September 11.

Summary

The adversarial relations that prevailed between Marxists and Christian Democrats were initially mitigated by good will and prudence on both sides. Forces seeking confrontation ultimately prevailed in each, however, due to the logic of partisan political competition and to the inability of either side to control its members and/or supporters, thereby placing both its intentions and credibility in doubt. With the PDC's abandonment of constructive opposition in September 1971 went all practical hope of significant collaboration. At the time economic conditions were still seemingly good, UP popularity still high, and antigovernment mobilization not yet underway. Although party leaders had become discouraged, the enmities brewing among party loyalists had not yet coalesced. In fact, the subsequent development of open conflict was encouraged by party leaders, although it was also in response to the continuing sectarianism of Communist and Socialist militants, something that more conciliatory spirits might have reduced.

In stressing the interaction of class and political factors, I have challenged the views of both left critics and Christian Democratic apologists. The PDC was simply not a bourgeois political force committed to the existing order and determined to displace Allende whatever he proposed or did nor was it a potentially willing collaborator forced to the right solely by UP sectarianism and the pull of its own passionately anti-Marxist constituency. Neither of these views gives sufficient play to the contradictions within each camp nor to the contingent political character of their relations over time.

The PDC was a petit bourgeois political force that enjoyed a strong following among both blue and white collar workers. Given their class experiences and political loyalties (the two were invariably interrelated), each of these forces had reason to fear the ascendancy of the Communists and Socialists. And as the Chris-

173

tian Democratic party began to oppose the Allende government more frontally, its support within these sectors grew apace.

The party's dominant petit bourgeois elements were nonetheless ideologically and strategically divided. All were upset by the manner and tactics of UP militants, but some would have opposed Allende's government however tactful or discrete it might have been. The latter were unwilling to trust Marxists under any circumstances, and as members of a self-proclaimed intellectual and technocratic elite they were also averse to any sort of worker-run economy or society. Others, in contrast, were willing to embrace a controlled and democratic form of socialism but were convinced from early on that this was not what parties supporting Allende had in mind. Even here, however, there was further division of opinion. Some Christian Democrats believed that no Marxist socialist, Chilean or otherwise, could be a sincere democrat; others contended that while some Marxists (e.g., followers of Gramsci) might well be democratic, Chilean Communists and Socialists were fundamentally Leninists whose interest in democracy was entirely instrumental and opportunistic.[52]

In fact, at crucial points throughout Allende's term the issue of greatest concern to the social democratic faction, and with it the party as a whole, was not the social or economic status quo but rather the intentions of the Communist and Socialist parties. Even as relations with the UP deteriorated, Christian Democrats were able to reach agreement on specific policy issues but could not overcome their feelings of doubt and mistrust. For some it did not matter what the parties or Allende said or did, "trusting them" was inconceivable. They believed, for example, that Communists would promise anything to buy time or achieve immediate goals but would not honor commitments unless forced by countervailing power. For others the lack of strong leadership or consensus within UP ranks made them wonder whether even sincere offers of compromise or concession could or would be carried out.

It would be wrong, finally, to depict the PDC as a party being

---

[52] In separate interviews in June 1981, two high-ranking *freísta* leaders spoke favorably of what they termed non-Leninist "Gramscian" Marxists and cited the Italian Communists as a Marxist party with which they would be quite willing to work closely. My impression at the time was that they were sincere but were expressing abstract personal sentiments and not the political disposition of their faction or its following.

dragged to the right by its increasingly militant anti-Communist or reactionary base. Through early 1973, at least, there was no upheaval at the base level and no notable disparities among party leaders, activists, and supporters. The views of the the rank and file were generally balanced and as varied as those of the leadership. Moreover, although most Christian Democratic workers opposed socialism and were little inclined to think of themselves as leftists, they were generally less hostile to the government than were their largely petit bourgeois party leaders.

Following the March 1973 elections, the social and political climate did polarize at virtually all levels. The dynamic of conflict and mistrust of which the Christian Democrats were initial beneficiaries quickly escaped their control, cutting off options and ultimately destroying the country's social consensus and democratic institutions. In the end the party played an important role in Allende's overthrow by refusing to compromise with Allende and by encouraging military authorities to take action.

At this point compromise with Allende was inconceivable given the experience of the preceding three years. But to many whose notions of the Chilean military were extraordinarily naive it also seemed to be unnecessary. A "clean" coup and a quick return to democratic rule under their leadership was an infinitely more attractive, if utterly unrealistic, option.

UNDER THE JUNTA

The years since Allende's overthrow have been difficult ones for Christian Democrats. Under military rule members and activists have been harassed, more than a few have been dismissed from private and public sector jobs, and some have been forced into exile. In addition, the party's means of communication frequently have been muffled and/or eliminated and its visibility and influence in national life sharply reduced. While political restrictions and repression have affected the Communists, Socialists, and smaller UP parties even more persistently and intensely, military rule has had an especially debilitating effect on the multiclass PDC, whose vitality and capacity for influence were always more dependent on an open political arena.

Today, after more than ten years of military dictatorship, Chileans are actively pressing for a return to civilian and democratic rule. The Christian Democrats are sure to play an important part in such a transition, if and when it comes. But they are not the party they once used to be. The years of military rule have taken their toll, as have the party's own internal contradictions.

The PDC remains, at this point, a decisive political force, but it will have difficulty holding its present political ground and even remaining intact once the military leaves. With political activity severely restricted, the party's traditional labor and other constituencies have become more autonomous, developing their own agenda and working with other groups as never before. Divisions between Christian Democratic and leftist workers have diminished significantly, reflecting more uniform class situations and experiences and the absence of countervailing ideological and partisan political pulls.

Most Chileans assumed that the period of military rule would be temporary and that power would revert to civilian hands as soon as was feasible. Assurances were given to that effect,[1] and although no deals were made, most anti-Allende civilians, in-

---

[1] Frei is said to have written to his son of military assurances of new elections within six months of the coup. See Christopher Roper's article in the *Washington Post*, September 15, 1973.

cluding leading Christian Democrats, were willing to accept military rule for a transitional period of one to three years. Since then, however, the military has not only retained power but has imposed radically conservative socioeconomic policies despite the country's strong labor movement and seemingly high level of political consciousness. Three factors in particular have facilitated its draconic but nonetheless remarkable political ascendancy: 1) the accumulation of deeply seated anxieties and enmities during the Allende years; 2) the military's effective exploitation of these sentiments in an atmosphere unencumbered by countervailing arguments or criticism; and 3) persistent division and lack of political imagination among center and left opposition forces. Since 1976, however, a new, more militant, and yet broadly based labor movement has emerged. With the dramatic economic downturn beginning in 1981 the regime's once considerable support has eroded very sharply, while the political stock of its opponents, including the Christian Democrats, has risen proportionately. The government's fate, and the future of Chilean politics as well, may be decided soon, and the PDC will have an important say in both.

Christian Democratic relations with the military government have evolved much as they did with the Allende regime. An initial period of limited collaboration or "constructive" opposition was followed by outright, though still circumspect, opposition. More recently the party has strengthened its ties with other opposition forces, including some on the left. As during the Allende years, internal factions have been of several minds, with sentiments shifting in accord with government initiatives and policies and changing economic and political conditions. The basic lines of division remain remarkably intact and familiar: a minority favoring closer ties with the left confronts a mainstream current that supports the reestablishment of a party-led center-right alliance.

Critical Support

Christian Democrats could be found welcoming, lamenting, and condemning Allende's overthrow. For most, socioeconomic and political conditions had become unbearable, and the blame was entirely Allende's. In their view the military was doing the party and the country a favor in bringing to an end the Chilean road to socialism. For others, responsibilities were less clear, but things could not have gone on as they were. Finally, a handful of social democratic leaders and a scattering of working-class activists looked at the coup with both guilt and apprehension. In public gestures and statements they decried the party's complicity as much as the coup itself. They quickly incurred the enmity and wrath of military authorities, and their leaders were forced into exile. Despite their stature and prestige they played only a minor role in the period immediately before and following the coup.[2]

Freístas and disillusioned social democrats offered "patriotic" support to the military government and its task of "national reconstruction." Although disturbed by the severity of postcoup repression, they were willing to accept a period of military rule during which normal political activities would be suspended. During this period, they hoped to prove their party's good faith and to suggest progressive or conciliatory ways for the military to achieve its goals. They sought to play the role of loyal or constructive critics who might then be asked to assume power at the head of a center-right alliance.

Under the policy of collaboration party members were not allowed to accept positions of political (policy-making) responsibility with the government but could hold technical posts in areas of their expertise. In suggesting policy adjustments or corrections party leaders went to considerable pains to show how the changes would help the government achieve its goals more effectively. They were publicly optimistic and deferential despite the widespread arrests, detentions, and allegations of torture and summary execution of the early postcoup period. Many, it seems, considered these to be "one-time measures" for which the need would dissipate; others felt that in any event private representations would be a more effective means of mitigating the repression. Although the military itself was a largely unknown quantity, the party did have friends or friendly contacts within its ranks and apparently assumed it could turn to them if such practices persisted.[3]

In fact, however, PDC-junta relations deteriorated steadily from the beginning. The statements and actions of military authorities quickly made clear that they would hold power indefinitely, maintain their own radically right-wing agenda, and have no

[2] Leighton and Tómic were expelled in October 1973, Fuentealba in November 1974.

[3] Army generals with whom Christian Democrats were on seemingly close terms included Sergio Arrellano, Oscar Bonilla, and Hernán Brady.

interest whatever in Christian Democratic suggestions or collaboration. Within the junta itself, Army Commander-in-Chief Augusto Pinochet quickly emerged as the dominant figure. Although reportedly pro-Christian Democratic,[4] he immediately sided with those who blamed both the PDC and the UP for the country's crisis. In fact, they saw other parties and forces as self-interested, divisive, and without a legitimate role in the political process at this point.

During the first six months of military rule, the PDC's radio voice (Balmaceda) was silenced frequently, its newspaper *La Prensa* shut down, and its leading spokesmen reprimanded, threatened with sanctions, and arrested and exiled for engaging in political activity.[5] The party was thus effectively removed from the public eye and stripped of its access to and influence over erstwhile supporters and sympathizers. As a result, it could do little to resist or dilute junta policy. It failed, for example, despite strenuous effort, to prevent implementation in early 1975 of antiinflationary measures that would bring on recession, dramatic price hikes, and increased unemployment and hardship for the poor. Nor was it able to prevent or mitigate the violations of human rights occurring at virtually all levels of society or the harassment and mistreatment of its own members and militants. Finally, without a public platform the party was powerless to counter the government's propagandistic reconstruction of recent history and of current political and social options. The most it could do was to direct carefully worded letters expressing concern or hopes for the resolution of this or that problem, letters that were generally dismissed by junta authorities as further evidence of the party's demagogic and ambitious character.

The junta's rejection of its conciliatory gestures pushed the party into an opposition stance. It sobered the early optimism of both *freístas* and timid social democrats, while lending greater credibility to the radical social democratic minority. By late 1974 virtually all were agreed that the junta was in fact a dictatorship with fascist or quasi-fascist leanings, whose policies they were

---

[4] Pinochet was generally regarded as favorably disposed towards the Christian Democrats and was said to have supported Tómic in the 1970 election.

[5] *La Prensa* discontinued publication in February 1974, citing "financial" reasons. These were ultimately political, however, provoked as they were by the government's withdrawal of advertising contracts, on which most Chilean newspapers depended for solvency.

powerless to affect.[6] But the various factions were not agreed on what to do about this. One problem was that many of the party's traditional electoral supporters backed the government, its policies, and actions. Another was that some Christian Democratic leaders and militants were willing, if not eager, to collaborate with military authorities.

The "collaborationists" made their views known in November 1974 in a letter that was published in both Chilean and leading foreign newspapers.[7] The letter was drafted by conservative Christian Democrat and former Senator and Minister of Mines (under Frei) Juan de Dios Carmona and signed by former members of the Left Radical party. The signers endorsed the military's broader objectives, its purification of the political arena, and the exclusion of Marxist elements. Most, it seems, were ardent anticommunists who, although acknowledging certain "abuses" of authority, defended the repression of the left as essential to the restoration of the country's social health. Others were technocrats anxious to join the government and to work in a setting in which plans and policies were not subject to popular acceptance. One such *técnico*, Jorge Cauas, Frei's central bank director and a lifelong party member, had accepted a cabinet post and was effectively in charge of economic policy. Other Christian Democratic technocrats were expected to follow his example in the ensuing months.

Party leaders and most party activists strongly opposed collaboration, and disciplinary action was taken against those calling for it without party authorization. In the judgment of party leaders military authorities were not likely to moderate their economic or political views, and their policies would aggravate existing problems and compromise the country's future. These Christian Democrats were not about to cast their lot with the left either, however, and continued to believe in the viability of a centrist movement supported but somehow not crippled by right-wing forces. And so they resolved to oppose the junta but to avoid antagonizing "moderate" or democratic rightists currently supporting it.

[6] *Keesings Contemporary Archives* 1975, 27124, reports on a secret PDC Congress in March which concluded that the military *junta* was "a right-wing dictatorship with fascist manifestations" and their policies were "erroneous, unjust, and incompatible with our principles regarding human rights."
[7] The letter appeared (as an advertizing supplement) in newspapers in Chile and abroad. See the *Washington Post*, November 24, 1974.

Most social democratic elements went along with this thinking, although others rejected the notion of alliance with right-wing elements of any sort. They feared that an overly nuanced opposition stance would be taken for support or approval and argued that the party's natural allies were forces on the left, without whose reconciliation no progress toward solving socio-economic or political problems was possible.

As in the past this was a distinctively minority view. In a poll taken at a party plenum in April 1975 most of the roughly five hundred leaders and militant activists in attendance endorsed either "active critical independence" (party policy at the time) or "critical collaboration." The breakdown can be seen in Table 5-1.

Practical considerations favored the middle ground position. For one thing, the junta continued to enjoy considerable popular support, if public opinion polls of the day are any indication. In a Gallup Poll taken in June, 76 percent of those responding supported Pinochet and only 20 percent expressed hostility.[8] Though one might have questioned the poll's reliability, few Christian Democrats did. Their own hostility toward Allende and the UP years made them more indulgent if not supportive of Pinochet and the military, and they apparently thought that most Chileans felt the same. Others in the party challenged these impressions and their relevance in choosing a course of action but were outnumbered by those wishing to stay in step with prevailing public opinion and to avoid association with forces they took to be roundly and widely discredited.

TABLE 5-1
Strategic Preferences among Christian Democrats, April 1975

Full collaboration	4.6%
Critical collaboration	28.8
Active critical independence	68.2
Outright opposition	9.1
Resistance (presumably armed)	1.5

SOURCE: *Qué Pasa* 1975, 15.
NOTE: The percentages total over 100, suggesting that the respondents were allowed to select more than one answer.

[8] See *Latin America Political Report* 1975b, 203.

Constructive Opposition

The period between 1975 and early 1980 was one of sharply contrasting trends and fortunes. In the beginning the Pinochet government was subjected to substantial criticism and uncertainty, and yet by the end of the decade it was in a stronger position than at any time since the coup. During the period, the Christian Democrats sought to arrest their growing margination from political life and to piece together a "democratic" center-right coalition as an alternative to military rule. They were not successful in either regard, despite considerable effort and seemingly auspicious socioeconomic and political conditions.

Following its April plenum, the party moved into outright opposition, doing its best to maintain a moderate tone and to steer clear of leftist groups, several of which were urging the formation of an antifascist front.[9] For many Christian Democrats the notion of constructive opposition was a reflection of their own mixed feelings. For others it was the most practical way of avoiding military sanctions and not alienating either longstanding followers or potential right-wing allies.

A major concern for both groups was the reopening of the political arena. Organizationally, the party had remained relatively intact. Although it had been formally suspended ("in recess"), its basic structures continued to operate. Through its various functional and administrative bodies it managed to stay in touch with most of its militants and activists, but as a multiclass party whose broader following was varied, dispersed, and not readily accessible (e.g., in factories or working-class neighborhoods), it was more reliant on the electoral process and an open political arena than other parties (Garretón 1981, 28).

At this point, then, its most serious weakness was its lack of ideological and political influence at the level of the general public, where military propagandists had unfettered sway. Unless it made inroads here, the party's still respectable organizational strength might not matter very much. In the short run the cohe-

---

[9] See *Latin America Political Report* 1975a, 20. The Communist party was not represented, however, at a July 1975 meeting in Caracas between Christian Democrats Renán Fuentealba and Bernardo Leighton and assorted representatives of the Socialist, Radical, and Christian Left parties, at which possible common opposition to the military government was discussed. See *Latin America Political Report* 1975c, 228-229. More conservative Christian Democratic leaders in Chile denounced the meeting and upbraided Fuentealba and Leighton for having attended and for endorsing the idea of a united center-left opposition.

sion and functional capability of its organizational units could be neutralized by military authorities, and over the longer term, unless it could publicly refute junta characterizations of pre-1973 parties and political life, it could not hope to challenge the military government's "mandate" or to affect policy in any significant way.

A key element in the party's effort to regain ideological and political hegemony was Eduardo Frei, who began to speak publicly against the military and its policies. While his image in some circles had been tarnished by his actions during the Allende years,[10] Frei was still an authoritative and credible figure. As president of the senate he had been highly visible during Allende's last six months. When the coup came, he endorsed it, urged "patriotic" collaboration in the reconstruction effort, and then withdrew, saying virtually nothing for the next twenty-one months. While his silence appears to have reflected his own genuine ambivalence, it was also a political strategem. Hoping to return to power in the relatively near future, Frei did not wish to antagonize the military or its many supporters at this point. But if he was to return to power, the anti-Christian Democratic views of military and civilian hard-liners would have to be countered and his party's base shored up. Frei was thus forced to play a more active political role,[11] which he began to do in mid-1975 by agreeing to an extensive interview in a national news magazine and by later publishing a lengthy essay, "El Mandato de la Historia," in which he attacked the junta's economic and human rights policies.

In the interview (*Ercilla* 1975, 20-22) he made circumspect but explicit criticisms of junta economic policy, with which his longtime friend Jorge Cauas was closely associated. His remarks had a greater impact, it seems, on highly sensitive junta officials,

[10] Frei was caught in a crossfire between right-wing critics for whom his opposition to Allende was insufficiently forthright and left-wing critics who saw it as uncompromising and determining.

[11] Initially Frei hoped that this could be done indirectly through the activities and good offices of party spokesmen other than himself. By tradition past presidents were expected to remain above partisan contention and debate following their terms. This seemed even more advisable in Frei's case because one of his perennial strong points had been his image as one above party politics. But with restrictions on political activity, the apparent force of lingering postcoup trauma, and the secondary stature of other Christian Democrats, the party's views were neither widely heard nor warmly received during the first eighteen months of military rule.

who immediately attacked Frei as one of the "local demagogues," than on the public at large. The Gallup Poll previously referred to showed 50 percent of the respondents to be "satisfied" with junta economic policy at the time.

Disappointed but not discouraged Frei wrote "El Mandato" in an effort to spell out his views more fully and explicitly. Published in December 1975, the essay was extensively circulated within and outside the country. In it Frei defended the record of his own administration. This was both self-serving and an attempt to demonstrate the possibility of progress, development, and justice without resort to dictatorship, be it of the left or right. His tone was notably defensive, however, that of one worried that the junta had succeeded in distorting both the country's past and its options for the future.

In a second section he attacked the junta's economic and social policies and accused it of engaging in the very practices that had led to the discrediting and overthrow of the Popular Unity government, i.e., chaotic economic policies, extralegal methods, excessive concentration of power, and encouragement of violence and hatred (Frei 1977, 31-33). He also argued that continued enforcement of restrictions on parties, labor unions, and grassroots organizations whose motives were neither narrow nor sectarian (he appeared to be excluding the Marxist left) would simply increase the likelihood of clandestine political activity and actually favor the left (p. 68).

Finally, Frei made a point of reaching out to other "democratic sectors" and to "moderate" rightists in particular. He spoke favorably, for example, of the right's democratic convictions and expressed regret that he had not sought out "a broader consensus from other political and social sectors," by which he certainly did not mean the left (p. 51).

Frei's efforts came during a period in which the economic circumstances of most sectors of the population were deteriorating: 1975 and 1976 were years of consciously provoked recession. Official rates of unemployment rose from 9.2 percent in 1974 to 16.8 percent in 1975 and 17.7 percent in 1976. Purchasing power for virtually all income-earning strata fell sharply, as did industrial production and overall GDP. Many families were reduced to begging for a living and forced to live on survival diets of low-grade wheat bread and other grains. Soup kitchens and food distribution programs sponsored by the Catholic Church and other charitable institutions kept many alive who would not otherwise have survived.[12]

These conditions gave rise not to partisan political activism but to agitation and maneuvering within the military, to increased labor unrest and activism, and to increased religiosity and involvement in socioreligious activities at the neighborhood level. In effect Frei failed to give the PDC the renewed stature or credibility that party leaders had hoped for. Indeed, his views were not widely discussed. People, it seemed, although respectful of Frei personally, considered him part of an earlier political era of which they remained weary and cynical. Such political instincts and energies as they had were pointed in different directions and pursued within different organizational settings, i.e., labor organizations and religious institutions.

Organized labor had been extraordinarily quiet during late 1973 and 1974.[13] It had been thoroughly purged and restructured following the coup, with virtually all UP union leaders and activists jailed, exiled, or killed. New, officially sanctioned union organizations had emerged, headed, in most instances, by veteran anti-Marxist union leaders. Among those given prominent roles in the new labor "movement" were Christian Democrats Ernesto Vógel of the Railway Workers Union, Eduardo Ríos of the traditionally conservative Maritime Workers Union, textile workers union head Manuel Rodríguez, Bernardino Castillo and Guillermo Medina of the Copper Mine Workers Union, and peasant leader Héctor Alarcón.[14]

During the first eighteen months of junta rule, these leaders

[12] Per capita food consumption nationally dropped 4.8 percent in 1974 and 14.8 percent in 1975. See Wilkie and Haber 1981, 7.

[13] The following discussion of the Chilean labor movement under the junta draws on Hirsch 1977 and on various issues of *Latin America Economic Report*, *Latin America Political Report*, and *Hoy* for the years 1975 to 1979.

[14] Ríos was chosen to head the Chilean delegation to the November 1974 meeting of the International Labor Organization in Geneva where he defended the coup and the new labor movement emerging under military auspices. Joining him at the conference were Public Sector Employees Association (ANEF) president Tucapel Jiménez, fellow Christian Democrat Vógel, and Freddy Mujica of the Private Sector Employees Confederation (CEPCh). On their return they continued to work together, initially supporting although later turning against the government and its policies. Medina resigned from the PDC in 1969 in order to devote himself more fully to union activities. Since then he has had little to do with the party or its leaders and has been consistently supportive of the military government and its policy, even at the cost of his leadership of the copper mine workers.

defended the coup and the new "depoliticized" union movement. After years of marginal status and frustration within the CUT they seemed more interested in holding power within the new structures than in who was offering them the opportunity. Nonetheless, most were in sympathy with the government's overall efforts. Many had been trained in the tradition of anticommunist, bread-and-butter unionism of the American Institute for Free Labor Development (AIFLD) and were veterans of earlier efforts to develop alternative (i.e., parallel) union organizations in opposition to the Marxist dominated CUT. Endorsement of the junta and a willingness to cooperate in its program of "national reconstruction" thus seemed a small price, if any at all, for the opportunity afforded.

These antileftist unionists later (1975) formed the Group of Ten, a coalition of ten major union federations that claimed a total membership of more than five hundred thousand workers organized in several hundred locals. Its leadership met every two weeks with the government's Coordinadora Nacional de Gremios to offer "constructive criticism" on current policy questions. Their chief concerns during this early period were wage levels and recent dismissals of workers for political reasons.[15]

Few Christian Democrats remained junta supporters for long, however. In pressing for wage increases and other concessions, they argued that these would help to undercut the appeal of more radical union elements. Unfortunately, military authorities were not persuaded by such reasoning and refused to make concessions or compromise in any way. With the waning of the initial honeymoon period, the onset of the 1975 recession, and continued rebuffs at the hand of the military government, "moderate" union leaders found themselves on increasingly precarious terms with their rank-and-file members and were forced to adopt a more critical position.

An important factor in the reemergence and strengthening of more progressive elements within the labor movement was the junta's refusal in mid-1976 to loosen restrictions on labor activity and enter into institutionalized dialogue. In making these requests the Group of Ten had contended that the constraints made things difficult for those willing to collaborate and actually

---

[15] Most of the union leaders were affiliated with the PDC, although former Radical Tucapel Jiménez (of ANEF) and several independents were also involved.

worked to the advantage of the left.[16] Labor Minister Díaz rejected such notions, apparently not thinking that the government's lines of defense and support needed shoring up and not wanting to set the precedent of bargaining for such support whether needed or not. His decision was costly. It heightened antigovernment sentiment among the unions involved, pushing them into less constructive and circumspect opposition.

Although demonstrations and strikes remained "illegal," their incidence rose sharply in 1977 and 1978. In most instances workers protested wage levels and government efforts to weaken labor organizations through new regulations and restrictions. During the period, Christian Democratic unionists worked with Communist and Socialist party militants in cosponsoring illegal May Day celebrations in 1977 and 1978, which were attended by large numbers of workers and students (between five and ten thousand).

The government responded by stepping up its harassment and persecution of dissident elements, particularly Christian Democrats. These moves intimidated some but emboldened many more. Traditional union leaders generally opposed the new militance as overly political and sure to provoke further repression. They were pulled along, however, by their increasingly restive memberships and by the imperious and insensitive responses of government authorities. Under these circumstances the need and desire for greater solidarity among union groups forced them to downplay their ideological fears and antipathies.

With stepped up harassment, four of the original member unions of the Group of Ten withdrew, one (the Private Sector Employees Confederation) to a more docile or compliant stance and the other three (the textile workers, construction workers, and mine workers confederations) to form the Coordinadora Nacional de Sindicatos with Communists, Socialists, and other leftist groups. The Coordinadora's first leader was AIFLD-trained Christian Democrat Manuel Bustos.

During 1978 and 1979, the union movement developed organizationally at both local plant and national coordinating levels. As they showed greater strength and cohesion, they began to win modest concessions in their separate negotiations efforts and to achieve a fairly broad consensus on the importance of political

[16] See *Latin America Political Report* 1976, 308-309.

reform and democratization to their social and economic struggles. As Bustos put it in May 1979:

> Now the rank-and-file worker realizes that it is not the fault of this or that entrepreneur who pays miserable wages but of the system that forces us into the category of cheap labor. ... They understand that it is necessary to change the system.[17]

The success of the new organizations was remarkable, given the limitations under which they were forced to operate, i.e., their lack of legal status and collective bargaining prerogatives, the loss of many of their most effective leaders, and the virtual absence of any organizational or financial support from the political parties on which the country's unions had traditionally depended. And yet they enjoyed a number of important advantages over the political parties in the present context. In the first place, their status as "natural" social organizations made them difficult for even conservative military authorities to outlaw. In the second, their "legitimate" social and economic concerns could be more readily and plausibly extended to include political issues. And finally, they had constant and much less conspicuous contact with their constituents. As Chilean labor sociologist Gonzalo Falabela has noted:

> Unions are the only ones ... with the ability to organize demonstrations and analyze the country's problems in the open. [They are the only ones that can] confront the government on all kinds of issues which are at the very basis of the economic and political model of the junta, and they have done so.[18]

Although Communists (though not Socialists) had for some time been urging formation of a broad opposition front to include the entire PDC and not just (as in the past) its "progressive" sectors,[19] most Christian Democrats still did not trust the Marxist left and in any event were committed to an alliance with "progressive" rightists. Among union activists (long the party's most anti-Marxist sector), however, interest in overcoming divisions and coordinating energies was growing steadily, and Bustos and

---

[17] *Hoy* 1979, 27.
[18] Quoted in Dinges 1983, 23.
[19] See *Latin America Political Report* 1977, 2.

other younger Christian Democratic labor leaders had moved left despite the strenuous objections of party officials. Helping in this regard was the fact that the political parties with which unionists on both sides were affiliated were neither in power nor as dominant as they might be in normal times. As a result unionists were freer to act on their own and less fearful of manipulation at one another's hands.

A second and somewhat less direct setting of political organization and activity was the Catholic Church. Since the coup the Church has enjoyed unprecedented visibility and appeal in both its sacramental and broader social ministries. Church attendance and vocations to the priesthood have risen sharply,[20] and in the face of hardship and repression the Church has become an indispensable social agency and refuge for all in need.

Immediately following the coup parish churches and communities offered support and consolation for those whose husbands, children, or relatives had been arrested and/or were "missing." Legal services and representation were also available to those in need. Later, with rising unemployment and food prices, church buildings and resources were used to support food banks and soup kitchens. In some cases these activities were organized by already functioning base Christian or base ecclesial communities that had begun to crop up around the country during the later 1960s and early 1970s. They were stimulated, sustained, and coordinated by the Comité Pro Paz, an ecumenical project of the Archdiocese of Santiago, several Protestant denominations, and Jewish community leaders.[21]

Through its various activities, most of which were of a public, albeit genuinely religious character, the Comité became a symbol and rallying point for those wishing to oppose the dictatorship because of their own circumstances or in connection with broader issues. Its credibility and moral authority were considerable thanks to the humanitarian character of its work, the strong support it received from Santiago Archbishop Raúl Silva

[20] The number of seminarians enrolled in 1973 was 100, in 1977, 208, and in 1979, 659. See Wilkie and Haber 1981, 158.

[21] Its full name was Comité de Cooperación para la Paz en Chile. It was responsible to an ecumenical board of seven religious leaders cochaired by Catholic Bishop Juan Ariztía and Lutheran Bishop Helmut Frenz. Its first two executive directors (*secretario ejecutivo*) were Catholic priests, and two of its four departments were headed up by priests as well (the other two by lay persons).

Enríquez, and its nonpartisan and nonself-interested character (Smith 1982, 334).

In their public statements and appeals Comité spokespersons were constructive, deferential, and yet forcefully critical of the junta, and in this regard they resembled the PDC. In fact, although committed to serving all Chileans in need, whatever their backgrounds or persuasions, many of the Comité's lay employees were one-time Christian Democrats or Christian Democratic sympathizers who had drifted away from the party.[22] But because in their work for the Comité they were not associated with the pre-1973 era, nor perceived as serving partisan or political interests, they were more visible and credible than Christian Democrats who were saying much the same things. In fact, the Comité helped to uncover and legitimate among the general public surprisingly extensive and intense misgivings regarding military rule. And this, in turn, suggested to some that the junta's real strength was the absence of a credible political alternative and not popular endorsement of its policies or practices.

In any case, the Comité's functional and political success prompted government authorities to demand its dissolution. Cardinal Silva resisted for more than a year but in a conciliatory gesture agreed to a reorganization under tighter archdiocesan control in November 1975. The Comité resurfaced almost immediately, however, as the Vicaría de Solidaridad, and became an even more powerful social and moral force. Although higher-ranking Comité officials were let go and in some cases forced to leave the country, the organization's core remained intact and resumed its activities with even greater dedication, albeit in a lower key.

Among the Vicaría's more important projects over the next several years were educational programs covering occupational (plumbing, carpentry, sewing, etc.), functional (neighborhood organizations), and strictly religious subject matters. Its organizers or promoters were not always socially conscious or motivated,

[22] The head of the Comité's Human Rights Department, which gathered information on human rights violations and provided legal services to political prisoners, was José Zalaquett. Like many others who worked for the Comité, Zalaquett had been a Christian Democratic party supporter during the 1960s but had subsequently moved to the left and was generally sympathetic to the Allende government and to MAPU, although he was never a member or activist of any party. He was arrested and held for two months in late 1975, and later for a week, before being expelled from the country in April 1976.

nor did they only attract constituencies searching for an organizational setting in which to become politically active. But in the absence of other outlets the programs provided "public space" in which people were able to come together to speak their minds and openly express their fears and hopes and in which they could develop a sense of solidarity with others like themselves throughout the country. Whatever their focus, sacramental, social, or educational, they became vehicles of socialization, consciousness raising, and even mobilization for substantial numbers of people.

The new organizations attracted the attention of both military authorities and their partisan critics. The former sought to stifle and obstruct their development, the latter to appropriate their credibility, their resources, and the loyalties of their constituencies. Neither group was very successful, as the popular organizations managed to escape both suppression, thanks to the protective auspices of the Church, and political colonization. If anything, in fact, they succeeded in drawing activists and militants away from the various party groups.

Christian Democratic efforts at political revitalization were further stymied by the party's formal dissolution in March 1977 and by the suppression of rivalries and divisions within projunta ranks. Although formally "in recess" since September 1973, the PDC, together with other non-Marxist parties, retained its legal personality and financial resources. Now, however, it was stripped of these as well and would have to function clandestinely, with all the risks and limitations which that entailed.

As he moved to weaken actual or potential opponents to his government, Pinochet also strengthened his own personal power position. The period between 1973 and 1976 saw him move from one of four coequal junta members (the Air Force and Navy had been more directly involved in coup planning than the Army) to chief of the junta, and later head of state. In early 1977, however, questions regarding his leadership began to affect the deliberations concerning the shape and powers of future political institutions. Factions and apparent factions emerged and in turn began to threaten, if not actually limit, Pinochet's discretionary power.

During the next two years, a good deal of speculation and maneuvering attended these deliberations. So-called *blandos* (or "softliners") favored an early return to civilian rule, a more open political process, and more restraints on presidential power, al-

191

though they also urged a continuation of the current radically free market economic policies. *Duros* (or "hard-liners"), on the other hand, preferred a much longer period of transition to civilian rule, authoritarian rather than democratic political institutions, and active state intervention in defense of "national" interests and unmet social needs. Outside groups sought to exploit these divisions to their advantage. The Christian Democrats pursued closer ties with the *blandos* in hopes of resurrecting a center-right alliance. Association with the right could enhance the party's acceptability within military and civilian circles, and while the economic inclinations of most *blandos* were troublesome, they were far more congenial politically.

Unfortunately many of the party's military friends or potential allies died, fell from favor, or were forced into retirement, leaving it virtually unrepresented in military circles.[23] Moreover, with the passage of time, the party had less and less to offer its moderate rightist "friends." No longer the vital, mass-based political force of early years, it was unable to reach former electoral supporters, many of whom were either sympathetic to the military government or had drifted into passive conformity. In addition, a good many of its own members and militant activists had become involved in labor and religious organizations that seemed more vital and more promising politically. In doing so they neither abandoned nor repudiated the party but did move beyond its immediate reach or jurisdiction.

The PDC had never been a credible or attractive alternative for either the political or economic right. While their distrust of the Christian Democrats often focused on the party's radical left wing, Chilean rightists had never trusted its mainstream either: "moderate" Christian Democrats, though more congenial, were still too ideological and too disdainful of other political forces. In fact, to Chileans identifying with the right, an alternative to existing and assertedly outmoded divisions could never be terribly appealing and almost invariably conveyed a threat to displace and not a genuine desire to work together (Garretón 1981, 27).

[23] Manuel Torres de la Cruz, a right-wing army general with reputedly close ties to the party, was forced to resign in early 1974. In March 1975 Frei's former aide-de-camp, General Oscar Bonilla, died in a helicopter accident amidst persistent rumors of an overthrow of Pinochet by "progressive" military elements aligned with him. Arrellano was forced to resign in January 1976 and Hernán Brady in 1977.

Finally, and perhaps most importantly, several years of partial economic revitalization helped to smooth over some of the differences among junta supporters. After a drop of 12.7 percent in 1975 GDP grew by 2.7 percent in 1976, and by more than 6 percent per year from 1977 to 1979. Of equal significance in terms of popular perceptions, the rate of inflation (as measured by the official Consumer Price Index) went from 374 percent in 1975 to 92 percent in 1977, 40 percent in 1978, and 33 percent in 1979 (Wilkie and Haber 1981, 16). This recovery, coupled with reductions (to 10 percent) in duties on imported goods, fueled a consumer boom with the appearance or feeling of generalized prosperity, although it was confined to middle-and-upper income levels and although unemployment remained uncommonly high: 17.7 percent in 1977, 18.3 percent in 1978, and 17.5 percent in 1979 (Aldunate 1982, 407).

Failing to promote its center-right alliance or alter government policy, party leaders concluded that neither *duros* nor *blandos* wanted democracy or social integration and that allies in these regards would have to be sought elsewhere. In addition, they resolved to take thorough stock of their party, which they did in harsh and candid terms at a secret plenary session in April 1980. There they acknowledged that things were, in fact, at an all-time low.

> The organization exists but at this point is not important. To recover that condition, two things must be done: reorganize the base, inasmuch as support from the masses is minimal; and introduce a new style, change the image of the old party politicians, who only sought to amass a following when they should be serving their fellow citizens.[24]

Party leaders also conceded that the government still had considerable support among the people, particularly when viewed against memories or images of the Allende period. Frei told the plenary, for example, of a visit he had made to the south where he informally probed popular attitudes and opinions. All of the one hundred or so people with whom he spoke indicated a preference for life under the junta, even under current conditions, to a return to Allende and the UP. And when Frei asked the same

[24] The remark was made by party president Andrés Zaldívar. See *Ercilla* 1980, 13.

question of Christian Democratic party delegates, 80 percent of them responded in kind (*Ercilla* 1980, 13).

Concerted Opposition

With such evidence of institutional weakness and waning influence over its own militants the party turned its attention to revitalization efforts. It also began to explore the possibilities of cooperation with other "democratic" groups, including some on the left, thus moving in the direction taken by some Christian Democratic trade unionists several years earlier.

The first significant instance of cooperation occurred just prior to the September 1980 plebiscite. In early August, with projunta groups still divided on key provisions of a proposed new constitution, Pinochet suddenly imposed a "compromise" that could leave him in power through 1997 and ordered it submitted to a plebiscite within a month. In the face of this unexpected challenge Christian Democrats and leftists met repeatedly in an effort to galvanize opposition. Although there were some who were inclined to abstain, in the end the PDC, the Communists, and several smaller leftist parties resolved to press jointly for a "no" vote.[25] Among other joint activities, Communists and Christian Democrats appeared together at the one public rally permitted during the month-long campaign, which took place at the politically legendary Caupolicán theater.

Their efforts failed to mobilize enough votes to reject the constitution and left both parties with bad tastes in their mouths.[26] The plebiscite had asked for a yes or no vote on a package of three propositions: 1) the terms of the constitution itself (with a dominant executive and severely restricted legislature); 2) a nine-year period of transition (ending in 1989); and 3) the designation of Pinochet to succeed himself for an additional eight-year term (ending in 1997). It was approved by what authorities claimed was a two-to-one margin.

[25] Socialists and *mapucistas* urged abstention instead. Also calling publicly for a no-vote were forcibly retired air force general and original junta member Gustavo Leigh, anti-Allende activist León Vilarín (of the Independent Truckers Federation), and right-wing political activist María de la Cruz, one of the organizers of the "march of the empty pots" of December 1971.

[26] One source of controversy was the the speech given at the Caupolicán theater meeting by a Communist party spokesman whose extensive use of leftist terms and slogans from the Popular Unity era evoked widespread booing and hissing.

Although the margin may not have been as broad,[27] and may not have indicated solid ideological support for either the military or Pinochet, it is still significant that only a minority of those participating were willing to publicly oppose Pinochet or his government. Under the prevailing conditions of widespread repression, intimidation, and limited information, discussion, and debate most Chileans either approved of the junta, preferred it to what they took to be the alternatives, or were unwilling to oppose it for fear of reprisal. Whatever the underlying mix of fraud, intimidation, and genuine sentiment the results were grim testimony to the government's organizational and political capabilities (Garretón 1982a, 332) and greatly strengthened Pinochet's hand.

Christian Democrats and leftists alike were shaken by the results, although the Christian Democrats were somewhat less surprised, as they had known for some time of their own dwindling support and impact.[28] The two groups agreed that the returns reflected and further enhanced the strong position of the Pinochet government and made changes in it in the relatively near future extremely unlikely. They disagreed, however, on what to do in view of this. According to the PDC, the opposition should think realistically:

> For the next four or five years it won't be able to change this government. At first we thought that in Chile such crude authoritarianism would never stand a chance. Then during the 1975-76 economic crisis people said: It won't survive. Then we thought that international pressure would bring it down. In September it managed to quash such dreams entirely.
>
> From now on we have to set long range objectives, try to get society to evolve in depth—in universities, factories,

[27] According to the Ministry of Interior, 4.2 million voted in favor and 1.9 million voted against the proposed constitution, but there is good reason to question these figures. Irregularities in both voting and tallying were denounced during and following the campaign. For one thing, there were no electoral rolls against which to check alleged votes. For another, if the government's figures are correct there would have been no abstentions whatsoever, something highly unlikely in a country whose abstention rate under normal political circumstances was generally between 15 and 25 percent. See the analysis of Christian Democratic lawyer Ignacio Balbontín in *Hoy* 1980, 17.

[28] Frei (1977, 15) had anticipated as early as 1975 that the military would have broader support among the public at large whose information and thinking it could control more effectively than from people active in labor, neighborhood, or other social organizations.

neighborhoods, army barracks—while patiently working to renew and reinvigorate party doctrine and organisation. That's not defeatism, it's realism. Politics is the art of the possible, not a way to compensate for the dullness of daily life by dreaming. [Clerc 1981, 12]

To those on the left, however, the plebiscite showed the futility of moderate or discreet opposition and the need for more "forceful" forms of resistance. Although this was variously understood by the different groups, Communists and *miristas* were no longer as inclined to regard one another as antagonists, and in the months following September a convergence developed in support of more militant antijunta activities.

The prevailing mood in both camps was of confusion and discouragement that bordered on despair. This could be seen in the sharp terms with which normally circumspect Christian Democrats like party president Andrés Zaldívar denounced the plebiscite as "fraudulent." Zaldívar's charges earned him immediate and indefinite exile, which his party colleagues angrily but helplessly protested. And for the next eighteen months the party languished in indecision and inactivity, as it searched for ways to oppose a hypersensitive but otherwise impervious and seemingly unstoppable government.

Despite the government's relatively secure position, labor, student, and religious organizations continued vigorously to oppose its polices and practices. There had been no economic upturn for lower income groups between 1977 and 1980. Wage increases had been modest, and effective purchasing power continued to decline (Aldunate 1979, 731-738). As a result, lunchroom boycotts, slowdowns, and even strikes became increasingly common occurrences among copper mine workers and other highly skilled, well-paid workers. Moreover, the imposition in January 1979 of a new labor code designed to depoliticize the revitalized movement had precisely the opposite effect, providing militant leaders with yet another banner around which to rally their once mutually hostile and skeptical rank-and-file members. In fact, in seeking to exclude leaders of longstanding or with known political ties the government effectively forced the holding of elections in which younger, more aggressive elements, usually Christian Democrats and Communists, emerged victorious.[29] As

[29] Opposition slates did particularly well among copper workers, steelworkers, and textile workers. Union leaders were under increasing pressure from their

a result, it faced even more determined and substantial opposition than before.

In addition, student, slum dweller, and peasant organizations also came to life. In university student elections held in 1979, the first permitted since the coup, progovernment candidates received 28.7 percent of the vote, while opposition candidates won 59.2 percent. In the cities and countryside the new popular organizations, nurtured and developed under the protective auspices of the Church, began to make their voices heard in connection with government policies and practices. But while these various phenomena indicate substantial opposition sentiment, that sentiment was limited to specific issues and policies and tended to remain localized. Restrictions on both political activity and reporting helped to prevent conflicts and controversies from extending beyond their own immediate levels and constituencies and thus from engaging or agitating wider audiences.

In fact, "public" opinion, such as it was, remained favorably disposed toward the government. And although many of the labor and other popular leaders who were being harassed were both admired and sympathized with, most Chileans continued to support the junta's overall enterprise, in effect giving it the benefit of the doubt, i.e., the doubt that there was any other way of avoiding the upheavals associated with the Allende years. They did not think of the labor or religious movements as political alternatives, and unless opposition parties offered something new and promising, something other than traditional slogans and recipes with their seemingly fatal consequences, military authorities would continue to have their compliant, if unenthusiastic, support.

The bleakness of the political landscape was further underscored for the Christian Democrats in January 1982 with the death of Eduardo Frei. To be sure it led to an extraordinary outpouring of sympathy and to expressions of solidarity toward both Frei and the democratic tradition with which he was identified. As many as seven hundred thousand people are said to have attended his funeral. Party leaders were visibly heartened and no doubt strengthened in their determination to carry on in his stead. But Frei's death nonetheless robbed the party of its principal national figure, the one with whom it had risen to political

---

members on matters of wages and were themselves resentful of junta efforts to undermine existing organizations and leaders.

prominence and who, alone among its leaders, was capable of rivaling Pinochet in stature at this point. It thus cast a cloud over the party's future appeal and would certainly reduce its leverage in bargaining relations with other forces. In fact, although Frei's absence made the PDC a less threatening coalition partner for both right- and left-wing groups, it also made it a less valuable one as well.

In a matter of months, however, the gloom that had descended began to lift, thanks to the deepening of an economic recession that had begun in mid-1981. The collapse was the consequence of worldwide recession, higher energy costs, stifling debt service obligations, and the government's own radical free-market, free-trade polices. Minimal external tariffs led to ruinous foreign competition and to sharp drops in industrial production, record levels of bankruptcy, skyrocketing interest rates, even higher levels of unemployment, and resurgent inflation. The gains of the 1977 to 1979 period were quickly wiped out, and the country confronted an economic crisis comparable to that of the last two years under Allende.[30]

With the collapse, fragmented and near despairing opposition parties, including the Christian Democrats, won a new and unexpected lease on life. They regained their badly shattered confidence and began to consult and coordinate with one another. Although divisions remained, a new openness on the part of virtually all groups was apparent. *Mapucistas*, Left Christians, Socialists of varying orientations, and even the Communists discovered new merit in democratic politics and began to speak of the Christian Democrats and other "bourgeois" forces in positive terms. Christian Democrats, in turn, hailed the new democratic tendencies of the left, and some even endorsed Tómic's views of a decade earlier, i.e., that the party could not and should not govern except in alliance with popular (read "left-wing") forces (*Hoy* 1981, 9).

With its economic model in shambles the junta's cohesiveness unravelled as well. The economic and political groups supporting it urged conflicting remedies and began looking for separate ways to safeguard their respective interests. Once again there was talk

---

[30] Unemployment was 16.1 percent in 1981 and 22.3 percent in 1982 (Aldunate 1982, 407). By October 1982 it had jumped to over 30 percent on an annual basis. Inflation in October, again projected over the entire year, was estimated to be 57.6 percent in Consumer Price Index terms and 88.8 percent in producer (wholesale) price terms (see Ruíz-Tagle 1982, 668).

of *blandos* and *duros* and of *aperturistas* (those supportive of an "opening") favoring a broader center-right alliance that would include the Christian Democrats and other pre-1973 parties. Most traditional rightists (those associated with the National party, the Democratic Radical party, and Patria y Libertad) stayed with Pinochet, although they disagreed on the issue of reconciliation with other political forces. A smaller segment actually abandoned the government, formed the new Republican party, and would later join with Christian Democrats, Social Democrats (formerly PIR), Radicals, and Socialists to form the Democratic Alliance.[31]

Among Christian Democrats a search was launched to find a leader and national figure to take Frei's place. This was a difficult task because Frei had played a dominant and absorbing role even when not directly involved in party affairs. It was doubly so, however, given the persistence of opposing ideological and strategic tendencies among leaders and activists. In fact, "social democratic" forces have broadened their ranks and extended their following in recent years. Known colloquially as *los chascones*, or "long-hairs," they have attracted social democrats, younger party activists, and some former *freístas* to their ranks. They appear to hold a slight edge over the *guatones*, or "fat-bellies," who consist largely of ex-*freístas* and other more conservative elements (*Latin America Regional Reports Southern Cone* 1982a, 7).

The *guatones* have long favored a center-right alliance, being more comfortable with the political and economic right. During the years of military dictatorship, they have come to support what one spokesman termed a "socially sensitive, but tempered liberalism" that operates within existing capitalist structures.[32] In their view, capitalism makes better economic and political sense not because of any intrinsic worth but because socialist

---

[31] After a number of false starts, and with the Communists excluded, the long-awaited "Democratic Alliance" (Alianza Democrática) was formed in August 1983, thanks to the work of the PDC's Gabriel Valdés and Socialists Julio Stuardo and Hernán Vodanóvic. The Alliance would subsequently endorse and help to organize antigovernment activities, although initially member parties remained active in such organizations or coalitions as the Popular Democratic Movement (MDP), the National Development Project (Prodén), and the *multipartidaria*, which often appeared to be working at cross-purposes strategically and tactically. In time, the multitendency Alliance and leftist MDP emerged as the two major, competing opposition groups.

[32] Interview with Claudio Orrego, May 31, 1981.

alternatives do not work, are prone to destructive politicization, and in any case are unacceptable to most Chileans. To advocate socialism under current and foreseeable circumstances would be both inappropriate and "politically stupid."[33] And yet at the practical level these conservative Christian Democrats readily concede the need for some sort of understanding with the left and with organized labor if they are to achieve power and exercise it effectively.

Chascones, on the other hand, would prefer to avoid the right altogether and to join with other social democrats and democratic socialists in a strong center-left alliance. They remain committed to the replacement of capitalism by more just and participatory economic structures, although they claim to be aware of the dangers and difficulties of building a democratic socialism and propose to move slowly and cautiously.

These positions reflect countervailing normative convictions. They also rest on varying assessments of the political strengths and prospects of other forces. *Guatones* see the right as politically strong and likely to remain so despite the current economic crisis. They are therefore more willing to defer to and join with its more moderate or democratic elements. The *chascones*, on the other hand, credit the right with less support and a less rosy future and think that the left still has considerable following among workers, peasants, and popular forces generally.

The two agree on a number of important points as well. Neither believes, for example, that the PDC can presently govern alone or effectively displace either right- or left-wing forces. Both accept the need to form coalitions with forces with whom they are in less than full agreement. And while they would choose differently, neither is indifferent nor completely opposed to the groups or interests favored by the other. It seems unlikely, however, that left- *and* right-wing parties will agree to join with the Christian Democrats in a three-way bloc. Indeed, they seem to be having enough trouble with the idea of joining with the Christian Democrats alone. Beyond the initial dividend of throwing off military rule it is hard to see what either right- or left-wing forces would have to gain from such a combination, and it seems, therefore, that the party will have to choose one or the other.

Because the *chascón* and *guatón* factions could not agree on a

---

[33] These views were gleaned from conversations with several *guatón* leaders and with a Christian Democratic economist close to them during late May 1981.

candidate, the party presidency went unoccupied for more than a year following Zaldívar's expulsion. In April 1982 Gabriel Valdés, foreign minister under Frei and later a United Nations Development Program official, was chosen as a compromise candidate. Under his leadership the party has become more outspokenly critical of Pinochet's government and has sought to build a broad opposition front from which only "nondemocratic" Marxist-Leninists like the Communists and the MIR would be excluded. In this regard Valdés has publicly made conciliatory references to Allende, taken favorable note of the democratic tendencies emerging within the once staunchly Marxist-Leninist Socialist party, and defended the right of the Communist party to exist, even as he rejects the possibility of working with it in any formal or institutionalized way.[34]

The prospects for alliance with either right- or left-wing forces will depend on developments within the labor movement and the country at large, the disposition of forces and sentiments within other parties, and the attitudes of key sectors of the PDC. With respect to the first of these, one must note the extraordinary mobilization of opposition forces begun by the labor unions in May 1983 and continuing on a monthly basis for the rest of that year. Working with students, neighborhood committees, and later political parties, the unions staged strikes, work stoppages, demonstrations, and acts of protest that condemned government policies and called for Pinochet's resignation. They began with the calling of a national work stoppage (*paro nacional*) by the powerful but normally cautious Copper Workers Confederation (CTC), of which little-known Christian Democrat Rodolfo Seguel was the president.[35] The plan was immediately embraced by hun-

---

[34] In an interview with *El Mercurio*, when asked about relations with left-wing parties, Valdés is quoted as saying that "he respected the memory of Salvador Allende, but believed that the policies of the Popular Unity government had been 'profoundly mistaken.' He added that the Communist Party should be legal, the first time this position has been taken in public in the country since the military took power in 1973. Valdés said that 'every idea has a right to exist,' insisting that parties should be judged by their actions and not their ideas alone. . . . " See *Latin America Regional Reports Southern Cone* 1982b, 4.

[35] Seguel is the young (twenty-nine), relatively obscure Christian Democratic labor leader who was thrust into the national spotlight in February 1983 when the military government forced Emilio Torres to resign as president of the powerful Copper Workers Confederation. With Torres unable to function, and with the Coordinadora's Manuel Bustos exiled to Europe, Seguel assumed leadership of the antijunta labor movement. His first crucial decision was to organize a

dreds of other organizations and expanded to become a Day of National Protest (*jornada de protesta nacional*), in which over seven hundred thousand people took part in Santiago alone. In subsequent months, and in the face of almost certain arrest and reprisal, similar events were carried out, with proportionately large participation and support.[36]

These actions succeeded in integrating dissident movements and sentiments previously unaware of and/or politically hostile to one another. They brought together Marxist and non-Marxist workers, petit bourgeois suburbanites and shantytown marginals, merchants and small businessmen and university students, all demanding a return to democratic rule. The broader agendas and concerns of these groups were by no means identical and will constitute a formidable problem in any transition to democracy. But they had begun to work together and for the first time could see the power of which they were capable.

In regard to other political parties things are in flux everywhere. On the right one can broadly distinguish between three groupings: traditionalist or extreme rightists who reject democratic values and remain staunchly supportive of Pinochet; "democratic rightists" who have abandoned the government and formed the new opposition Partido Republicano or Republican

---

massive protest of the government's refusal to permit traditional May Day activities. Although threatened with reprisal by authorities and urged to pursue a more conciliatory path by more conservative Christian Democratic labor leaders and party officials, Seguel persevered and the protest became an overwhelming success, involving hundreds of thousands of participants. Seguel has been arrested and jailed on several occasions since this first Day of National Protest but has continued to press for trade union unity and to call for an immediate return to civilian rule.

[36] Large demonstrations were held in Santiago and other cities on or about the eleventh of each month through the end of the year. The extent of popular support and involvement varied from month to month for a variety of reasons. The largest demonstration was in August, when eighteen thousand army troops were called in to "restore" law and order. Seventeen people were killed on that occasion alone, and there have been casualties, albeit fewer, in each of the demonstrations since. The PDC has endorsed some of the demonstrations but opposed others. Most of the support for them has come from the unions, from students, and most notably from neighborhood organizations in the outlying slum areas where barricades have been set up and organized resistance activities carried out. The militance of some of these groups has alarmed segments of the antijunta movement, and pressure has been put on Christian Democratic party leaders to repudiate them and their confrontational agenda.

party; and those in between these two who seem to be waiting to see how things turn out before committing themselves.[37]

In the middle, along with the perennially divided Christian Democrats, are the Radicals, minus their more left-wing elements, and the Social Democrats, who are former members of the Party of the Radical Left, the group that broke away from the Radical party and the UP in 1972. Although other forces are also involved, the center's major organizational expression is the Democratic Alliance, formed in August 1983 to succeed the broader *multipartidaria*, or "Multi-Party Formation."[38]

On the left there are the Communists, multiple factions of the former Socialist party, the Popular Socialists, two fractions of MAPU, the Izquierda Cristiana, left-wing Radicals, and the MIR. To date the groups have clustered around two broad tendencies: the Communists, several Socialist factions, left Radicals, and the MIR, on the one hand, and both MAPUs, the Izquierda Cristiana, and more moderate Socialists, on the other. The former group appears to feel that the military will only be removed from power by force and that the popular movement should be developing capabilities of this sort. The latter espouses a non-Leninist-Marxist perspective, is committed to building socialism democratically, and stresses the need for accommodating and working with petit bourgeois forces like the Christian Democrats. Unfortunately, at least from the standpoint of clarity, the various groups move within and between a number of alliances, fronts, umbrella groups, and consultative committees (e.g., the Democratic Popular Movement, the Bloc for Socialism, the Socialist Conver-

[37] Right-wing groups have split into a number of factions. The National party has at least three distinct subgroups: the progovernment National Unity Movement, the moderately oppositionist Phillips group, and the more resolutely oppositionist Frias group. In addition, there is the new Republic party, consisting of former National party members who left the party several years ago in order to work more freely for a return to civilian rule, and the pro-Pinochet Independent Democratic Union, led by traditionalist ideologue Jaime Guzmán.

[38] The Alianza Democrática consists of the PDC, the Social Democrats (formerly PIR), the Radicals, the new Republic party, and several factions of the Socialist party. Its leadership rotates among the member groups and usually reflects their respective orientation. On the whole the Alianza has sought to project a "moderate" image and a willingness to negotiate differences with the military government. It appeals to petit bourgeois and white collar elements who are worried about more militant groups but has been undermined by Pinochet's unwillingness to respond.

gence, and the Democratic Unity Command), in which they co-operate, debate, negotiate, make public statements, and attempt to out-maneuver one another and other political groups.[39]

Ideological and strategic divisions have been common in Chilean parties for most of the twentieth century but are more pronounced today given the difficulty of estimating strength and likely trends and because the parties themselves have lost touch with their former bases and must literally speculate as to how their experiences under the military government have affected their political dispositions. This is particularly true in the case of the Christian Democrats, whose former supporters have been difficult to reach through restricted media and without the benefit of electoral campaigns. Moreover, under military rule the party's various functional organizations have acquired considerable autonomy and are not as likely to consult with its leaders or do their bidding in political matters. It is also true that among the party's still faithful constituencies there is considerable diversity of opinion. The Christian Democrats who have worked with Marxists and other leftists in Church-sponsored social programs, within labor organizations, and in university and secondary student movements favor some form of quasi-permanent alliance or collaboration with the left. Their own experiences have been positive, if not in accomplishments at least in terms of group relations. However, these relationships involved issues (wages, organizing rights, and general economic conditions) of a direct, straightforward, and ultimately self-interested character, on which it was enough to criticize military policies or practices. Moreover, they developed among people who for the moment did not have to worry about their party's interest or those of anyone else's. Cordial relationships thus were formed under relatively ideal "can't-miss" circumstances. But there is no indication that they have moved beyond the negative consensus of which they were born (to a definition of positive political or socioeconomic programs, for example), or that they would survive the resumption of competitive partisan politics.

In addition, these cooperative relationships did not include all Christian Democratic or Marxist workers. In fact, it was because most Christian Democratic union leaders refused to work with

[39] The Convergencia Socialista represents an alliance between the Christian Left, the two MAPUs, and remnants of the Socialist party. It has sought, as yet unsuccessfully, admission to the Alianza Democrática and is critical of Communist party support for armed struggle.

Marxist groups that Bustos and the others left the Group of Ten to form the Coordinadora. Since 1977 these more conservative elements have adopted a firmer opposition stance, complaining as they did that junta intransigence had forced them out of the "moderate" center,[40] and continuing to criticize Bustos and the left as overly confrontational. Most of them had been been attracted to the party initially because of its progressive ideals *and* its firm opposition to the Marxist left. Theirs had been, in effect, an anti-Marxist and anticommunist political formation. They might support an alliance that included social democrats, non-Marxist socialists, and even former Christian Democrats, but it is difficult to imagine them embracing Communists or Socialists under any circumstances.

In addition to workers and labor leaders one must also remember the petit bourgeois professionals, merchants, small farmers, businessmen, civil servants, and technical functionaries that made up the core of local-level party activists throughout the country. Most were newcomers, former Conservatives, or ex-ibañistas who had been drawn to Christian Democracy as part of Frei's "national and popular" alternative to Marxist revolution. In their case, too, antileftist sentiments had been part of their political identity and purpose from the first moment and were simply reenforced during the Allende years. They held abstractly progressive ideological and political views but opposed ties with the left even more adamantly then some Christian Democratic workers. What they did not fear in terms of their social status, their economic and social stability, and their leading (and controlling) role in the process of change, they did fear in terms of partisan identities and rivalries.

The further evolution of pro- and anticollaboration forces will be shaped by developments among left-wing parties and groups and by public opinion generally. Since 1977, and particularly since mid-1981, some leftist forces have been reexamining the Allende years somewhat more self-critically and have shown growing interest in more "democratic" conceptions of class struggle. Intellectuals associated with the moderate Gazmuri wing of MAPU have played a leading role in these efforts and have lent them greater credibility in the eyes of some Christian Democrats.[41] Concurrently, factions of the Socialist party have down-

[40] See the interview of Eduardo Ríos in *Hoy* 1982, 13.
[41] The work of Garretón and Moulián has been particularly important in this

played, if not abandoned, the strident conceptions and strategies of earlier years and have expressed a willingness to work with nonrevolutionary elements and within bourgeois democratic institutions.[42] Were these trends to persist and leftist groups to effectively abandon their traditionally Leninist positions, the anti-Marxist sentiments of many Christian Democrats might lose their warrant and force, and a center-left alliance would be far more acceptable to some. Others, however, are likely to dismiss such moves as calculated and will remain opposed to any and all rapprochement.

These matters will also depend on evolving public opinion regarding the junta and pre-1973 parties and politics. The Allende years brought renewed credibility and appeal to the right. The junta's efforts to inculcate nationalist, authoritarian, and conservative economic principles have met with some success, and prior to the recent economic crisis the right appeared stronger than at any time since the late 1950s, a fact that strengthened the hand of Christian Democrats who were pushing for a center-right alliance. But the right's appeal was largely conjunctural, a function of the relative success of the 1977 to 1980 period and of the absence of viable political alternatives. It would decline sharply with the economic crisis and the revival of center and leftist forces that it helped to spawn.

Even so, Pinochet or a charismatic successor might still rally bourgeois, petit bourgeois, and even popular forces under the banner of right-wing populist nationalism. Assuming some attenuation of the economic crisis, such a movement might draw away support from the Christian Democrats, the center would

---

regard. Garretón's essays on the general subject of "democratization" (return to civilian rule) have been published regularly in the Jesuit monthly *Mensaje*, and for several years he was one of a number of leftist thinkers associated (along with many Christian Democrats) with the Archdiocese of Santiago's Academia de Humanismo Cristiano.

[42] It is difficult to know what is going on within the Socialist party. One leader who has remained in Chile, Julio Stuardo, has worked actively to persuade party leaders and militants to abandon the harder-line concepts and strategies of earlier years and to work for incremental goals within bourgeois democratic institutions. At times he has had the support of the Aniceto Rodríguez and (surprisingly) the Carlos Altamirano factions. Forces identified with former Foreign Minister Clodomiro Almeyda, on the other hand, take a more militant stance, agreeing with Communists and *miristas* that Pinochet will only be removed by force and stressing revolutionary social as well as democratic objectives. Some efforts have been made to bring the various factions together again but as yet without success.

lose its remaining political viability, and the party might be forced into alliance, in a considerably weakened condition, with either the new movement or its leftist critics.

The left, on the other hand, is weak. Many of the top Socialist and Communist party leaders were either killed or forced into exile shortly after the coup. Conscious of this lack of leadership and organization, leftists readily concede the need to rebuild their political credibility within the country as a whole. A liberalization of views and strategic perspective would probably help in this regard, although antipathy toward the Popular Unity experience is still sufficiently widespread to preclude a majoritarian leftist movement, at least for now. It does not rule out a center-left coalition with the Christian Democrats, however. In fact, the experience of labor, student, and Church-based organizations during the last five or six years points promisingly in this direction. Nonetheless, if these liberalizing trends do not endure, and if leftist parties retain their Leninist conceptions, they will continue to be unacceptable to large segments of the populace. And if this is the case, the number of Christian Democratic leaders and followers willing to support a center-left alliance will be much smaller.

Summary

At present, support for the military government is at its lowest ebb since the coup. The economy lies in semiruin, incapable of providing either employment or minimal well-being for 30 percent of the country's population. Political support for the regime is limited to the military and to the hard-line civilian right. Pinochet's fall, however, is neither imminent nor inevitable. The terms of his withdrawal and of the transition to civilian rule are equally unclear. Pinochet could conceivably weather the current storm without making major adjustments. Alternatively, he could be replaced by a more accommodating military government that could either survive or prepare the way for a return to civilian rule on a very restricted basis. Finally, Pinochet himself could be forced to give way to a relatively unfettered civilian regime.

A return to civilian rule is nonetheless a distinct possibility.[43]

[43] Political risk analysts Frost and Sullivan give Pinochet a 55 percent chance of surviving the next eighteen months and predict that he will be replaced within five years (see *Latin America Weekly Report* 1984, 12).

Also predictable is the leading role that the Christian Democrats are almost certain to play in the transition process. As a centrist force with a still substantial following, it will be a crucial factor in the maneuvering against Pinochet and will bring moderation and respectability to any transitional alliance.

But the Christian Democrats are not likely to dominate more than the initial stages of this process. Their problems are many. First, they are still not trusted by either the right or the left, each of which suspects the party of seeking to displace it and absorb its following. Second, they are now without Frei, a founding father and leading personality for over forty years. Third, during the years of military rule, the party lost touch with its electoral following, and many of its militants and activists were drawn away to organizational involvements beyond its control and influence. And finally, the party remains, as always, deeply divided on questions of basic ideology, strategy, and alliance. Of these problems the lack of unity may constitute the party's greatest liability during the postjunta period.

Over the longer run the strength of the right and sheer survival of the left preclude the party's going it alone. Similarly, their antagonism rules out any possibility of the PDC serving as the axis of a multitendency coalition for any appreciable length of time. Beyond a commitment to democratic rule at this juncture forces of the left and right have little in common. Their basic outlooks, social bases, and policy views differ radically. They are certain to turn on one another once military authorities have retired to their barracks. At that point, it seems, the Christian Democrats will have to choose between them. And whether it chooses a center-left or center-right direction, the decision will be both traumatic and costly.

In the past the party has almost always chosen the alternative likely to attract or hold the largest electoral following. More often than not this was the center-right, and it could be the case again today. Many Chileans now critical of the junta's performance would probably support a "milder" or more protectionist version of authoritarian capitalist development. They would also endorse a center-right alliance of the sort favored by conservative Christian Democrats. But at the same time the socioeconomic policies of such a government would be unacceptable to more progressive *chascones* and to Christian Democratic workers who for ten years have struggled against the policies of the military government. In the past otherwise progressive Christian Democrats usually went along with the center-right strategy, albeit with reservations. Lacking confidence in themselves and trust in other groups, there was little they could do and nowhere they could go. Since 1973, however, Christian Democratic workers have acquired both confidence and autonomy and have developed solid relationships with other workers and popular forces. They are less docile and compliant, less fearful of either absorption or manipulation by parties of the left, and newly appreciative of the importance of worker unity. They are not likely to put up with either center-right alliances or conservative economic policies. And without their political support the party itself is unlikely to dominate a center-right coalition.

It is conceivable, of course, that party leaders would move to the left in order to accommodate these forces. But conservative leaders, traditional labor activists, and petit bourgeois and other middle sector elements are certain to resist. In fact, some have already bolted party ranks,[44] and more may follow their lead, either leaving the party in the hands of progressives or taking control and forcing them to leave. And if significant numbers were involved, of course, progressives would find it more difficult to bargain with or restrain their leftist allies and could easily become yet another minor leftist force.

The Christian Democrats moving to the left have suffered from deteriorating economic conditions (wages, working conditions, etc.) and political repression. They have developed a greater sense of the oppression and exploitation they share with other workers and popular elements. To this point their solidarity is largely oppositional, i.e., focused against the junta. They are calling for a return to democracy, for labor code reforms, and for structures giving workers greater control of their work places. But there is no agreement as yet on the character of these structures or on how they are to be brought into being. Disagreements on such questions are bound to arise among these former Christian Democrats and between them and others on the left. The more broadly based consciousness and solidarity of the current period have emerged in the absence of normally antagonistic ideological and partisan political influences. Such circumstances may or may not

[44] Conservative Christian Democratic figures Juan de Dios Carmona and William Thayer, both cabinet officers under Frei, have recently established the Movimiento Socialcristiano para Chile. They have reportedly accused the Alianza Democrática of being led by "well known marxist leninists." See *Latin America Weekly Report* 1983, 12.

endure, but to the extent that they do ideological disagreements may be more easily managed and resolved than in the past.

The Christian Democrats who are still active within or supportive of the party remain divided along perennial center-left and center-right lines. The PDC itself will likely remain stable and intact as long as no moderate right- or left-wing alternative appears. But if or when one does the party will have to choose, and the choice will almost certainly alienate leaders and supporters of the other side.

« 6 »

CHRISTIAN DEMOCRACY IN
COMPARATIVE CONTEXT

This chapter attempts to resolve a number of unanswered questions regarding Chilean Christian Democracy. Why, for example, did the PDC not possess greater ideological cohesion? What accounts for its various political shifts? Why were most of its leaders and followers never willing to consider alliance with the Marxist left? Why did the party's left wing remain a minority faction within its ranks? What accounts for the anticommunism and general ideological moderation of Christian Democratic workers, peasants, and marginals. And finally, how have the Christian Democrats remained together, and why have their various internal factions not realigned themselves with ideologically more congenial forces? Answers to these questions are to be found both in the nature of Christian Democracy as a political phenomenon and in particular features of its Chilean expression. A brief look at other Christian Democratic experiences, Latin American as well as European, will be useful in connection with the first of these factors.

Other Christian Democratic Parties

In Latin America there are politically significant Christian Democratic parties or movements in Venezuela, El Salvador, and Peru, three of the eight countries in which political parties are able to compete for public favor and political office. The absence of significant parties or movements in the other five, Costa Rica, Colombia, the Dominican Republic, Mexico, and Brazil, is puzzling but can only be noted here. In the remaining Latin American countries autonomous parties are either illegal or so restricted as to be incapable of meaningful political operations or appeal. In four of these, Chile, Uruguay, Panama, and Guatemala, however, Christian Democrats would certainly play an important role in any postmilitary political process.

Of the three Latin American parties Venezuela's Comité de Organización Política Electoral Independiente (COPEI) is one of its country's two leading political forces, capturing the presidency in two of the last four presidential elections. The Partido Demócrata Cristiano is El Salvador's largest single political group, although it is presently outflanked by military and right-wing civilian forces. Finally, Peru's Partido Popular Cristiano has carved out a place for itself on the right, thanks to its association with a popular national figure.

In Europe Christian Democratic parties are leading members of ruling coalitions in Belgium, Ireland, West Germany, Italy, Luxembourg, and the Netherlands. They are a major political force (enjoying more than 20 percent of the national vote) in Switzerland and marginally significant (with between 5 percent and 10 percent of the vote) in France, Norway and Portugal. Parties exist, but are relatively insignificant in Finland, Denmark, Spain, and Sweden.

VENEZUELA

Next to the PDC, COPEI of Venezuela has been Latin America's most prominent and successful Christian Democratic party. In thirty-five years of existence it has risen from provincial obscurity to become one of the country's two leading political forces. Under President Luís Herrera Campíns (1978-1983), it enjoyed a near majority of seats (98 of 205) in the national Congress.

With a social base once confined to western provincial elites, traditional Catholic conservatives, and their respective retainers, COPEI has become a "catchall" party drawing support from all classes and strata. The bulk of its following comes from students, the marginal populations of major urban areas, urban blue and white collar workers, the urban petite bourgeoisie, and disgruntled segments of the industrial and financial bourgeoisie.[1]

Like the PDC, COPEI has suffered from left-right divisions within its ranks. Its right wing is stronger and more explicit than the PDC's, its left wing less radical. The right includes both traditionalist Catholic and more pragmatic conservative groups. Several congressional representatives and members of former

[1] Only once, in 1961, did the party's support within the Venezuelan Confederation of Labor reach even 30 percent. In general, it has remained under 20 percent and has been concentrated among white collar workers in the public sector (Herman 1980, 78-81). *Copeyanos* have done much better, on the other hand, among entrepreneurial elements. Although the largest commercial and industrial organizations have usually backed Acción Democrática candidates, COPEI enjoys the preferred support of a number of powerful family firms and consortia and maintains cordial relations with virtually all others. Its success in this regard is at least partially due to the absence of a conservative alternative to which the bourgeoisie could turn.

President Rafael Caldera's cabinet were active in the Opus Dei movement. Far more numerous and influential, however, were the party professionals with close ties to industrial, commercial, or financial circles. With little or no ideological compunction they embraced and defended a brand of free enterprise and "trickle down" economics relatively untempered by broader social values or concerns.[2] The left wing consists of younger intellectuals and labor leaders. It emerged during Caldera's presidency as various factions of the party's youth sector, the so-called "astronautas," "avanzados," and "auténticos," declaimed against the government's temporizing policies.[3]

COPEI has long been dominated by more conservative elements, although individual leaders like Herrera Campíns have made gestures and concessions to the left from time to time. On the whole the party has been markedly pragmatic in its policy and political outlook. Like its Acción Democrática rivals it has never considered initiatives that would strike against the interests of important constituents or potential support groups. It has proceeded on the basis not of preconceived programs but of the possibilities offered by the shape of forces and sentiments at the time. In the short term this has probably enhanced the country's still tenuous political stability but has precluded efforts to deal with some of its more serious social and economic problems. In the process it has perpetuated the disparity between what is said and done and thereby reenforced already widespread cynicism regarding parties and political life.[4]

PERU

The Peruvian Christian Democratic movement has also suffered from left-right ideological divisions, splitting into separate parties in 1967. Whether united or divided, however, its social

[2] For a useful overview of the party's various ideological tendencies see Handelman 1978. One group playing a dominant role within the party under Caldera was the so-called *desarrollistas*, some of whom (e.g., banker Pedro Tinóco) have since left COPEI in search of a more conservative political vehicle.

[3] Like "*rebeldes*" and "*terceristas*," these groups disagreed on how to deal with the party mainstream but shared a commitment to communitarian or Christian socialist structures in which capital and labor were no longer in separate hands and the workers themselves made decisions regarding the work place, production levels and priorities, and income distribution.

[4] In their 1978 survey Baloyra and Martz (1979, 211) found that 74 percent of all respondents thought that political parties were always controlled by small groups concerned with their own interests and that 71 percent felt political parties were concerned with winning elections and nothing more.

composition and base have been narrower than those of its Chilean and Venezuelan counterparts. It has had no natural constituency among progressive, socially conscious Catholics and has been unable to develop a following among working-class or other popular forces.

One problem was that most middle- and lower-class forces were already spoken for when (in the late 1950s) the party emerged as a political force.[5] During the 1960s, the party made repeated appeals to working-class groups but without success. Their social Christian views and positions struck most Peruvian workers as overly abstract and more suitable as matter for philosophical discussion than as bases of political appeal. Despite these failures most progressives were prepared to redouble their efforts, while conservatives and the more pragmatically inclined thought that the more viable option was to turn to classes and forces who were fearful of social change. For the next several years the party's orientation oscillated. With the progressive Cornejo Chávez faction dominating party councils, moderately reformist positions were adopted, and when the Bedoya Reyes group prevailed, a more conservative posture was struck.[6] Bedoya and other conservatives left the party in 1967 to form the Popular Christian party, hoping to appeal to bourgeois and petit bourgeois groups less ambiguously and to build on the popular following Bedoya had enjoyed as mayor of Lima.

The Cornejo Chávez faction went on to support the Velasco and Morales Bermúdez military governments. It appears to have been hurt politically by this association and is presently mired in relative obscurity among a number of small left-wing critics of the current Belaúnde government.[7] Bedoya, on the other hand,

[5] Much of Fernando Belaúnde's large Catholic following comes from association with his uncle, Víctor Andrés Belaúnde, a philosopher who was the country's leading Catholic intellectual figure.

[6] The first of these groups was led by Héctor Cornejo Chávez who garnered only 5 percent of the vote in the 1962 presidential elections. Conservatives, led by corporate lawyer Luís Bedoya Reyes, blamed Cornejo's poor showing on his "radical" platform. Bedoya, who was a close friend of the victorious Fernando Belaúnde, was named minister of justice, tying the party more closely to the new government. By 1965, however, unhappiness with the government's failure to carry out pledged reforms enabled the Cornejo forces to regain control and again orient the party in a more progressive direction.

[7] Many military officers holding important posts in the Velasco government were reform-minded Catholics and were receptive to Christian Democratic proposals. Cornejo Chávez was well received in government circles and was named

won the support of important right-wing financial and media interests and for several years was a major national figure. He was soundly beaten by Belaúnde for the presidency in 1980, however, and appears to have lost much of his personal following as well.[8]

EL SALVADOR

Salvadorean Christian Democracy (PDC) has been its country's most broadly based political force for more than twenty years. It too has been plagued by ideological divisions, however, and today is outflanked by right-wing civilian and military forces.

Since its founding in 1960 the PDC's principal social constituency has been the urban middle and popular sectors, i.e., merchants, professionals, small businessmen, white collar workers, and slum-dwelling marginals. It has been less successful among skilled and semiskilled blue collar workers, most of whom have supported either military sponsored-labor organizations or those of the Marxist left.[9] Although it has sought support in rural areas in recent years, it has not had much success here either. With the power of large landowners and their ties to local National Guard and Treasury Police authorities it has been difficult to recruit organizers to work in rural areas, difficult for those willing to go to survive and continue organizing, and difficult to convince farm workers and small plot holders to risk supporting party candidates or positions.

The movement's ideological divisions resemble those of other Christian Democratic movements. "Popular" Christian Demo-

---

editor of the influential daily *El Comercio* when the government seized control of the country's newspapers in 1974. He was influential in helping to define and defend the military government's ideological orientation and in drafting laws regulating social property and the new "industrial communities." Other Christian Democrats, particularly young technocrats, also found niches from which to promote ideas and influence policy makers. Had it broken with the government when Velasco was overthrown by the more conservative Morales Bermúdez, the PDC might not have been as badly discredited. But it did not and in effect went down with the military over the next four years. In the 1978 constituent assembly elections it won only two seats and in the congressional elections two years later failed to win even one.

[8] With Belaúnde's Acción Popular not in the running, Bedoya's PPC won 26 percent of the vote in the 1978 election of a constituent assembly. When Belaúnde ran two years later, Bedoya's support dropped to less than 10 percent.

[9] According to White (1973, 215), the Christian Democratic Unión Nacional de Obreros Cristianos made little headway in challenging either the right-wing Confederación General de Sindicatos or the left-wing Federación Unitaria Sindical de El Salvador.

crats, including those who left the party in 1980,[10] envision an egalitarian society founded on the redistribution of power and wealth. They have made common cause with leftist groups and embraced "popular" forces (workers, urban slum dwellers, small plot holders, and agricultural laborers) as a principal constituency and concern. Moderates, in contrast, have urged spreading the party's net to include all social forces, even those with minimal objections to the status quo. They see the party's ideal society as one in which all forces are effectively and democratically represented and in which the interests of capitalists, middle sectors, and workers alike would be respected and preserved (White 1973, 199). The moderates have generally prevailed, and from its inception the party has been one of "respectable opposition," a "catchall" for various and sundry regime opponents.

Traditionally, the party has done well in the electoral arena, although it has often received support that would have been given to parties prevented from functioning at the time or in a particular part of the country.[11] In March 1982 Christian Democratic candidates won 40 percent of the vote in constituent assembly elections. With the left excluded, however, they were out-polled by their combined right-wing rivals, who proceeded to form a bloc within the assembly to force Christian Democrat José Napoleón Duarte's resignation as president. With this, the party was relegated to a secondary level, as Magana, conservative army generals, and the right-wing bloc in the assembly emerged as major power brokers. In the process, it would seem, the party has learned the difficulties of playing the role of a moderating centrist force in a system without a legal left wing.

WEST GERMANY

West German Christian Democracy (CDU-CSU) has been its country's dominant political force since the end of World War II.

---

[10] These included Rubén Zamora, Héctor Dada, and others who served in either the first or second of the civil military cabinets following the overthrow of the Romero government in October 1979. They resigned from the government charging that their military allies were blocking promised reforms and sanctioning continued widespread violations of elementary human and civil rights; they resigned from the PDC in March 1980 in protest against Duarte's willingness to join the government despite evidence of military complicity in the deaths of a number of Christian Democratic politicians.

[11] During the later 1960s for example, the party gained considerable support from those who normally would have backed candidates of the banned Partido de Acción Renovadora. See White 1973, 203.

It represents the fusion of several Catholic groups—the liberal democratic Christian Democratic Union (CDU), the pre-Nazi Zentrum, and Bavaria's conservative Christian Social Union (CSU)—although it appeals to Protestant groups as well.[12]

In terms of membership and electoral base the CDU-CSU is a predominantly Catholic petit bourgeois and white collar party.[13] It offers yet another example of a Christian Democratic party whose dominant neocapitalist and politically cautious majority is confronted by a smaller left-wing minority. Like Venezuela's COPEI, its majority is probably more conservative and more pragmatic and its minority less radical than those of other Christian Democratic parties.

Also like COPEI, the CDU-CSU entered a political arena that lacked an established conservative party and so became a repository of right-wing hopes and support despite efforts to project a reformist image. Also pushing the party rightwards was the intensification of the cold war, with its attendant disparagement of socialist and leftist ideas,[14] the party's close association with its imperious, strongly anticommunist and enormously popular leader, Konrad Adenauer, and the left of center orientation of the rival Social Democrats (SPD).

The later 1940s and 1950s were years of phenomenal recovery and expansion of the German economy. Here the key figure was Adenauer's Economics Minister Ludwig Erhard, who was the

[12] Ideologically it was a coalition of diverse elements that was, in the words of one observer, "socialist and radical in Berlin, clerical and conservative in Cologne, capitalist and reactionary in Hamburg, and counter-revolutionary and particularistic in Munich" (Pridham 1977, 12).

[13] Among party members the percentage of white collar workers has gone from 44 percent in 1956 to 53 percent in 1976, while that of the self-employed has dropped slightly from 45 to 32 percent. Blue collar workers rose from 11 percent in 1956 to 15 percent in 1976. In terms of electoral support, white collar workers and the self-employed also predominate, comprising 40 and 32 percent respectively in 1976, compared to 28 percent for blue collar workers. See Feist et al. 1978, 174.

[14] Within the prevailing cold-war atmosphere of the 1940s and 1950s democratic social and political values were given a markedly liberal cast. In such a context capitalism was seen as assuring economic freedom and thus bolstering freedom generally. Moreover, the experience of Nazism left many German intellectuals and political figures with an aversion to government control of the economy and to any dilution of individual rights and freedoms. In their view communism and socialism were as perverse as Nazism and far more threatening in the postwar era. Many agreed with Schwering, it seems, that the party should provide a "spiritual dam" against the "socialist and collectivist ideas" (Pridham 1977, 14).

principal architect of the so-called social market economy. The resulting "German miracle" of growth and prosperity enhanced the party's political standing and further consolidated its rightward orientation.[15]

Within CDU-CSU ranks entrepreneurial and petit bourgeois elements have become increasingly dominant. The Economic Council, or Wirtschaftsrat, an employers' group representing conservative business interests, and the *mittelstandsvereingung*, or "middle-class associations," have been particularly influential on issues of social and economic policy.[16] Workers, on the other hand, have lost much of their once substantial leverage despite their still large numbers (about one hundred thousand) and organizational resources. The party's "left wing" consists of intellectuals, students, and trade unionists from the social committees who espouse "Christian socialism" and at one time apparently considered forming a united democratic labor party with the SPD. Despite their socialist tendencies, however, they are strongly committed to maintaining harmony and partnership with other classes. And even outspoken social committee leader Norbert Blum insists that he could never join a party like the SPD because of its "utopianism" and "militant spirit" and because of his own

[15] According to Erhard, the choice facing Germany was not between capitalism and socialism; these were outdated terms and options. It was rather between a free and controlled economy, or better yet, between a socially conscious free market economy and a cynical laissez-faire market economy. Why, other than for reasons of rhetorical image, such an economy should not be considered capitalist, however, is not clear. Ownership and administration of the means of production would remain in private hands, and the state would use regulatory powers to assure effective competition and general well-being (Erhard 1963, 7-10). The market was considered a faithful voice or reflection of economic society. Social well-being, on the other hand, was thought to be most effectively preserved by free initiative and competition. Controls, if any, would be indirect rather than direct, i.e., social spending programs, tax incentives, etc., rather than price controls, wage controls, production quotas, and the like. Strains, stress, and/or mistakes, which in a controlled economy invariably escaped notice until too late, would be readily detected and resolved by legal action and social programs.

[16] Over the years entrepreneurial elements have placed their people in key policy-making positions, such as the ministry of economics, and have made effective use of the financial support they have provided, or arranged for others to provide, the party. A telling reflection of their influence has been the council's successful resistance of the efforts to extend worker participation in firm and factory management, even though the notion was an ideological hallmark of the Christian Democratic movement. The extent of their influence has generated resentment among party progressives and has prompted calls (as yet unheeded) for policies and programs of a more principled character.

218

commitment to the "liberal" values for which the CDU stands (Pridham 1977, 213).

ITALY

The Partito Democrazia Cristiana (DC) has been the dominant force in Italian politics since World War II. It is less a party, however, than a "heterogeneous collection of groups with differing views held together by their religious identification, their thirst for power, and their suspicion of the Marxists" (Kogan 1981, 3). Its members and electoral supporters are divided into internal factions (*correnti*), each with its own political line, organizational structure, financial base, and media. Its leaders have generally been guided by considerations of partisan political expediency, with occasionally benign but often unfortunate consequences for the country's economic and political life.

The social distribution of the party's voting base follows that of the general population, although recently its following among industrial workers has declined.[17] Support for the DC appears to be a function of religious identification and patronage and not class identity or interest. The strength of religious identification emerges clearly from survey data. In Barnes' 1968 survey (Barnes 1974, 90), for example, the Christian Democrats enjoyed the support of 38.6 percent of all Catholic workers. Of these, 61.1 percent described themselves as churchgoing and only 22 percent as nonchurchgoing. Figures for middle-class voters show similar patterns.[18] The importance of patronage, on the other hand, can

[17] Labini (1972, 400) hypothetically divides the party's 1968 vote into 53.6 percent petite bourgeoisie, 44.8 percent industrial and agricultural workers and marginals, and 1.6 percent bourgeoisie but does not include the "inactive," i.e., housewives, pensioners, etc. Unfortunately, his projections are based on the highly questionable assumption that voting support for 1968 broke along the same occupational lines as did the general population. The 1976 survey cited by Allum (1979, 147), on the other hand, uses the categories of old and new middle classes and includes those not economically active. If the latter are excluded, and the old and new middle classes lumped together as the petite bourgeoisie, the 1976 breakdown would have been 62.6 percent petite bourgeoisie and 32.2 percent working class, confirming a shift away from a working-class base. These impressions are reenforced if one looks at data concerning the party preferences of voters. Labini's figures for the DC in 1968 are 43.5 percent among the petite bourgeoisie and 35.6 percent among workers (Labini 1972, 401), while Allum's figures for 1976 are 37.2 percent and 23 percent respectively (Allum 1979, 164). The downturn in working-class support may reflect the workers who left the party in 1974 and the anticommunist flavor of the 1976 campaign.

[18] Some authors (Irving 1979b) consider dependence on a Catholic constituency

be seen in the behavior of the party's various *correnti*. Each of them can be described in terms of its leading personalities and ideological orientation, but with the possible exception of left-wing groups their primary purpose is to deliver specific favors to their respective clienteles, thereby retaining their support.[19]

The party's public positions and statements tend to be general so as not to alienate constituencies or upset its internal balance. Individual *correnti* choose sides and define priorities but tend to focus on specific policies and programs, not general propositions. Moreover, all appear willing to take what the system will give them. While right-wing groups insist on incentives and subsidies to encourage private sector investment and initiative, for example, only a few are willing to abandon the politically secure ground of the center-left. Similarly, while leftist groups oppose further concessions to "already privileged" social forces, they are more than willing to remain part of a multiclass party with a substantial business constituency. All forces, finally, are committed to sustaining the party's electoral base and control of state power and to periodically adjusting positions in accord with changing public moods and sentiments.

Although notably nonideological, the Italian Christian Democrats have pursued more consistently progressive policies than any of the parties here examined. Expenditures for social services and programs together with the real income of workers have risen steadily vis-à-vis the cost of living during the postwar period. Income distribution has become quite "respectable" for a country of Italy's per capita income level.[20] And, finally, the Ital-

---

a liability given recent trends toward secularization. Others (Pasquino 1979) argue that any loss of Catholic votes will be compensated for by stronger clientelistic relationships and general political factors. The decline in working-class support remains noteworthy, however, and at the least secularization is producing class realignment among party members and voters.

[19] Pasquino (1979, 96) groups the factions along a left to right continuum, with Force Nuove and Base on the left, Nuovo Cronache and Iniziativa Democrática in the middle, and Impegno Democrático and Force Liberale on the right. Zuckerman (1979, 110) characterizes the breakdown among the three as being roughly 12 percent, 83 percent, and 5 percent between 1954 and 1973. Even the "principled" anticommunism of some, however, has a largely pragmatic underpinning. While ethical and religious concerns weigh heavily on voter opinion of the Communists, party members are far more troubled by the possible loss of patronage opportunities and electoral support.

[20] The bottom 40 percent of Italian income-earning households earn a higher percentage of the national income (5 percent) than do their French or United States counterparts (whose per capita income is three times larger) but lower than Germans of the same category. See Bertsch et al. 1978, 61.

ians have been one of the few Christian Democratic parties to accept alliances or understandings with either Socialist or Communist parties for any length of time.

These progressive stances or initiatives are less the result of principled politics than of pressure from other sources. One such source has been organized labor, consisting of the Communist controlled CGIL, the Socialist CISL, and the independent though formerly DC affiliated ACLI.[21] The labor movement as a whole is stronger because of the willingness of these organizations to work together in support of common causes. The Christian Democrats, concerned with both their own labor sector and their broader political position, have found it costly to resist labor on major policy questions. In Italy, it seems, the party responds to political and class phenomena that originate elsewhere rather than providing the terms and context of class and social force development.

FRANCE

Following World War II, French Christian Democracy enjoyed political prospects as promising as those of its German and Italian counterparts.[22] Over the past three decades, however, its once substantial constituency has been sharply undercut and its efforts to build up and defend the political center have failed to prevent the exodus of followers toward right- and left-wing affiliations. Once a major party it is now reduced to secondary tendency in opposition to the current Socialist government. Its decline has been the result of several factors, among them the charismatic appeal of Charles de Gaulle, the structure of political competition under the new Fifth Republic, the secularization of French life since the mid-1960s, and related upswings in class consciousness and polarization.

In their initial electoral ventures, French Christian Democrats (the Mouvement Républicain Populaire, or MRP) won close to 30 percent of the total vote, drawing support proportionately from

[21] During the 1960s, the ACLI moved away from the DC and began working closely with both Socialists and Communists on a variety of issues. See Kogan 1981, 57-67.

[22] French Christian Democrats entered the postwar period with impressive credentials and lofty aspirations. Many of their top leaders and spokesmen had been active in the Resistance (e.g., Maurice Schumann, George Bidault, Henri Bouret, and Max André) and brought its prestige and promise with them; others came from more traditional Catholic backgrounds with little in common but their religion, a sense that it must somehow inform their political action, and an acceptance of republican political institutions. See Irving 1973, 74-78.

all social strata. Twenty to 25 percent of their electorate came from industrial working-class backgrounds, while white collar workers, professionals, small businessmen, and bourgeois elements were also well represented. Much of this support was a function of the MRP's perception as a Catholic, and therefore anticommunist, force. It was widely regarded as "the party of the Catholic faithful" and like the Italian DC did disproportionately well among churchgoing Catholics from all strata.[23]

Support levels dropped dramatically (to about 12 percent) when, in 1951, Charles de Gaulle reentered national politics and rallied traditional right-wing and anticommunist forces. They remained more or less stationary through the early 1960s, at which point they were again cut in half as the result of growing secularization[24] and the political structural changes introduced with the Fifth Republic.[25] With de Gaulle's preemption of much of its constituency, French Christian Democracy sought alliances with groups to its left, as with the coalition proposed by Socialist Gaston Deferre during 1964 and 1965, and to its right, with both Radicals and Independent Conservatives.

None of these initiatives bore their hoped-for political dividends, and in the ensuing years party leaders drifted rightward in search of a secure political niche. In the process they have

[23] In 1952, although its support had fallen to less than 12 percent, the MRP continued to enjoy the support of 54 percent of the country's church-going Catholics (compared to 20 percent for the Conservatives and 18 percent for the Gaullists [Irving 1973, 90]). By 1958 that figure had fallen to a still disproportionately high 33.9 percent of "practicing Catholics" (Janda 1980, 340). In this instance, moreover, such Catholics comprised a much larger segment (84.8 percent) of its overall support than they did for any other party (the next greatest degree of dependence was 53.6 percent), although some Catholics did support the Gaullist and Conservative parties (Janda 1972, 341).

[24] In the mid-1960s evidence of powerful secularizing trends and forces began to surface. There was a sharp drop, for example, in the number of persons attending church regularly and/or describing themselves as believers. Another trend, thanks to the Second Vatican Council, was the more progressive social orientations of those that still worship regularly. These developments were at once causes and consequences of both the radicalization of French Catholic workers in the mid-1960s and and the ferment arising within groups like the Young Catholic Workers, Young Catholic Action, and the Young Catholic Students.

[25] In supporting the constitutional changes embodied in the new Fifth Republic the Christian Democrats contributed to their own undoing as a significant political force. The granting of emergency powers to de Gaulle, the introduction of a system of two-round voting, and the later emergence of a popularly elected presidency all helped to encourage a process of political polarization that undercut centrist forces like the MRP.

ceased to exist as an independent political force, lost much of their earlier Catholic flavor and constituency, and become a mere *tendence* within a broader center-right front.[26] The drift rightward was reflected at the ideological level. Although once espousing a "third-way" alternative to capitalist and socialist structures, they have reembraced the more timid social Christianity of earlier Catholic movements (e.g., the Parti Democratique Populaire) and cast their lot with the capitalist status quo.[27] In addition to alienating more progressive followers, these changes failed to retain or increase support from more conservative sectors, and in effect the Christian Democrats continued to lose ground to both a resurgent Popular Front and a remarkably resilient right. While former bourgeois and small business supporters were lured away by Gaullists and Giscardians, one-time student and working-class activists have broken away to either the Communist or Socialist parties or to independent political activity.[28]

Like the Italians, French Christian Democrats have been will-

[26] In 1967 the MRP itself was formally dissolved, with most of its members moving into a Centre Democratique (CD) alliance with right-wing Radicals and Independent Conservatives. This organization split into independent (Centre Progressiste Démocratique et Moderne, or CPDM) and pro-Gaullist (Centre Democratique et Populaire, or CDP) movements on the eve of the 1969 presidential election. Both groups supported Independent Republican Valéry Giscard against Socialist François Mitterand in the presidential election of 1974 and were reunited along with Giscardians, dissident Radical, and other "moderates" in a Centre Démocratique et Social (CDS) as "the left conscience of a rightist government." During Giscard's presidency (1974-1981), Christian Democrats helped to draft several moderate reform programs but for the most part fought inconclusively with rightist (Gaullist) elements for the president's ear and favor. Under the current Mitterand government they remain allied with centrists and moderate rightists in the opposition Union Démocratique Française, or UDF.

[27] During the late 1960s and early 1970s, Christian Democrats embraced a socially responsible form of capitalism of the sort espoused by Erhard. They began to speak of reform and progress *within*, not in place of, capitalism, in effect abandoning the "third way" and calling instead for greater income equality, worker participation in factory management, expanded social programs, limited state involvement in the economy, and active encouragement of the private sector.

[28] In 1964 its radical wing captured the once strongly Christian Democratic Confédération Française de Travailleurs Chrétiens, renamed it the Confédération Française Democratique du Travail, and moved it into an openly left political posture. Left-wing students and workers who later abandoned Christian Democratic ranks remained committed to the notion of humane and decentralized socialism. They accept the cause of class struggle and call for the overthrow of capitalism and its replacement by public ownership and worker control of the means of production.

ing to take what their political system offered. Early in the post-war period this was the progressive center from which the party battled left and right in classic Christian Democratic fashion. Later, with de Gaulle's preemption of much of its initial constituency, it sought alliances to its left and right. A relationship with the Socialists along Italian lines might have been possible during the 1970s had Mitterand not been committed to resurrecting the Popular Front (the Union de la Gauche) or had the French Communists rejected an alliance that was certain to be dominated by the Socialists. Cut off from the center-left, however, the Christian Democrats lost their popular base and were reduced to being a species of social conscience for a new united right.

Christian Democracy Generally

The patterns emerging from these overviews reflect basic characteristics of Christian Democracy and may shed light on the Chilean case. Despite their many different contexts the six movements share a number of common features. First, all are parties whose leadership and most enduring social constituency have been petit bourgeois. Second, each has been plagued by ideological divisions along fairly standard left-right lines. Third, despite such divisions each has been dominated by pragmatic leaders determined to achieve or retain power and willing to settle for what public opinion and the political process will offer at any given juncture. Fourth, in each of the cases, including Italy, this has meant that the Christian Democratic alternative to the traditional left and right assumes, in practice, a center-right orientation. Finally, all have been generally hostile toward the Marxist and non-Marxist left. A brief exploration of each feature will help to define Christian Democracy's nature as a political phenomenon.

An initially common feature of the six cases is the predominantly petit bourgeois character of party leaders and electoral supporters. From their earliest days each of the movements sought to attract the broadest possible following of social and political forces. In predominantly Catholic countries (all except Germany) Christian Democracy's explicitly Catholic character helped it to cut across class, regional, and other lines of division. Each party has achieved significant levels of support among blue and (especially) white collar workers, farmers and farm workers, civil servants, small businessmen, technicians, professionals, and even bankers and industrialists.

Despite their broadening appeal, however, the parties remained, as in Chile, under the control of a relatively small but determined petit bourgeois leadership (e.g., Caldera, Cornejo Chávez, Bedoya Reyes, Duarte, Adenauer, Erhard, de Gasperi, Fanfani, Schumann, Lecanuet, and the like), one that was distinctively Catholic, from an academic or intellectual background, and possessed of notable personal qualities. Such leaders gave Christian Democracy a distinctively favorable image or stature in the political arena but at the same time inhibited more effective participation or representation of other sectors in party or policy decisions. In several of the cases, moreover, petit bourgeois leaders, although adept at analysis and political formulation, were less concerned with or skilled at organizational tasks, strategy building, and political stumping and infighting. Their lack of such skills has hurt the party most notably in Peru and France, although it may not have been as marked or as much a liability elsewhere.

Christian Democracy's petit bourgeois character is amply reflected in the content of its reformist ideology, with its abstract and complex notions (e.g., "communitarianism"), its rich philosophical framing, its efforts at formal reconciliation of seemingly contradictory concerns and interests, its pushing of painless reforms, and so on. Such notions were helpful in providing moral reassurance or justification for those (petit bourgeois sectors) needing to think of their party as doing the right thing but probably not needing the policies to succeed as much as did other social classes. Thus, while polarization has drawn away working-class and bourgeois supporters in four of the six countries, it may not affect the movement's petit bourgeois following, most of which thinks of itself as progressive and yet is both jealous of its social status and threatened by the specter of a worker-led popular movement coming to power.

Another feature of the six cases is the persistence of deep-seated ideological divisions. In each the dominant center-right majority has been opposed by a "radical" minority of intellectuals, students, and labor leaders and activists. The call for a "third-way" between capitalism and socialism has taken various forms and emphases, and broad left-right cleavages have emerged. Thus far the German and Venezuelan parties have contained their left wings, but French, Italian, Peruvian, and Salvadorean radicals have abandoned their party ranks in considerable numbers.

That left-right divisions should characterize a movement claiming to transcend such distinctions and conflicts prompts one to ask why Christian Democracy has not enjoyed greater ideological cohesion. The answer must be sought in the specific class situations, economic conditions, and cultural and political contexts in which the movement's leaders, members, and supporters have operated. Class differentiation and cohesiveness are products of objective class interests and of political developments that condition class relations and either foster or retard consciousness. In Italy and France, for example, working-class consciousness and solidarity among Catholic trade unionists appears to have been enhanced by the cooperative attitudes and strategic positions of their Marxist counterparts.

It is also clear, however, that Christian Democratic thought has failed to give the movement an adequate ideological foundation. This is because neither of the sources from which it is drawn, i.e., contemporary papal encyclicals and Catholic social philosophy, provides such a base.

Ideologies diagnose reality and orient action. They rest on foundational values (e.g., freedom, justice, community, the classless society, etc.) of the sort articulated in Catholic social teaching and philosophy. But commitment to such values cannot determine how they are best served in practice. This requires an understanding of social forces and processes, how they function, how they can be countered, accelerated, or otherwise affected, and with what consequences. It requires, in other words, a "sociological" perspective, and this neither the Church's social teaching nor Catholic social philosophy provide.

In its teaching the Church endorses fuller participation of the poor and underprivileged in social, economic, and political affairs. It also stresses that such goals should be pursued in a spirit of love and harmony, with full respect for the legitimate rights and interests of all. Strictly speaking, however, the Church takes no political or ideological stands. Its statements and admonitions are made in highly general terms and, if specific, are offered as nonbinding illustrations. The Church's teaching remains politically and ideologically noncommittal because of the general nature of moral principles and because its jurisdiction excludes the technical and contingent matters on which political and ideological choices rest (Schillebeeckx 1968).

The social theories of Maritain and Mounier, although linked to European and Latin American Christian Democratic movements, failed to provide sociological perspective either. Maritain was a cautious liberal who emphasized the nonmaterial dimensions of social relations and was hopeful of voluntary cooperation among social classes. Mounier was a more ambitious and critical "radical" who stressed structural factors and relationships. Yet they were alike in several respects. Their preferences and priorities were couched within larger dualistic frameworks that blunted much of their force. Thus, Maritain gave sufficient importance to material factors to allow for just about any approach in a particular case, while Mounier's insistence on the "primacy of the spirit" and the duality of human nature left more than a hint of ambivalence as well. Moreover, both were political philosophers, not ideologues or strategists. They were concerned with the nature and purposes of political society, the standards in light of which political life should be structured, not the means or methods with which to achieve them. The internal workings of a society and its concrete options and prospects were political and ideological questions on which neither was inclined to embark. Though each was willing enough to make such assessments in his own personal life, neither would commit himself at the general theoretical level.[29]

Without an authoritative sociological perspective with which to mediate basic values, Christian Democrats have turned to other sources. These have included a variety of Marxisms and neo-Marxisms, democratic elitism, the structuralist perspectives of the United Nations Economic Commission for Latin America, and neoclassical, Keynesian, and more recently neoconservative economics. Ludwig Erhard, who believed in the freedom and justice of the marketplace, and the leaders of the Confederation Française Democratique du Travail, who call for class struggle and public ownership of the means of production, invoke the same Christian Democratic tradition. Given its aspirational and dualistic character each makes only modest adjustments in order to press that tradition to its service. Clearly, however, their views are rooted in fundamentally opposing conceptions of politics, history, and the social process.

[29] Mounier was highly critical of French Christian Democracy for both its pragmatism and its timid and moralistic critique of capitalism (see Rausch 1974). Maritain, on the other hand, moved in a liberal democratic direction, particularly after coming to the United States following the end of World War II.

227

Liberal pluralist and Marxian class analyses were two of the more influential perspectives in most parties through the 1970s. Their strong appeal reflects an ambivalence within the Christian Democratic tradition, one by which most members and supporters are psychologically, if not theologically, conditioned.[30] It is an ambivalence that sees historical social reality as a vale of tears to be endured and yet resisted, as an expression of fallen nature, not to be whole until the final judgment and yet the object of transformation beginning now.

The ambivalence sustains both conservative and radical orientations. The more dominant conservative tendency grants social phenomena an importance less for their own sake than for the opportunity they afford for personal spiritual development. In this view social progress is desirable, but major transformations are unlikely and, in any event, of passing significance in relation to spiritual ends. This idealism is one of high standards but low expectations, and is therefore politically blunted: historical achievements are less important than the motives or ends for which they are pursued; political involvement is a question of intent or aspiration, not actual accomplishment; Christians are to fight the good fight, to *attempt* to make the world over, but are not expected, nor to expect, to actually do so.

Radicals, on the other hand, reject dissociation of the temporal and spiritual. In their view historical social reality is not simply a context in which personal qualities are displayed or honed, it is the object and medium of the salvation process. Achievements are important, and one must do more than merely aspire or struggle. Radical idealism is idealism of a different sort, the frustration of which leads to the reaffirmation of high expectations and a redoubling of efforts to transform people and structures. In keeping with their more favorable view of the status quo pluralist Christian Democrats have stressed the diversity and reconcilability of most interests. In their eyes, powerful groups effectively compete with and restrain one another, providing representation for most social forces, whatever their resources and circumstances. With proper safeguards and reforms the interests of all groups, and those of society as a whole, could be preserved and promoted.

[30] The ambivalence affects not just those who remain faithful and who live and act in the light of that faith but also those who, while they may not retain or practice that faith, are intellectually and psychologically conditioned by the sensibilities that early inculcation generates.

Radical Christian Democrats have rejected such claims. They saw economic and political power concentrated in the hands of capital at the expense of working people. In their view the interests of capital and labor were irreconcilable. One had to choose labor over capital and to work for labor's emancipation by expropriating the owners of capital, i.e., the capitalist class. Only then, they insisted, could society's potential and the interests of the majority be realized.

One must ask, of course, which elements in a given party are drawn to which tendency, and why. In no single case, however, do the tendencies break consistently along class situational lines. Bourgeois elements that support Christian Democratic parties do have a fair degree of class consciousness (although some differ sharply from their non-Christian Democratic colleagues) and are invariably aligned with the more conservative tendency. But petit bourgeois forces can be found in equal numbers in both camps, as can workers, labor leaders, peasants, and marginals. Much depends, it seems, on the nature of their experience and relationships with others in the same class situation.

These ideological alignments divide forces internally and pit one or more of them against others outside the party as well. They are important because they generate political rivalries and antagonisms that overshadow common relations of exploitation and because they tend to perpetuate themselves.

During the 1970s, diverse political and economic crises prompted shifts in assumptions and positions within each of these camps.[31] Many erstwhile "liberals" became less certain that all interests could be reconciled, or that prosperity was within the reach of all. Concurrently, they grew more impressed with the value and precariousness of "progress" already made and were inclined to accept current conditions rather than persist in well-intended but ultimately futile and possibly disastrous efforts to change

[31] The difficulties of the Italian economy, continued high inflation and stagnation in most "western" industrial countries, and the fall of the Allende government in Chile have stimulated rethinking on both sides. The first two directly challenged the liberal (and Christian Democratic) assumption that growth and reform were both compatible and mutually reenforcing, while the latter made it harder to believe that once "in power" the undertaking of economic transformations would automatically yield political and cultural transformations. These views have contributed, at least in part, to the emergence of a less hopeful and less liberal pluralism and a more patient and restrained socialism, both of which have cut into ideological and political ground on which Christian Democratic parties have traditionally stood.

them (Fleet 1981). Along with this neoconservatism, however, a more politically oriented socialist analysis also emerged, one accepting the contingent character of class consciousness, the consequent need to struggle for control of both the productive process and popular consciousness, and the need to recognize the laws of bourgeois political economy and rationality even as one attempted to transform them. With these changes in perspective, left-wing Christian Democrats, including many who left their parties, became more tolerant of and willing to work with more conservative colleagues and/or former colleagues, although for their part the latter were often less interested in making concessions to left-wing elements within or beyond party ranks.

Despite their ideological divisions each of the six parties is dominated by pragmatic leaders who favor a center-right orientation. In many instances this was also the position to which these leaders were ideologically inclined, but the decisive consideration appears to have been the belief that a center-right orientation assured the achievement or retention of power. In effect, Christian Democratic parties seem more concerned with practical political success than with either ideological principles or particular policies or programs. This befits their character as electoral coalitions and patronage mechanisms whose lack of ideological cohesiveness makes the concern for power both possible and essential.

This concern need not be as cynical as it might seem. In pluralistic systems majority support is necessary if policy is to be made and goals achieved. It is simply not possible to hold out for one's own preferred position in all cases. One must be willing to settle for less, i.e., to make concessions and agree to compromises in order to win or hold the majority. A striking but representative example of this was COPEI's concessions to private sector groups in exchange for their support of Caldera in 1968. When asked what effects such deals might have on the party's commitment to economic reform, one party leader conceded that

COPEI had to make these arrangements in order to win the election. Once the party controlled the executive branch, it could build its strength through labor, peasant, and various organizations. The Copeyanos would also have the opportunity to realize their program, something which they could never do without control of the government. [Herman 1980, 65]

The need to make concessions in order to build or sustain coalitions is particularly incumbent upon catchall parties like the Christian Democrats that seek to attract and aggregate diverse social and political forces. What appeals to such groups, it seems, is not that their views will be integrally defended and promoted (they will not) but that the party has influence with other groups and that such influence assures effective realization of at least some of its goals and concerns. In fact, it is the catchall party's ability to strike bargains or work out compromises with diverse constituencies and forces, not its commitment to particular interests or causes, that makes it politically attractive. For such a party the possession or perceived possession of power breeds additional power, just as the loss or perceived loss of support from one force or faction leads readily to loss of support among others.

Christian Democratic party leaders have understood and accepted these facts of political life. They have retained their leadership positions largely because they were willing, and in most cases able, to keep their constituencies and their political power intact. Their successes can take surprising twists, as in Italy where the party's support among industrialists is less a function of concessions to them than to organized labor whose continuing support makes Christian Democracy an attractive and formidable political force.

Despite varying trajectories and fortunes all six movements continue to offer a reformist alternative to traditional left- and right-wing forces. In all cases, including the Italian, however, this has assumed a predominantly center-right flavor, as criticism and concern have focused primarily on socialist theories, planned economies, demagogic labor movements, hidden totalitarian agenda, and other sinful predilections of the left. Although claiming to share their goals and concerns, Christian Democrats reject both the manner in which leftist groups have conceived these goals and their methods for pursuing them.

Christian Democracy also attacks the right for its indifference to the social costs of laissez-faire economics and for its opposition to reforms that would produce a more just and a more stable social order. In practice, however, Christian Democrats have been much more willing to negotiate and ally with parties and forces of the the right, giving their vaunted reformism a distinctively conservative hue. There have been several reasons for this preference. One has been the belief that right-wing forces would not be as formidable a rival in the years to come. Care had to be exercised with the left, with its potential mass appeal and its designs on the party's popular base, but the right posed no such threat. Another reason was that Christian Democracy's largely Catholic, petit bourgeois, and white collar following would be far less uncomfortable in association with the right than with the fearsome left. Finally, in the 1970s many party leaders and activists were attracted to neoconservative perspectives on questions of economic growth and social order. As they became more concerned with creating an "adequate" climate for investment, so too were they increasingly skeptical regarding the cost-effectiveness of social programs and of concessions to workers. On both counts they found it easier to bargain with the right than with the "short-sighted" and "narrowly self-interested" unions and parties of the left.

The German and Venezuelan parties have been the most successful practitioners of center-right politics, the French the least. This may mean that "moderate" Christian Democracy will prosper where there is no established conservative movement or strong Marxist tradition. Where such parties do exist, as in Italy (where the left is strong), and in France, Peru, and El Salvador (where both right and left parties are present), Christian Democratic parties will have greater difficulty retaining their multiclass followings and dominant political influence.

A final characteristic of Christian Democracy has been hostility toward the organized left at both leadership and constituency levels. This orientation, which has kept most Christian Democratic parties looking to their right for support, has deep ideological, psychological, and institutional political roots.

Ideologically, Christian Democracy arose as a critique of traditional conservatism, on the one hand, and communism and fascism, on the other. It found little to differentiate between the latter two and frequently treated them in the same breath. The social encyclicals and Catholic philosophy on which first-generation Christian Democrats were intellectually nourished condemned communism as "intrinsically evil" for its atheistic materialism and for its lack of respect for the religious, political, and economic rights of the human person. Most Catholic authorities either counselled against or simply forbid collaboration of any sort. These strictures were informally suspended within the antifascist resistance during World War II but were revitalized in the postwar period as in Europe and later Latin America the Church launched a major anticommunist offensive through Catholic Action and Christian Democratic party channels.

This offensive involved promotion of parallel mass organizations of Catholic students, workers, and young people to combat growing leftist influence and to help orient lay thinking on social, economic, and political matters. Institutes were established, and publications started to carry the Church's social teaching to the grass roots through channels other than Sunday mass. The results of these efforts included an upsurge in electoral support for Christian Democratic parties and the inculcation of strong anticommunist sentiments among the members of a new generation of party activists. In many instances these sentiments would endure for thirty years and more; in others they would weaken in the face of changing economic and social conditions. But even in these cases they helped to poison Christian Democratic-left relations at a formative stage of postwar political development.

For their part Communist parties in Europe and Latin America did little to allay Christian Democratic fears and prejudices. In most cases they were aggressively critical of these "new reactionaries" and sought to discredit party leaders and strategies in the eyes of their working-class and student supporters. Such tactics yielded meager dividends but intensified enmity between the two groups, particularly at the rank-and-file level. Marxist sectarianism was much more pronounced and Marxist leadership much less flexible in some countries (France) than in others (Italy). But in every case Communists and Christian Democrats became antagonists in virtually every mass-organizational and political context. The conflicts and hostilities engendered by this political antagonism would have been troublesome even for parties that were ideologically congenial (as it has been for Socialists and Communists themselves in several of the six countries). But with the Christian Democrats, they merely compounded ideologically rooted concerns.

An additional factor operating at the party leadership level had less to do with psychological rivalry than with institutional political interest. Whatever one thought of the Communist party, anticommunism was an electorally potent force and a sure basis of support among certain working-class, peasant, and petit bourgeois sectors in each of the six countries. It was seldom militant support, and there were limits beyond which it could not be extended, but it could be lost and the party's political position weakened if its anticommunist credentials were questioned for any reason. To guard against such a possibility party leaders were inclined or willing to raise the anticommunist flag from time to time, making it more difficult, though not impossible, to reach agreements or understandings with communist and other leftist forces.

During the 1960s and 1970s, there was a weakening of anti-communist sentiment among Christian Democrats in trade union and student circles. This was due to declining religiosity, to the more progressive content of Catholic social teaching,[32] and to increased economic difficulties and a sharpening of class identity and conflict. In those countries where these latter phenomena were most clearly in evidence (El Salvador, France, Peru, and to a lesser extent Italy) they pushed workers and students together in common, if not joint, opposition to more aggressive and more powerful threats from the right.

The radicalization of these Christian Democrats led to the emergence of left-wing Christian Democrats calling for formal ties with traditional leftist forces, but they remained a small minority, and many later abandoned party ranks. Most of these "left wingers" have been intellectuals and labor elites without large followings in mass organizations. They tend to be more sophisticated ideologically than the average Christian Democratic activist or sympathizer, whose theoretical views reflect the more traditional social Christianity of earlier days. Nor are their numbers likely to grow much. Those Christian Democrats sufficiently radicalized to embrace the newer perspectives may not be willing to do so within the context of a party that (not wrongly perhaps) they identify with petit bourgeois and bourgeois interests. The party's ties to these groups are at once the source of its political strength and a major liability. Its petit bourgeois and bourgeois support makes it an important national political force and affords Christian Democratic workers leverage they would not have otherwise in dealing with other workers, and yet it is an obvious weakness as well in that it makes them the object of diffidence and of efforts to lure them away from party ranks. The liability seems likely to grow in those polarizing contexts in which

[32] Official Catholic attitudes towards Marxism and Communism softened considerably in the encyclicals of Pope John XXIII and Pope Paul VI, while liberation theologies based on quasi-Marxist class analysis of church and society and calling for collaboration between Christians and other "popular" forces also began to exert influence.

the party's bourgeois and petit bourgeois constituencies, and with them party leaders, are moving to the right.

Concerning the political implications of these characteristics one might ask if Christian Democracy is likely to remain, or again become, a united or dominant political force. As of early 1984 the German, Italian, and Venezuelan parties were holding their own. The prospects for the Salvadorean party, on the other hand, are no clearer than those for El Salvador itself, while the French and Peruvian parties appear doomed to relative insignificance, at least as Christian Democratic formations.

During the 1970s, Christian Democratic reformism lost its appeal to many bankers, small and large businessmen, professionals, farmers, and middle-class taxpayers previously attracted to it. Drawn to more conservative views they were followed, in many instances, by party leaders and militants. Some of these were apparently determined to preserve their own bourgeois or petit bourgeois interests. Others were convinced (*a la* "trickle down" theory) that concessions and incentives to the private sector would mean greater well-being for all. And finally, yet others simply accepted the need for making "strategic concessions" in order to retain the leverage (with these and other groups) needed to mitigate policies and conditions that otherwise might be worse.

Where parties are prospering, they form a center-right alternative to social democratic rivals burdened by economic recession and other problems (the case of Germany and Venezuela), or a center alternative between a divided and uncertain left and a smaller and much weaker right (Italy). At the moment there is no clear party option (other than Christian Democracy) for progressive Catholic workers in any of these countries.[33] If a strong, moderate left party were to emerge, however, and if the Christian Democratic leadership were to continue its neoconservative drift, that could change.

As parties lose Catholic workers to the left, they drift rightwards, embracing policies and positions that will make it more difficult both to hold the workers they still retain or to avoid becoming a relatively conservative party with a narrow petit bourgeois and bourgeois base. In fact, one can relate the movement's difficulties in recent years to the strong secularizing and polarizing forces afoot in both European and Latin American

---

[33] Many Italian Catholic workers devoted most of their energies to independent trade union, not party, activities.

countries. The combination of cyclical expansion and recession has weakened the influence of traditional religious values and sentiments, strengthened and unified the left (which has moderated its views considerably), caused normally loyal petit bourgeois and bourgeois forces to ask whether more traditional approaches to problems might not be more effective, or at least less risky, than reformist ones, and pushed many Christian Democratic leaders into neoconservative reappraisals of their own views.

The Chilean Case

The experiences of Latin American and European Christian Democratic parties, the factors and forces they reflect, and their implications for the future help to clarify the nature and future prospects of the Chilean movement. The parallels and common elements are striking. Like the parties just surveyed, the PDC has been a relatively pragmatic, strongly anti-Marxist, and predominantly petit bourgeois political force. Similarly, its various wings and tendencies have been drawn in wide-ranging if not conflicting ideological directions. Finally, although seeking to transcend left-right distinctions, it too has steered a center-right course, preferring understandings with the right as less risky and/or more likely to bear fruit.

Much like other Christian Democratic movements, the Chilean party has shown itself to be generally pragmatic, although occasionally this pragmatism has been diverted or reenforced by ideological inclinations and antipathies. During the Allende period, the overriding concern for party leaders was maximization of institutional interests and leverage. As Allende took power, their expectations of his government varied considerably. Most anticipated problems and insisted on dealing with the UP from strength. From early on they were concerned with blocking Allende and expanding their electoral base. More progressive and less skeptical elements went along with the second of these goals even though they opposed the first. Unfortunately, the pursuit of political and electoral advantage embittered spirits and helped to undermine Christian Democratic-Popular Unity relations. By mid-1972 Christian Democrats and Marxists had become each others principal antagonists, and from this point on the party's principal concern was with holding Allende in check and staying in step with its own increasingly anti-UP activists and followers.

Under the junta, the PDC has had to confront both the government and its own former supporters. Not wishing to alienate the latter it has moderated its criticism of the junta, attempting to steer an even course between intransigent opposition and tacit complicity. Until 1980 it tried to be critical of economic and political policies without appearing to challenge the government itself or the process of "national reconstruction." And to this day it has tried to remain credible with former activists and followers who are now suspicious of reformism, not unsympathetic to authoritarian rule, and anything but averse to capitalist structures and practices.

The party was not always so opportunistic. Frei himself was a determined, some would say stubborn, political figure who stood against the country's tradition of bargaining and compromise. Between 1964 and 1967 he was unwilling to share power or alter his program, and when he later did make concessions he found no takers. His meager offerings to the right in 1967 were rejected as insufficient, and those the following year came too late. By this time his economic program had been defeated, and both the left and right had begun to look beyond him to the elections of 1970. It might be noted, however, that the program from which Frei initially refused to waver was one that appealed to the practical interests of various groups. And though it failed to win them over and thus did not "work," he clearly believed that it could and would.

These experiences caused most Christian Democrats to see new merit in the traditional give-and-take of Chile's party politics. Tómic's center-left platform and campaign were exceptions confirming this trend. Most party leaders privately decried them and blamed them for his poor showing. Their frustrations carried over to the Allende period, during which practical political interests predominated. Exclusion from power, it seems, fostered a greater appreciation of its advantages and of the need to pay the price for achieving it. The similarity in Christian Democratic and Popular Unity programs, a potential basis for collaboration between the two groups, was quickly forgotten in the pursuit of partisan advantage and in view of the increasingly antagonistic sentiments of militants and supporters on both sides. By late 1971 what mattered to most Christian Democrats was defeating Allende and regaining power, and whatever posturing and/or concessions that were needed to do so should be adopted. When, and only when, power was achieved should the party turn to its own ideals and agenda. This orientation remains in effect under the current military government, although there is considerable division within party ranks as to what is in its best interests and how that can best be achieved.

Another feature the PDC shares with other Christian Democratic movements is its hostility toward the left. Always strong, this intensified during the Allende years and has continued to dominate party thinking and action in the period since 1973. Although opposing the military government, it has steadfastly refused to form an antijunta front with the left and even now insists on an Alianza Democrática that includes the right but excludes the Communist party, thus maintaining its longstanding preference for an independent centrist stance. Most party leaders and sympathizers place the blame for what happened under Allende on the Communist and Socialist parties. While conceding the need to distinguish among personalities and factions on the left, they view recent expressions of political moderation and respect for democratic principles by leftist leaders with considerable distrust, and in any event appear determined to isolate and draw off only certain "respectable elements" but to avoid dealing with the parties or their constituencies as such.

The party's continuing hostility toward the left has been undercut, however, by the extensive grass-roots contacts and collaboration between Marxists and Christian Democrats since 1973. In countless neighborhoods, factory unions, schools, and small communities throughout the country militants and supporters of the two groups can be found working together. Economic hardship and political repression have united them much in the manner of the European resistance movements during World War II.

Thus far activities have centered around immediate and practical concerns, e.g., food distribution, shelter, and working conditions. They have not raised "larger" political questions, and they have taken place virtually free of considerations of partisan interest and agenda. It has been individuals rather than the parties themselves who have been involved. No one has had to worry about what the parties hope to gain, what designs they might have on one another's following, or what other party members are doing in other areas. These, of course, are considerations that often have undermined collaborative work between groups and would come into play when the parties again resume their normal activities.

The experience nonetheless suggests that the party's anticommunism may be as much of an institutional political as an ideological nature. In other words it may be less Marxism as such than particular Marxists in a position of power that party leaders have feared. Christian Democrats have often been willing to work with Marxists on an individual basis where, it seems, they pose no real threat. They have no "ulterior" interests or power and can readily cooperate, compromise, and work with others. Linked to the party, however, they take on institutional interests and the power to defend and promote them.

The PDC's anticommunism thus has a straightforward and arguably practical basis: these particular Marxists could not be trusted with power and should not be helped to obtain it. This fear cannot be dismissed out of hand. First, despite their often practical outlook and conciliatory manner, the Chilean Communist party remains an orthodox Marxist-Leninist party with little sympathy or tolerance for neo-Marxist or other contemporary Marxist currents that might sustain more democratic convictions or practice. Second, the Communists have been very clear for some time that they view collaboration as a means of bringing about a polarization of Christian Democratic militants and followers and thus winning over the party's "popular" sector.[34]

The basic problem, however, has been one of credibility. Within political circles, friendly and otherwise, the Communists have long been known for their "flexibility," i.e., their willingness to say or promise virtually anything to achieve an objective or reach agreement with others. Unfortunately, the party's congressmen, trade union officials, and local organizers have often reversed their positions and broken these arrangements and commitments on the instructions of higher authorities, leaving their friends, allies, and foes to pick up the pieces. In light of this historical experience the problem of Christian Democratic-Communist relations is less one of the terms (here, in fact, Christian

[34] Thus, for example, Communist party strategist Carlos Cerda (1971, 161) had argued during the Frei administration that "the bulk of the proletariat and the most developed popular sectors know that Christian Democracy is not the solution. But the same cannot be said of other popular sectors, who first began to participate in politics voting for it. They have to go through their own experience. Now in order that this be as brief as possible, that they not fall into indifference or despair, that they not serve as a social base for any new adventure or any new bourgeoisie, and that they come quickly to the conclusion that what is needed is a revolutionary government led by the working class. The working class has to win their confidence through a broad and combative policy of common action among all popular forces."

Democrats and Socialists are usually much further apart) than of the credibility of any agreement. And this will remain a problem for some time to come, since even if the Communists were to embrace a more open, Gramscian style of theoretical and strategic orientation, it could be seen and dismissed as a tactical maneuver.

A third feature that the PDC shares with other Christian Democratic movements is its petit bourgeois character. Through 1973 its leadership and most consistent and proportionately dominant electoral support came from the petite bourgeoisie. Furthermore, the PDC's policies and strategic orientation have long been petit bourgeois as well. Resisting the overtures of particular commercial, industrial, and financial interests, they have approached development as a messianic but largely technical undertaking in which their own talent, expertise, and vision would warrant them the right to exercise tutelary control over the ascent of the masses.

Among its various effects, this petit bourgeois orientation has made relations with the left, and particularly the Communists, very difficult. On the one hand, it gave PDC leaders further reason to feel threatened by the organized working class, which not only rejected tutelage but considered itself the country's sole legitimate class. And on the other hand, it fueled the left's suspicions that Christian Democratic reformism was merely a more artful and presentable means of opposing real change.

Like their European and Latin American counterparts, the Chilean Christian Democrats have been ideologically divided since their inception. The basic split has been between neocapitalist and democratic socialist wings, although many party members and activists would place themselves somewhere between these poles. The neocapitalist wing has long been the dominant force, although for most the attachment was more to Frei than to his ideas or programs. The radical wing, although a minority, has played a crucial role at several key junctures and remains a force within party circles today.

The division has gone through several stages. Debate was overt and explicit prior to Frei's election and during the first four years of his term. Opposing views of society and of socioeconomic and political structures confronted each other directly. Subsequently, attention shifted to questions of electoral strategies, attitudes towards Allende, and relations with the right. As these matters involved issues of broader analysis and outlook, debate continued, albeit in implicit form.

That the left-wing tendency survives today is remarkable in view of the defections by radicals in 1969 and 1971. In each instance their departure left the party a somewhat more unified and more conservative force, but only temporarily. In time the defectors were replaced by those (like the "social democratic" faction and a number of once strongly anticommunist trade unionists) radicalized by subsequent crises or experiences. Chilean life, it seems, periodically does this to a segment of the socially and politically committed Christian population. The issues, contexts, and organizational expressions change, but the phenomenon itself persists.

At the same time, however, many "moderate" or conservative Christian Democrats have apparently stopped working for reform on grounds that it is impossible and/or inappropriate at this time. Others continue to call for change but have lowered both their expectations and the risks and/or sacrifices they will endure in pursuit of it. And yet Christian Democracy continues to reproduce radical dissenters for the reasons having to do with its fundamental ambivalence towards social reality. The radicals of the 1980s have experienced the same frustration and disappointment that other Christian Democrats have but will not give in or settle for less. In many cases they have lived and worked with the poor, be they industrial workers, marginals, or peasants. Their commitment is less to human dignity in the abstract than to the struggles of people and communities with whose fates and fortunes they are wholly identified.

Finally, like other Christian Democratic movements, the Chilean party has steered a generally center-right course. The neocapitalist views of Eduardo Frei were a source of orientation and appeal in this regard. Most of the party's bourgeois, petit bourgeois, and popular activists looked to him for guidance and readily followed his lead in both policy and political strategy matters. Frei and his views helped the party to become the country's principal political force after only six years of formal existence and brought the Christian Democrats resounding victories in the 1964 and 1965 elections.

The party's dramatic rise in the late 1950s and early 1960s came with the sudden political decline of its centrist and right-wing rivals. Thanks to Frei's popularity and to concern that the left might actually come to power, its electoral base broadened

241

socially and expanded numerically. Frei's efforts to build a reformist movement on an anti-Marxist, center-right base nonetheless failed. He was unable to allay the fears or retain the
support of a nervous and skeptical right but in the attempt managed to alienate many of his party's most progressive elements.

The PDC thus failed to avert the breakdown of the antileft
alliance that brought it to power in 1964. During the subsequent
Allende government, the party helped to resurrect the center-
right alliance but under circumstances in which confrontational
rightist elements played the dominant role. The result was economic and social disintegration and a violent seizure of power
by a repressive and socially reactionary military regime under
which the party's political position and influence have diminished sharply.

In Chile, as in other Christian Democratic experiences, the
center-right strategy prospered when the right was either weak
or discredited and the left neither well-organized nor acceptable
to most voters. These conditions were met during the late 1950s
and early 1960s. But with the economic difficulties and growing
unrest of subsequent years the right proved resilient. It recovered from its temporary eclipse and again became a major
political force, helping the left to undermine Frei's program and
foiling the consolidation of his center-right majority.

The Christian Democrats clung to their center-right posture
under Allende but were pulled in opposite directions by powerful
polarizing currents. Progressives left the party over its collaboration with the right. And yet its peasant, female, student, and
trade union sectors fully supported the move into ever more intense opposition. The polarization of 1972 and 1973 eroded the
middle of the road, and as it was pulled rightward the party lost
its once dominant role to military conspirators and other more
intransigent opposition elements. The coup itself was the culmination of a process of social and political disintegration that
had begun during the last two years of the Frei government.

The takeover brought to power a brutal military dictatorship
and led to Pinochet's emergence as an authoritarian personality
around whom right-wing and some popular forces have rallied.
For the next seven years the party maintained its center-right
course, attempting to play the role of the loyal or respectable
opposition. In the country's sharply if not evenly polarized environment, however, its views found little echo. Many Chileans
considered its "moderately critical" stance a form of tacit com-

242

plicity with the junta, while others accused it of seeking to undermine a government that they believed the country badly needed. The PDC thus continued to lose support to the right and to a lesser extent the left. Many former activists and supporters, although not formally disavowing their party ties, have become absorbed in autonomous and increasingly assertive labor and popular organizations.

In early 1980 the party abandoned the center-right course and intensified its opposition to the military regime. This move brought few dividends until the economic crisis of late 1981, at which point its political fortunes began to rise again. Little is known of current public sentiment regarding either Pinochet or the various parties opposing him, although it seems unlikely that the PDC can recover its lost constituencies and again dominate Chilean politics. Its organizational and outreach capabilities are today extremely limited. Influential leaders and activists have been forced into exile and if they return are prevented from resuming social and political activity. And among the better known figures now back, images have been tarnished and appeal has waned with the passage of time.

More importantly, the party lacks access to former electoral supporters and the public at large. Without radio and television outlets, without a newspaper of appreciable circulation, and without a national figure whose even ordinary activities command public attention, the PDC is cut off from erstwhile supporters and constituents. In this respect Frei's death may prove a particularly costly loss. Though his prestige had declined since leaving office, he remained a respected and highly visible figure. His presence would certainly have assured the party continued stature and credibility as a political force. In electoral terms it would have meant additional support if or when elections were held and would have helped to introduce and legitimate a new generation of Christian Democratic political figures.[35]

Frei's departure may also weaken the position of Christian Democrats favoring the center-right strategy. In the first place, no other party figure appears to approach his appeal or credibil-

---

[35] The German and Italian parties survived the departure of their founding father-major national figures while they were still in power, when the transition to second-generation leaders was easier to make. Frei's death, in contrast, comes at a time when the party lacks the stature and patronage potential of incumbency, is organizationally dissolved, and can only prepare the terrain for its new leaders in very restricted ways.

ity in right-wing circles. In the second, there is no one to come to the aid of those opposed to negotiating with the left. And finally, leftist parties themselves may be more interested in living and working with a PDC free of Frei's overarching influence.

Summary

It is difficult to anticipate either the postjunta future or the party's fortunes therein. The disposition of class forces will be a determining factor, but in the short term this will depend on the relative appeal and organizational capabilities of pre-1973 forces and those that have arisen since. It will matter greatly, for example, which, if any, of the parties will retain their influence and support among former members and supporters, whether the PDC's electoral base will remain as anti-Marxist and conservative as it seemed from 1972 to 1976, and whether the post-1976 Christian Democratic-left collaboration within labor and other movements can survive a resumption of party politics as usual.

The years of military rule have been important for class development. Economic and political conflicts growing out of the military's radical free market strategy have divided a once solidly united bourgeoisie. Bankruptcies, mergers, and the realignment of economic and financial groups have radically altered fortunes and relationships, although the political implications are not yet clear. At the same time working-class and popular interests once pitted against one another have come together in defense of common civil and economic rights. Within labor and community organizations divisions persist, but harmony is greater than at any time in the last thirty years. What remains to be seen is whether unity born of adversity will endure once the clouds lift and partisan politics resume. Petit bourgeois elements have faired well since the coup but again seem politically fragmented, as does the peasantry, some of which the junta has raised to prosperous family farmer status but most of which has continued to languish in poverty, hopelessness, and confusion.

The evolution and ultimate consequences of these trends depend on the political channels and formulae available to them. Labor and other popular-based groups have kept up their organized activities despite military rule. They have developed a collective identity, a sense of common interest, and a joint agenda, albeit of a relatively limited, functional character. They will provide stimulus and direction to partisan political forces once these

244

resume activity, although they will also depend on these parties and the various arrangements they are able to make.

The majority of Chileans, of course, are not active in union organizations, neighborhood associations, base Christian communities, or political party networks. Their circumstances are quite different, and it is difficult to anticipate their political direction and impact. For more than ten years they have been a passive and captive audience for Pinochet and other junta spokesmen. They have been the objects of efforts to discredit traditional institutions and forces, which have been denied the right of response. The extent to which these efforts have succeeded will be clear only if and when open debate resumes and a fair test of public opinion can be had.

The party is likely to persist in its present centrist course only until moderate left- and right-wing blocs emerge. This might happen prior to or shortly after a return to civilian rule or to less dictatorial military rule. If and when this happens the party's political leverage and significance are likely to decline. Christian Democratic parties in West Germany, Italy, and Venezuela have become or remained dominant where there has been no strong right-wing force. These parties have been able to hold their various factions together and thus retain their broad electoral appeal because they can make concessions to left-wing and labor groups (especially in the Italian case) without fear of right-wing reprisals. Given the revival of the Chilean right, however, the PDC would seem headed for the fate of the once powerful but now virtually defunct French movement. It will have to choose, it seems, between right and left and will inevitably alienate a substantial segment of its activists and supporters whatever its choice.

The party's recent political revival is thus likely to be short-lived. Its days as a coalition of diverse class and social forces identifying with a common religious and philosophical tradition or with a new and promising political style appear at an end. On the one hand, class consciousness and conflict have greatly intensified during the last fifteen years. On the other, certain ideological and political rivalries have subsided, and Christian Democratic influence among workers, popular groups, and public opinion generally has declined in the last ten years. Under these circumstances working-class consciousness and solidarity have made significant inroads among erstwhile Christian Democratic supporters and activists. What this will lead to is difficult to know, although the emergence, as in Peru, of rival Christian Democratic parties, one a right-wing social Christian party[36] and the other with its roots in the organized working class and progressive petite bourgeoisie, would seem a distinct possibility. The two would dispute the patrimony of a once powerful tradition, although neither would approach the original PDC in either stature or extent of following. Each, in fact, would likely become a secondary or at best coequal force within its respective bloc.

[36] As indicated in Chapter 5, Juan de Dios Carmona and William Thayer have already established such a party. What remains to be seen is the extent of the support they are able to draw from the *guatón* faction. What seems most likely is that most *guatones* will hang on until the questions of party control and direction are resolved.

APPENDIX

The Hamuy Surveys

The survey data used in this analysis was generated by Professor Eduardo Hamuy and his staff at the Centro de Opinión Pública in Santiago. I have had access to three of these studies in their entirety—*Political Behavior in Chile*, August and September 1958, *Pre-Electoral Political Sociology*, August 1964, and *Research Project No. 45*, February 1973—and portions of two others—*Research Project No. 37*, August 1970, and *Research Project No. 39*, April 1972.

The Samples

The 1958 survey consists of two waves of interviews, the first of 807 respondents conducted prior to the presidential election of that year, and the second of 399 respondents (those who actually voted) taken after the election. The sample was designed to represent the three electoral districts of Greater Santiago and was drawn from households within the following communes of Santiago province: Cisterna, Conchalí, Las Condes, Nuñoa, Providencia, Quinta Normal, Renca, San Miguel, and Santiago. No information is available on how the sample was constructed, although it is possible that the procedures outlined below in connection with the 1970, 1972, and 1973 surveys were used. The similarity between the preelectoral expressions of preference and actual electoral behavior in the three districts has been noted in Chapter 2, note 26. It indicates a high degree of content validity for the instrument.

The 1964 survey consists of interviews of 1,095 respondents taken just before that year's presidential election. The sample was designed to represent the same three Greater Santiago districts but included households from three additional communes: Barrancas, Maipú, and La Granja. No information is available on how this sample was constructed either, although procedures outlined below may have been used. The survey was less accurate than Hamuy 1958 in predicting actual electoral behavior

247

(see Chapter 2, note 41) but was sufficiently close (off by 11 percent) to be considered valid in content.

The 1970 survey consisted of interviews of approximately 730 respondents conducted prior to the September 1970 presidential election. As indicated above in Chapter 3, note 37, however, the version to which I have had access contained data for only 629 of these interviews (i.e., those from the original sample whom the Centro Belarmino was able to interview again on additional matters). The original sample included households from the communes used in the 1964 survey, and from La Reina, La Florida, and Quilicura as well. It was constructed in various stages, using conventional mechanisms to insure randomness, and consulting mapping and demographic materials to insure proportional inclusion of households from different sectors (communes), block units, and social strata. In an initial stage the primary sectors were defined (areas or blocks of between 20 and 80 houses), from which 241 were randomly selected in such a way as to assure geographical representativeness. In a second stage each of the households in these sectors was characterized (as to number of people living in it) and numbered, and from each list the appropriate number of households to be selected (depending on the number of houses in the unit) was determined. Finally, this number of houses was randomly selected from each list, and one person in each of these households was then interviewed.

Although Centro Belarmino researchers attempt to vouch for the sample's reliability, they fail to point out the possible consequences of effectively reducing the sample by 100 respondents. As these 100 were simply those who were not available for reinterview, the sample loses its strictly random character and has its reliability at least partially compromised. This represents a significant problem and should be kept in mind when using the data. It may account, for example, for the bulk of my disagreement with Stallings (see Chapter 4, note 7) over the occupational statuses of Christian Democratic supporters. As noted in Chapter 3, note 37, however, this 1971 version of the 1970 survey was reasonably accurate in predicting actual behavior in the September 1970 election. Clearly it would be best to have the 1970 data in their original form, but that has not been possible, and I believe that a substantial portion of these data is more enlightening than no data at all.

The 1972 survey consisted of April 1972 interviews of respondents in Valparaíso, Concepción, and Greater Santiago and included a wide-ranging body of questions on social and political topics. The version to which I have had access contains data from interviews with 886 respondents from Greater Santiago alone and only on a small number of these questions. The sample of Greater Santiago included households from all communes used in the 1972 survey except Quilicura, and it added San Bernardo. It contained a distribution of 238 primary units (usually blocks of approximately 30 houses) from a total universe of 16,048. All houses in these 238 units were then characterized and numbered and from the resulting lists a total of 1,105 representative households were randomly chosen. Finally, individual persons in 886 of these households were actually interviewed. Because no data was provided on electoral preferences, the content validity of the instrument cannot be assessed in the way it was with other surveys. Data on party affiliation (see Chapter 4), however, corresponds to what is generally known concerning early 1972.

The 1973 survey consists of interviews of 754 respondents from Greater Santiago just prior to the March 1973 congressional elections. The sample was constructed in the same way as that of 1972. As indicated in Chapter 4, note 42, it accurately predicted subsequent electoral support for the government and opposition blocs, although it overstated support for the Christian Democrats at the expense of that for the right-wing Nationals.

Regarding the reliability of these various data collections, caution must be urged. This would be true with any data collection, even one generated by the person utilizing it. In this case, given the remoteness in time and space, caution would seem even more in order. Although each of the surveys attempts to provide a representative sampling of political attitudes in the same basic universe, they are not panel data and they approximate one another to varying extents. Moreover, no assurances can be offered as to the methods or practices of the actual interviewers, although Professor Hamuy's credentials in this area are widely respected.

SELECT BIBLIOGRAPHY

Abbott, William, ed. 1966. *The Documents of Vatican II*. New York: Guild Press.

Ahumada, Jorge. 1965. *En Vez de la Miseria*. Santiago: Editorial del Pacífico.

———. 1966. *La Crisis Integral de Chile*. Santiago: Editorial Universitaria.

Aldunate, Jose. 1979. "Más Acá de los Indices: La Situación Económica."*Mensaje*, no. 284.

———. 1982. "El Rostro de Nuestra Cesantía." *Mensaje*, no. 311.

Alexander, Robert. 1978. *The Tragedy of Chile*. New York: Greenwood Press.

Allum, P. T. 1979. "Italy." In *Political Parties in the European Community*, ed. Stanley Henig. London: Allen and Unwin.

Almeyda, Clodomiro. 1958. *Reflexiones Políticas*. Santiago: Prensa Latinoamericana.

Altamirano, Carlos. 1977. *Dialéctica de una Derrota*. Mexico City: Siglo XXI.

Althusser, Louis. 1969. *For Marx*. New York: Random House.

Angell, Alan. 1972. *Politics and the Labour Movement in Chile*. London: Royal Institute of International Affairs, Oxford University Press.

———. 1977. "Chile: From Christian Democracy to Marxism." *The World Today*, no. 11.

———. 1979. "Chile after Five Years of Military Rule." *Current History* 76, no. 444.

Aptheker, Herbert. 1968. *Marxism and Christianity*. New York: Humanities Press.

Aranda, Sergio, and Martínez, Alberto. 1970. "Estructura Económica: Algunas Características Fundamentales." In *Chile Hoy*, ed. Aníbal Pinto et al. Mexico City: Siglo XXI.

Aron, Raymond. 1967. *Ensayo sobre las Libertades*. Madrid: Alianza Editorial.

Arriagada, Genaro. 1974. *De la Vía Chilena a la Vía Insurreccional*. Santiago: Editorial del Pacífico.

Astiz, Carlos. 1969. *Pressure Groups and Power Elites in Peruvian Politics*. Ithaca: Cornell University Press.

Aylwin, Patricio. 1966a. "Carta en que Patricio Aylwin Acepta Repostular a la Presidencia del PDC." *Política, Economía, y Cultura*, no. 189.

————. 1966b. "El Ritmo de Nuestra Revolución." *Política y Espíritu*, no. 295.

————. 1967. "Carta de Patricio Aylwin a Rafael Agustín Gumucio en que Analiza el Informe de la Comisión Político-Técnica." *Política, Economía, y Cultura*, no. 253.

Ayres, Robert. 1976. "Electoral Constraints and the Chilean Way to Socialism." In *Chile: Politics and Society*, ed. Arturo Valenzuela and Samuel Valenzuela. New Brunswick: Transaction Books.

Baloyra, Enrique, and Martz, John. 1979. *Political Attitudes in Venezuela*. Austin: University of Texas Press.

Barnes, Samuel. 1974. "Religion and Class in Electoral Behavior." In *Electoral Behavior: A Comparative Handbook*, ed. Richard Rose. New York: Free Press.

————. 1977. *Representation in Italy*. Chicago: University of Chicago Press.

Bars, Henri. 1962. *Maritain en Nuestros Días*. Barcelona: Editorial Estela.

Belloni, Frank; Caciagli, Mario; and Mattina, Liberio. 1979. "A Mass Clientilist Party: The Christian Democratic Party in Catania in Southern Italy." *European Journal of Political Research* 7, no. 3.

Bertsch, G.; Clark, R.; and Wood, D. 1978. *Comparing Political Systems: Power and Policy in Three Worlds*. New York: Wiley.

Bigo, Pierre. 1968. *La Doctrine Social de l'Eglise*. Paris: Presses Universitaires de France.

Bodenheimer, Susanne. 1972. "Stagnation in Liberty." In *New Chile*, coord. Elizabeth Farnsworth. New York: North American Congress on Latin America.

Boizard, Ricardo. 1965. *La Democracia Cristiana en Chile*. Santiago: Editorial Orbe.

Boorstein, Edward. 1977. *Allende's Chile*. New York: International Publishers.

Bray, Donald. 1964. "Chile: The Dark Side of Stability." *Studies on the Left* 4, no. 4.

Brenner, Robert. 1976. "Agrarian Class Structure and Economic

Development in Pre-Industrial Europe." *Past and Present*, no. 70.

Bustos, Ismael. 1965. *El Sentido Existencial de la Política.* Santiago: Editorial del Pacífico.

Castells, Manuel. 1974. *La Lucha de Clases en Chile.* Buenos Aires: Siglo XXI.

Castillo Velasco, Jaime. 1963. *Las Fuentes de la Democracia Cristiana.* Santiago: Editorial del Pacífico.

———. 1966. "El Concepto de la Revolución en Libertad." Mimeographed. Santiago: Instituto de Estudios Políticos.

———. 1967. "Introducción." In *Seminario Internacional sobre una Visión Comunitaria de la Economía.* Mimeographed. Santiago: Instituto de Estudios Políticos.

Centro Belarmino. 1971. *CEDOP Research Project No. 37 and Study of the Public Image of Priests in Greater Santiago.* An adaptation of Hamuy's 1970 survey of greater Santiago.

Centro de Estudios para el Desarrollo Social de América Latina. 1965. *América Latina y Desarrollo Social.* Santiago: DESAL.

Cerda, Carlos. 1971. *El Leninismo y la Victoria Popular.* Santiago: Quimantú.

Chile, Election Fact Book. 1965. Washington, D.C.: Institute for the Comparative Study of Political Systems.

Chonchol, Jacques. 1965. *El Desarrollo de América Latina y la Reforma Agraria.* Santiago: Editorial del Pacífico.

———. 1971. "Poder y Reforma Agraria: La Experiencia Chilena." In *Chile Hoy*, ed. Aníbal Pinto et al. Mexico City: Siglo XXI.

Clerc, Jean Pierre. 1981. "Chile: A Second Wind for the Dictatorship." *Manchester Guardian-Le Monde Weekly*, March 29.

Connolly, William. 1967. *Political Science and Ideology.* New York: Atherton Press.

Converse, Phillip. 1965. "The Nature of Belief Systems in Mass Publics." In *Ideology and Discontent*, ed. David Apter. New York: Free Press.

Corvalán, Luis. 1971. *Camino de Victoria.* Santiago: n.p.

Cranston, Maurice. 1953. *Freedom: A New Analysis.* London: Longmans.

Cusack, David. 1970. "The Politics of Chilean Private Enterprise under Christian Democracy." Ph.D. dissertation, University of Denver.

Davis, Stanley. 1972. "The Politics of Organizational Development: Chile." In *Workers and Managers in Latin America*, ed. Stanley Davis and Louis Goodman. Lexington: Heath.

Dealy, Glen. 1977. *The Public Man*. Amherst: University of Massachusetts Press.

Departamento de Capacitación del Partido Democrata Cristiano. 1962. "Principios del Comunitarismo." *Política y Espíritu*, no. 272.

de Vylder, Stephan. 1976. *Chile under Allende*. New York: Cambridge University Press.

Diccionario Biográfico de Chile. 1967, 1970. 13th and 14th ed. Santiago: Empresa Periodística de Chile.

Dinges, John. 1983. "The Rise of the Opposition." *NACLA Report on the Americas* 17, no. 5, September/October.

di Palma, Guiseppe. 1977. *Surviving without Governing: The Italian Parties in Parliament*. Berkeley: University of California Press.

di Tella, Torcuato. 1965. "Populism and Reform in Latin America." In *Obstacles to Change in Latin America*, ed. Claudio Véliz. London: Oxford University Press.

Economic Commission for Latin America. 1970. *Economic Survey for Latin America, 1969*. New York: United Nations.

Edwards, Thomas. 1972. *Economic Development and Reform in Chile: Progress under Frei, 1964-1970*. East Lansing: Michigan State University Latin American Studies Center.

Einaudi, Mario, and Goguel, François. 1952. *Christian Democracy in Italy and France*. Notre Dame: University of Notre Dame Press.

Ercilla. 1949. Santiago. No number available, May 17, 1949.

————. 1968. Santiago. No. 1742, November 6-12.

————. 1971. Santiago. No. 1873, June 9-15.

————. 1973a. Santiago. No. 1975, May 23-29.

————. 1973b. Santiago. No. 1981, July 4-10.

————. 1975. Santiago. No. 2078, May 28-June 3.

————. 1980. Santiago. No. 2250, April 23-29.

Erhard, Ludwig. 1963. *The Economics of Success*. London: Thames and Hudson.

Espinosa, Juan, and Zimbalist, Andrew. 1978. *Economic Democracy: Workers' Participation in Chilean Industry, 1970-73*. New York: Academic Press.

Falange Nacional. 1948. *Declaracion de Principios del 5o Congreso Nacional de la Falange Nacional*. Pamphlet. Santiago.

Feist, Ursula; Gullner, Manfred; and Liepelt, Klaus. 1978.

"Structural Assimilation Versus Ideological Polarization: On Changing Profiles of Political Parties in West Germany." In *Socio-Political Change and Participation in the West German Federal Election of 1976*, ed. Max Kaase and Klaus von Beyme. Beverly Hills: Sage.

Ffrench-Davis, Ricardo. 1973. *Políticas Económicas en Chile, 1952-70*. Santiago: Editorial Universitaria.

Fitzgerald, E.V.K. 1979. *The Political Economy of Peru, 1956-78*. New York: Cambridge University Press.

Fleet, Michael. 1971. "Ideological Tendencies within Chilean Christian Democracy." Ph.D. dissertation, University of California, Los Angeles.

———. 1973. "Chile's Democratic Road to Socialism." *Western Political Quarterly* 60, no. 4.

———. 1981. "Neo-Conservatism in Latin America." In *Neo-Conservatism: Social and Religious Phenomenon*, ed. Gregory Baum. New York: Seabury Press.

Fogarty, Michael. 1957. *Christian Democracy in Western Europe*. London: Routledge.

Foxley, Alejandro; Ainant, Eduardo; and Arrellano, Pablo. 1979. *Redistributive Effects of Government Programs: The Chilean Case*. New York: Oxford Pergammon.

Francis, Michael. 1971. *The Allende Victory: An Analysis of the 1970 Chilean Presidential Election*. Tucson: University of Arizona Institute for Governmental Research.

———, and Lanning, Eldon. 1967. "Chile's 1967 Municipal Elections." *Inter-American Economic Affairs* 21, no. 2.

Frei, Eduardo. 1937. *Chile Desconocido*. Santiago: Ediciones Ercilla.

———. 1942. *Aún es Tiempo*. Santiago: Ediciones Ercilla.

———. 1946. *La Política y el Espíritu*. Santiago: Editorial del Pacífico.

———. 1951. *Sentido y Forma de una Política*. Santiago: Editorial del Pacífico.

———. 1955. *La Verdad Tiene Su Hora*. Santiago: Editorial del Pacífico.

———. 1956a. *Pensamiento y Acción*. Santiago: Editorial del Pacífico.

———. 1956b. "Un Discurso Conmemorando el 21 Aniversario de la Falange Nacional." *Política y Espíritu*, no. 167.

———. 1960. "Principios de Orden Político." In *Caminos de la Política*, ed. Guilisasti Tagle. Santiago: Editorial Orbe.

————. 1961. *Chile Tiene un Destino*. Santiago: Editorial del Pacífico.

————. 1964. *Dos Discursos*. Santiago: Editorial del Pacífico.

————. 1966. *Segundo Mensaje al Congreso Nacional*. Santiago: República de Chile.

————. 1977. *The Mandate of History and Chile's Future*. Oxford: Ohio University Center for International Studies.

Gall, Norman. 1973. "Oil and Democracy, Parts I and II." *American Universities Field Staff Reports*, East Coast South America Series 17, nos. 1 and 2.

Gallegher, Donald, and Gallegher, Idella. 1972. *The Achievements of Jacques and Raissa Maritain: A Bibliography, 1906-1961*. New York: Doubleday.

Galli, Georgio, and Prandi, Alfonso. 1971. *Patterns of Political Participation in Italy*. New Haven: Yale University Press.

Garaudy, Roger. 1965. *Perspectivas del Hombre: Existencialismo, Pensamiento Cristiano, Marxismo*. Buenos Aires: Editorial Platina.

Garcés, Joan. 1971. *La Pugna por la Presidencia en Chile*. Santiago: Editorial Universitaria.

————. 1976. *Allende y la Experiencia Chilena*. Barcelona: Ediciones Ariel.

Garretón, Manuel Antonio. 1981. "Problemas y Perspectivas de la Oposición en Chile." *Mensaje*, no. 296.

————. 1982a. "La Institucionalización Política del Régimen Militar Chileno." *Mensaje*, no. 310.

————. 1982b. "La Crisis Política en El Régimen Militar Chileno." *Mensaje*, no. 311.

————, and Moulián, Tomás. 1979. "Procesos y Bloques Políticos en la Crisis Chilena, 1970-73." *Revista Mexicana de Sociología* 41, no. 1.

Garretón Walker, Manuel. 1934. *Hacia un Ideal Político*. Santiago: Ediciones Lircay.

Geertz, Clifford. 1965. "Ideology as a Cultural System." In *Ideology and Discontent*, ed. David Apter. New York: Free Press.

Gil, Federico. 1962. *Los Partidos Políticos Chilenos: Génesis y Evolución*. Buenos Aires: Ediciones de Palma.

————. 1966. *The Chilean Political System*. New York: Houghton Mifflin.

————; Lagos, Ricardo; and Landsberger, Henry. 1979. *Chile at the Turning Point: The Lessons of the Socialist Years, 1970-73*. Philadelphia: Institute for the Study of Human Issues.

Gil, Federico, and Parrish, Charles. 1965. *The Chilean Presidential Elections of September 4, 1964: Parts I and II*. Washington, D.C.: Institute for the Comparative Study of Political Systems.

Gilson, Etienne, ed. 1954. *The Church Speaks to the Modern World: The Social Teachings of Leo XIII*. New York: Image Books.

Gold, D.; Lo, C.Y.H.; and Wright, E. O. 1975. "Recent Developments in Marxist Theories of the Capitalist State." *Monthly Review* 27, nos. 5, 6.

Goldrich, Daniel; Pratt, Raymond; and Schuller, C. R. 1967. "The Political Integration of Lower Urban Settlements in Chile and Peru." *Studies in Comparative International Development* 3, no. 1.

Grayson, George, Jr. 1968a. *El Partido Demócrata Cristiano Chileno*. Buenos Aires: Editorial Francisco Aguirre.

————. 1968b. "The Frei Administration in Chile." *SAIS Review* 2, no. 4.

————. 1969a. "Chile's Christian Democratic Party: Power, Factions, and Ideology." *Review of Politics* 31, no. 1.

————. 1969b. "The Frei Administration and the 1969 Parliamentary Elections." *Inter-American Economic Affairs* 23, no. 2.

Guilisasti Tagle, Sergio. 1966. *Caminos de la Política*. Santiago: Editorial Orbe.

Gumucio, Rafael Luís. 1932. *El Deber Político*. Santiago: Ediciones Ercilla.

Halperin, Ernst. 1965. *Nationalism and Communism in Chile*. Cambridge: MIT Press.

Hamuy, Eduardo. 1958. *Political Behavior in Chile*. Santiago: Centro de Opinión Pública.

————. 1964. *Pre-Electoral Political Sociology*. Santiago: Centro de Estudios Socioeconomicos.

————. 1972. *Research Project No. 37*. Santiago: Centro de Opinión Pública.

————. 1973. *Research Project No. 45*. Santiago: Centro de Opinión Pública.

Handelman, Howard. 1978. "Venezuela's Political System on the Eve of National Elections." *American Universities Field Staff Reports*, South America, no. 44.

Harris, Richard. 1979. "Structuralism in Latin America." *The Insurgent Sociologist* 9, no. 1.

Herman, Edward. 1980. *Christian Democracy in Venezuela*. Chapel Hill: University of North Carolina Press.

Hinklehammert, Franz. 1967. *Economía y Revolución*. Santiago: Editorial del Pacífico.

Hirsch, Fred. 1977. "An Analysis of the AFL-CIO Role in Latin America, or Under the Cover with the C.I.A." In *The C.I.A. and the Labour Movement in Chile*, ed. Fred Hirsch and Richard Fletcher. Nottingham: Spokesman Books.

Houtart, François, and Pin, Emile. 1965. *The Church and the Latin American Revolution*. New York: Sheed and Ward.

Hoy. 1979. Santiago. April 25-May 1.

———. 1980. Santiago. September 24-30.

———. 1981. Santiago. November 4-10.

———. 1982. Santiago. February 17-23.

Hubner, Jorge Ivan. 1959. *Los Católicos en la Política*. Santiago: Empresa Editora Zig-Zag.

Instituto de Estudios Políticos. 1966a. "Visión Comunitaria de la Economía." Mimeographed. Santiago: Instituto de Estudios Políticos.

———. 1966b. "Seminario Internacional sobre la Propiedad." Mimeographed. Santiago: Instituto de Estudios Políticos.

Irving, R.E.M. 1973. *Christian Democracy in France*. London: Allen and Unwin.

———. 1979a. "Christian Democracy in Post-War Europe: Conservatism Writ Large or a Distinctive Political Phenomenon." *West European Politics* 2, no. 1.

———. 1979b. *The Christian Democratic Parties of Western Europe*. London: Royal Institute of International Affairs, Allen and Unwin.

Janda, Kenneth. 1980. *Political Parties: A Cross-National Survey*. New York: Free Press.

Jobet, Julio Cesar. 1971. *El Partido Socialista* Vols. 1 and 2. Santiago: Editorial Prensa Latina.

Johnson, Dale, ed. 1973. *The Chilean Road to Socialism*. New York: Anchor Books.

Kaufman, Robert. 1972. *The Politics of Land Reform in Chile, 1950-1970*. Cambridge: Harvard University Press.

Keesings Contemporary Archives. 1975. London. May 12-18.

Kogan, Norman. 1981. *A Political History of Post-War Italy*. New York: Praeger.

Labini, P. S. 1972. "Sviluppo Economico e Classi Sociali in Italia." *Quaderni di Sociologia* 21, no. 4.

Labrousse, Alain. 1972. *L'Experience Chilienne: Reformisme ou Revolution?* Paris: Editions de Seuil.

Lagos, Ricardo. 1965. *La Concentración del Poder in Chile.* Santiago: Editorial del Pacífico.

Landsberger, Henry; Barrera, Manuel; and Toro, Abel. 1967. "The Chilean Labor Union Leader." *Industrial and Labor Relations Review* 17, no. 3.

Landsberger, Henry, and McDaniel, Tim. 1976. "Hypermobilization in Chile, 1970-73," *World Politics* 28, no. 4.

Larson, Oscar. 1967. *La ANEC y la Democracia Cristiana.* Santiago: Ediciones Rafaga.

Latin America Political Report. 1975a. London, No. 3, January 16.

―――. 1975b. London. No. 27, July 4.

―――. 1975c. London. No. 29, July 18.

―――. 1976. London. No. 39, October 8.

―――. 1977. London. No. 2, January 14.

Latin America Regional Reports Southern Cone. 1982a. London. No. 2, March 5.

―――. 1982b. London. No. 5, June 25.

Latin America Weekly Report. 1983. London. No. 49, December 16.

―――. 1984. London. No. 6, February 10.

Lebret, Louis Josef. 1947. "Carta a los Cristianos de Buena Voluntad." *Política y Espíritu,* no. 22.

―――. 1948. *Los Cristianos frente al Comunismo y al Anticomunismo.* Montevideo: n.p.

―――. 1950. *Guía de Militante.* Vols. 1 and 2. Santiago: Editorial del Pacífico.

Lechner, Norbert. 1970. *La Democracia en Chile.* Buenos Aires: Ediciones Signos.

Levine, Daniel. 1973. *Conflict and Political Change in Venezuela.* Princeton: Princeton University Press.

Lira Massi, Eugenio. 1968a. *La Cámara y los 147 a Dieta.* Santiago: Editorial Te-Ele.

―――. 1968b. *La Cueva del Senado y los 45 Senadores.* Santiago: Editorial Te-Ele.

Lircay. 1935a. Santiago. No. 31.

―――. 1935b. Santiago. No. 37.

―――. 1936. Santiago. No. 41.

―――. 1937a. Santiago. No. 52.

―――. 1937b. Santiago. No. 73.

———. 1938a. Santiago. No. 133.

———. 1938b. Santiago. No. 146.

———. 1938c. Santiago. No. 147.

———. 1938d. Santiago. No. 164.

Lyon, Margot. 1967. "Christian Democratic Parties and Politics." *Journal of Contemporary History* 2, no. 4.

McLaughlin, Terrence, ed. 1957. *The Church and the Reconstruction of the Modern World: The Social Encyclicals of Pius XI*. New York: Image Books.

Magnet, Alejandro. 1951. "Semblanza de Eduardo Frei." *Política y Espíritu*, nos. 62-63.

Mannheim, Karl. 1959. *Ideology and Utopia*. New York: Harcourt, Brace and Co.

Maritain, Jacques. 1947. *Christianity and Democracy*. Santiago: Charles Scribner's Sons.

———. 1951. *Man and the State*. Chicago: University of Chicago Press.

———. 1966. *Humanismo Integral*. Buenos Aires: Ediciones Carlos Lohle.

Mattelart, Armando, and Garretón, Manuel Antonio. 1965. *Integración Nacional y Marginalidad: Un Ensayo de Regionalización de Chile*. Santiago: Editorial del Pacífico.

Mazzella, Frank. 1972. "Party Building in the Modernizing Society: A Study of the Intermediate Leaders of the Chilean Christian Democratic Party." Ph.D. dissertation, Indiana University.

Meiksins Wood, Ellen. 1981. "The Separation of the Economic and the Political in Capitalism." *New Left Review*, no. 127.

———. 1983. "Marxism without Class Struggle?" In *The Socialist Register 1983*, ed. Ralph Miliband and John Saville. London: The Merlin Press.

Mello, Gerardo. 1965. *Eduardo Frei y la Revolución Latinoamericana*. Santiago: Editorial del Pacífico.

Mensaje. 1962a. Santiago. No. 113.

———. 1962b. Santiago. No. 114.

———. 1966. Santiago. No. 148.

El Mercurio. 1970. Santiago. October 3.

———. 1971a. Santiago. January 1.

———. 1971b. Santiago. January 7.

———. 1973. Santiago. March 10.

Metz, Johannes. 1968. "The Church's Function in the Light of Political Theology." *Concilium*, no. 36.

Miliband, Ralph. 1969. *The State and Capitalist Society*. London: Oxford University Press.

———. 1977. *Marxism and Politics*. London: Oxford University Press.

Moix, Candide. 1964. *El Pensamiento de Emmanuel Mounier*. Barcelona: Ediciones Estela.

Molina, Sergio. 1972. *El Proceso de Cambio en Chile, 1965-70*. Santiago: Editorial Universitaria.

Moreno, Francisco. 1969. *Legitimacy and Stability in Latin America: A Study in Chilean Political Culture*. New York: New York University Press.

Morris, David. 1973. *We Must Make Haste - Slowly: The Process of Revolution in Chile*. New York: Random House.

Mounier, Emmanuel. 1938. *A Personalist Manifesto*. New York: Longman, Greene and Co.

———. 1952. *Personalism*. London: Routledge and Kegan Paul.

———. 1954. *Be Not Afraid: Studies in Personalist Sociology*. New York: Harper.

———. 1965. *Manifesto al Servicio del Personalismo*. Madrid: Taurus Ediciones.

———. 1966. *Comunisme, Anarchisme et Personalisme*. Paris: Editions de Seuil.

Naudón, Carlos, and Bustos, Ismael. 1965. *El Pensamiento Social de Maritain*. Santiago: Editorial del Pacífico.

Nuestro Tiempo. 1945a. Santiago. No. 32.

———. 1945b. Santiago. No. 33.

———. 1945c. Santiago. No. 34.

———. 1946. Santiago. No. 41.

Offe, Claus. 1975. "The Theory of the Capitalist State and the Problem of Policy Formation." In *Stress and Contradiction in Modern Capitalism*, ed. Leon Lindberg et al. Lexington: Lexington Books.

Olavarría Bravo, Arturo. 1966-1971. *Chile bajo la Democracia Cristiana*. 6 vols. Santiago: Editorial Nascimiento.

Orrego Vicuña, Claudio. 1972a. *El Paro Nacional: Vía Chilena contra el Totalitarismo*. Santiago: Editorial del Pacífico.

———. 1972b. *Empezar de Nuevo, Chile Después de la UP*. Santiago: Editorial del Pacífico.

———. 1974a. *El Bién Común y Seguridad Nacional*. Santiago: Editorial del Pacífico.

———. 1974b. *Chile: O la Razón o la Fuerza*. Santiago: Editorial del Pacífico.

Pacheco, Luís. 1970. "La Inversión Extranjera en la Industria Chilena." Licentiate thesis, University of Chile.

Palacios, Bartolomé. 1932. *El Partido Conservador y la Democracia Cristiana*. Santiago: Ediciones Ercilla.

Parra, Bosco. 1966a. "Las Exigencias del Díalogo." *Política y Espíritu*, no. 295.

————. 1966b. *Las Tareas Inmediatas para la Construcción de una Nueva Sociedad*. Pamphlet. Santiago: n.p.

————. 1966c. "Una Vía No-Capitalista de Desarrollo." In *Una Visión Comunitaria de la Economía*. Santiago: Instituto de Estudios Políticos.

————. 1967. *Ganemos, pero Sepamos Que Hacer con la Victoria*. Pamphlet. Santiago: n.p.

Partido Demócrata Cristiano. 1966a. *El Programa de la Revolución en Libertad y su Cumplimiento*. Santiago: Talleres La Nación.

————. 1966b. *Participación del Gobierno y del Partido en la Revolución en Libertad*. Santiago: Talleres La Nación.

Pasquino, Gianfranco. 1979. "Italian Christian Democracy: A Party for All Seasons." *West European Politics* 2, no. 3.

Paupert, Jean-Marie. 1969. *The Politics of the Gospel*. New York: Holt, Rinehart, and Winston.

Penniman, Howard. 1977. *Italy at the Polls*. Washington, D.C.: American Enterprise Institute for Public Policy Research.

Perlman, Janice. 1976. *The Myth of Marginality*. Berkeley: University of California Press.

Petras, James. 1967. *Chilean Christian Democracy: Politics and Social Forces*. Berkeley: Institute of International Studies.

————. 1969. *Politics and Social Forces in Chilean Development*. Berkeley: University of California Press.

————, and Zeitlin, Maurice. 1970. "The Working-Class Vote in Chile: Christian Democracy vs. Marxism." *British Journal of Sociology* 21, no. 1.

Philip, George. 1978. *The Rise and Fall of the Peruvian Military Radicals, 1968-1976*. London: Athlone.

Pike, Frederick. 1963. *Chile and the United States, 1880-1962*. South Bend: University of Notre Dame Press.

Política y Espíritu. 1947. Santiago. Nos. 27-28.

————. 1953a. Santiago. No. 96.

————. 1953b. Santiago. No. 98.

————. 1954. Santiago. No. 123.

————. 1957. Santiago. No. 187.

Política y Espíritu. 1959a. Santiago. No. 220.
———. 1959b. Santiago. No. 221.
———. 1959c. Santiago. No. 222.
———. 1963a. Santiago. No. 277.
———. 1963b. Santiago. No. 280.
———. 1964. Santiago. No. 284.
———. 1967. Santiago. No. 303.
———. 1971a. Santiago. No. 320.
———. 1971b. Santiago. No. 321.
———. 1971c. Santiago. No. 325.
Portes, Alejandro. 1971. "Political Primitivism, Differential Socialization, and Lower-Class Leftist Radicalism." *American Sociological Review* 36, no. 5.
Poulantzas, Nicos. 1973. *Political Power and Social Classes*. London: New Left Books.
———. 1975. *Classes in Contemporary Capitalism*. London: New Left Books.
———. 1979. "The New Petty Bourgeoisie." *The Insurgent Sociologist* 9, no. 1.
Pridham, Geoffry. 1977. *Christian Democracy in West Germany*. New York: St. Martin's.
Punto Final. 1967. Santiago. Vol. 2, no. 44. December 19.
Qué Pasa. 1975. Santiago. No. 215. June 5.
Rahner, Karl. 1968. "Magisterium." In *Sacramentum Mundi*, vol. 3, ed. Karl Rahner et al. New York: Benzinger Brothers.
Rappaport, Ronald, and Langton, Kenneth. 1979. "Putting the Chilean Voter in Context." Paper prepared for delivery at Midwest Political Science Association Meeting, Chicago, Illinois, April 19-21.
Rausch, William. 1972. *Politics and Belief in Contemporary France. Emmanuel Mounier and Christian Democracy: 1932-1950*. The Hague: Martinus Nyhoff.
Rodríguez, Luis, and Smith, Brian. 1974. "Comparative Working-Class Behavior." *American Behavioral Scientist* 18, no. 1.
Roxborough, Ian. 1976. "Reversing the Revolution: The Chilean Opposition to Allende." In *Allende's Chile*, ed. Phillip O'Brien. New York: Praeger.
———. 1979. *Theories of Underdevelopment*. London: MacMillan.
Ruddle, Kenneth, and Odermann, Donald, eds. 1972. *Statistical*

Abstract of Latin America 1971. Los Angeles: UCLA Latin American Center.

Ruíz-Tagle, Jaime. 1982. "La Gestión Luders: Mantención del Modelo y Profundización de la Crisis." *Mensaje,* no. 284.

San Francisco Bay Area Kapitalistate Group. 1979. "Political Parties and Capitalist Development." *Kapitalistate,* no. 6.

Sartori, Giovani. 1969. "Politics, Ideology, and Belief Systems." *American Political Science Review* 63, no. 2.

Schillebeeckx, Edward. 1968. "The Magisterium and the World of Politics." *Concilium,* no. 36.

Sigmund, Paul. 1962. "Christian Democracy in Chile." *Journal of International Affairs* 20, no. 2.

———. 1977. *The Overthrow of Allende and the Politics of Chile, 1964-1976.* Pittsburgh: University of Pittsburgh Press.

Silva Bascuñán, Alejandro. 1949. *Una Experiencia Socialcristiana.* Santiago: Editorial del Pacífico.

Silva Solar, Julio. 1963. "Jacques Maritain." *Política y Espíritu,* no. 277.

———. 1968. "Católico o Marxista." *Documentación, Ideología, y Política,* no. 10.

———. 1969. "Aportes al Debate Ideológico de la D.C." *Documentación, Ideología, y Política,* no. 20.

———, and Chonchol, Jacques. 1951. *Hacia un Mundo Comunitario.* Santiago: Editorial del Pacífico.

———, and Chonchol, Jacques. 1965. *El Desarrollo de la Nueva Sociedad en América Latina.* Santiago: Editorial Universitaria.

———, and François, Jacques. 1948. *Qué es el Socialcristianismo?* Santiago: n.p.

Silvert, Kalman. 1965. *Chile, Yesterday and Today.* New York: Holt, Rinehart and Winston.

Skotnes, Andor. 1979. "Structural Class Determination." *The Insurgent Sociologist* 9, no. 1.

Smith, Brian. 1982. *The Church and Politics in Chile.* Princeton: Princeton University Press.

der Spiegel. 1970. Hamburg. Vol. 24. no. 20, May 11.

Stallings, Barbara. 1978. *Class Conflict and Economic Development in Chile, 1958-1973.* Stanford: Stanford University Press.

Steenland, Kyle. 1974. "Rural Strategy under Allende." *Latin American Perspectives* 1, no. 2.

Stepan, Alfred. 1978. *State and Society: Peru in Comparative Perspective.* Princeton: Princeton University Press.

Stephens Freire, Alfonso. 1957. *El Irracionalismo Político en Chile*. Santiago: n.p.

Stevenson, John Reese. 1942. *The Chilean Popular Front*. Philadelphia: University of Pennsylvania Press.

Stolz Chinchilla, Norma, and Sternberg, Marvin. 1974. "The Agrarian Reform and Campesino Consciousness." *Latin American Perspectives* 1, no. 2.

Strasma, John. 1975. "Agrarian Reform in Chile under Frei and under Allende: Some Problems in Evaluating Resources and Results." Paper prepared for delivery at the Pacific Coast Council on Latin American Studies Conference, Fresno, California, October 23-25.

Szulc, Tad. 1967. "Communists, Socialists and Christian Democrats." *The Annals of the American Academy of Political and Social Sciences*, no. 360.

Thayer Arteaga, William. 1968. *Trabajo, Empresa y Revolución*. Santiago: Empresa Editora Zig-Zag.

Unwin, Derek. 1974. "Germany: Continuity and Change in Electoral Politics." In *Electoral Behavior: A Comparative Handbook*, ed. Richard Rose. New York: Free Press.

Urdemales, Pedro. 1970. *Quién Ganará la Elección?* Santiago: Ediciones Desafío.

Valenzuela, Arturo. 1972. "The Scope of the Chilean Party System." *Comparative Politics* 4, no. 1.

―――. 1977. *Political Brokers in Chile: Local Government in a Centralized Polity*. Durham: Duke University Press.

―――. 1978. "Chile." In *The Breakdown of Democratic Regimes*, ed. Juan Linz and Alfred Stepan. Baltimore: Johns Hopkins University Press.

―――, and Wilde, Alexander. 1979. "Presidential Politics and the Decline of the Chilean Congress." In *Legislatures and Development: The Dynamics of Change in New and Old States*, ed. Joel Smith and Lloyd Musolf. Durham: Duke University Press.

Vitale, Luís. 1964. *Esencia y Aparencia de la Democracia Cristiana*. Santiago: Arancibia Hermanos.

von Lazar, Arpad, and Quiroga Varela, Luis. 1968. "Chilean Christian Democracy: Lessons in the Politics of Reform Management." *Inter-American Economic Affairs* 21, no. 1.

Vúskovic, Sergio. 1968. *Problemática D.C.* Santiago: Editora Austral.

Webre, Stephen. 1982. *José Napoleón Duarte and the Christian*

Democratic Party in Salvadorean Politics, 1960-72. Baton Rouge: Louisiana State University Press.

White, Alistair. 1973. *El Salvador.* New York: Praeger.

Wiarda, Howard. 1982. *Politics and Social Change in Latin America: The Distinctive Tradition.* Amherst: University of Massachusetts Press.

Wilkie, James, ed. 1977. *Statistical Abstract of Latin America.* Vol. 18. Los Angeles: UCLA Latin American Center.

————, and Haber, Stephen, eds. 1981. *Statistical Abstract of Latin America.* Vol. 21. Los Angeles: UCLA Latin American Center.

Williams, Edward. 1968. *Latin American Christian Democratic Parties.* Knoxville: University of Tennessee Press.

Wilson, Frank. 1971. *The French Democratic Left, 1963-69.* Stanford: Stanford University Press.

————. 1982. *French Political Parties under the Fifth Republic.* New York: Praeger.

Wolf, Daniel. 1960. "Emmanuel Mounier, a Catholic of the Left." *Review of Politics* 22, no. 3.

Worsley, Peter. 1969. "The Concept of Populism." In *Populism, Its Meaning and Character,* ed. Ghita Ionescu and Ernest Gellner. London: MacMillan.

Zammit, Joanne, ed. 1973. *The Chilean Road to Socialism.* Austin: University of Texas Press.

Zapata, Francisco. 1976. *Las Relaciones entre el Movimiento Obrero y el Gobierno de Salvador Allende.* Mexico City: El Colegio de México.

Zariski, Raphael. 1965. "Intra-Party Conflict in a Dominant Party: The Experience of Italian Christian Democracy." *Journal of Politics* 27, no. 1.

Zeitlin, Maurice; Ewen, Linda Ann; and Ratcliff, Richard Earl. 1974. "New Princes for Old? The Large Corporation and the Capitalist Class in Chile." *The American Journal of Sociology* 80, no. 1.

————; Neuman, W. Lawrence; and Ratcliff, Richard Earl. 1976. "Class Segments: Agrarian Property and Political Leadership in the Capitalist Class of Chile." *American Sociological Review* 41, no. 6.

Zuckerman, Alan. 1979. *The Politics of Faction: Christian Democratic Rule in Italy.* New Haven: Yale University Press.

INDEX

Acción Católica, 44
Adenauer, Konrad, 217
Aguirre Cerda, Pedro, 48-49, 77, 166n
AIFLD, 186
Alarcón, Héctor, 185
Alessandri, Jorge, 32, 60, 61, 77, 110, 113-114, 122, 137; presidential campaign of, 113-114
Alfonso, Pedro Enrique, 61
Alianza Democrática, *see* Democratic Alliance
Allende government, 129-131; agrarian reform, 145-146; bank reform, 141-142; budget proposals of, 140; and Chilean Congress, 173; civil-military cabinet, 159-160, 167n; economy under, 152, 158, 167; nationalization of copper mines, 141; and PDC, 138; proposal for nationalization of industries, 150; relations with PDC, 128-175; takeover of textile firms, 143-144; unrest under, 169; wage adjustment proposals of, 140, 152
Allende, Salvador, 3, 4, 59, 67, 113, 121, 126, 128, 138, 139, 144, 148, 150, 153, 154, 159, 166, 167, 172; agreement with PDC, 147; presidential campaign of, 114; prospects for success, 126; on relations with PDC, 128, 138, 139, 148
Altamirano, Carlos, 6, 129, 132, 206n; attitude toward PDC, 139n
American Institute for Free Labor Development, *see* AIFLD
ANEC, 44
Arriagada, Genaro, 6, 129, 133, 154n, 157, 164
asentamientos, 104, 105
Asociación Nacional de Estudiantes Católicos, *see* ANEC
Astorga, Samuel, 149n
Aylwin, Patricio, 65, 68n

banks, 23, 141-142
Barros, Alvaro, 147n
base Christian communities, 189
base ecclesial communities, 189
Bedoya Reyes, Luís, 214
Belaúnde, Fernando, 214
Belaúnde, Víctor Andrés, 214n
blandos (soft-liners), 191-192
Bloc for Socialism, 203
blue collar Christian Democrats, 136, 160, 208-209; and Allende government, 164-165; attitudes toward Marxist workers, 144-145, 204-205; and El Teniente mine strike, 170; experience since 1973, 204-205, 208-210; extent of unionization, 162; ideological and political views of, 164-165; ideological self-placement of, 136, 157, 161; religious practice of, 161n; response to *paro nacional*, 159
blue collar workers: domestic, 28; independent, 27; industrial, 27; and party preferences, 34, 155-156; presidential preferences, 78n
Blum, Norbert, 218
Boorstein, Edward, 141n
Bustos, Manuel, 187, 188, 201n, 205
Buzeta, Fernando, 146n

camino propio strategy, 110-111
Campaña, Eric, 91
carabineros (Chilean police), 169
Carmona, Juan de Dios, 180, 209n, 246n
Castells, Manuel, 81, 91; assessment of Frei years, 116
Castillo, Bernardino, 185
Catholic social organizations, 4, 190-191, 207
Catholic social teaching, 44, 226; and Marxism, 234n
Cauas, Jorge, 180, 183

Library of Congress Cataloging in Publication Data

Fleet, Michael.
The rise and fall of Chilean Christian democracy.

Bibliography: p.
Includes index.
1. Partido Democrata-Cristiano (Chile) 2. Christian democracy—Chile.
3. Chile—Politics and government—1920-1970. 4. Chile—Politics
and government—1970-   . I. Title.

JL2698.D4F54 1985   324.283'072   84-42885
ISBN 0-691-07684-7 (alk. paper)
ISBN 0-691-02217-8 (pbk.)

Michael Fleet is Assistant Professor of Political
Science at Marquette University.